"Here is an excellent, searching, full-length study on the moral and spiritual requirements of being a professional, evangelical, biblical scholar. This book will do great good to those of us who ply this trade."

J. I. Packer, Professor of Theology, Regent College

"Sadly, Christian scholarship often has more prima donnas than the New York ballet and more mediocrity than a Cuban car-making factory! In an age when scholars sometimes think of themselves as celebrities rather than as servants of the church, along comes Andreas Köstenberger with a great book on the virtues of the Christian academic. Köstenberger provides engaging reflections on how to turn your utmost scholarship to the highest ends of all: the glory of God. In this book, Köstenberger provides us with a pathway on how to cultivate the great virtues in the life of the Christian scholar. It is rebuking, moving, and inspiring!"

Michael F. Bird, Lecturer in Theology and New Testament, Crossway College, Brisbane, Australia

"Excellence is a lofty challenge and is most often measured in our culture by personal or financial gain. Dr. Köstenberger has given us a much-needed biblical and theological perspective on excellence, centered in the very character and works of God. The journey of excellence begins with God and is lived out in us in our own spiritual growth and development. This message has been a fresh reminder to me that I have no choice but to pursue excellence in all areas of my life because of the grace given to me in Christ."

Selma Wilson, President, B&H Publishing Group

"Andreas Köstenberger, who has a distinguished career in the world of scholarship, addresses a topic few have had courage to tackle in a kind-spirited tone—namely, the practical application of intellectual virtues in scholarship. Grounded in the biblical text and balanced by the realities of life, this clear, concise, compelling, and convicting work points the scholar to the more excellent way, where *conduct* in scholarship weighs as important as the *content* of scholarship. For those who long to see Christian graces and civility permeate the world of scholarship, this book deserves careful attention. It is not to be read and then left on the shelf, but taken to heart."

Bruce A. Little, Professor of Philosophy of Religion and Associate Dean of Theological Studies, The Southeastern Baptist Theological Seminary

EXCELLENCE

OTHER CROSSWAY TITLES BY ANDREAS KÖSTENBERGER

Understanding the Times: New Testament Studies in the 21st Century: Essays in Honor of D. A. Carson on the Occasion of His 65th Birthday (co-edited with Robert Yarborough)

God, Marriage, and Family: Rebuilding the Biblical Foundation

The Heresy of Orthodoxy: How Contemporary Culture's Fascination with Diversity Has Reshaped Our Understanding of Early Christianity (co-authored with Michael Kruger)

Quo Vadis, Evangelicalism?: Perspectives on the Past, Direction for the Future: Nine Presidential Addresses from the First Fifty Years of the Journal of the Evangelical Theological Society

Whatever Happened to Truth? (general editor)

EXCELLENCE

*The Character of God and the
Pursuit of Scholarly Virtue*

ANDREAS J. KÖSTENBERGER

::: CROSSWAY

WHEATON, ILLINOIS

Excellence: The Character of God and the Pursuit of Scholarly Virtue
Copyright © 2011 by Andreas J. Köstenberger
Published by Crossway
        1300 Crescent Street
        Wheaton, Illinois 60187

All rights reserved. No part of this publication may be reproduced, stored in a retrieval system, or transmitted in any form by any means, electronic, mechanical, photocopy, recording, or otherwise, without the prior permission of the publisher, except as provided for by USA copyright law.

Cover design: Faceout Studio
Interior design and typesetting: Lakeside Design Plus
First printing 2011
Printed in the United States of America

Unless otherwise indicated, Scripture quotations are from the ESV® Bible (*The Holy Bible, English Standard Version*®), copyright © 2001 by Crossway. Used by permission. All rights reserved.

The Holy Bible, New International Version®, NIV®. Copyright © 1973, 1978, 1984 by Biblica, Inc™. Used by permission. All rights reserved worldwide.

All emphases in Scripture quotations have been added by the author.

Trade paperback ISBN:	978-1-58134-910-8
PDF ISBN:	978-1-4335-3049-4
Mobipocket ISBN:	978-1-4335-3050-0
ePub ISBN:	978-1-4335-3051-7

Library of Congress Cataloging-in-Publication Data
Köstenberger, Andreas J., 1957–
    Excellence : the character of God and the pursuit of scholarly virtue / Andreas J. Köstenberger.
       p. cm.
    Includes bibliographical references (p. 233) and index.
    ISBN 978-1-58134-910-8 (tp)
    1. Christian scholars—Religious life. 2. Excellence—Religious aspects—Christianity. 3. Learning and scholarship—Religious aspects—Christianity. I. Title.
BV4596.S34K67 2011
248.8'8—dc23
                                                2011017074

Crossway is a publishing ministry of Good News Publishers.

VP	23	22	21	20	19	18	17	16	15	14	13	12	11
14	13	12	11	10	9	8	7	6	5	4	3	2	1

For
Robert Yarbrough and
David Köstenberger:
Men of integrity, models of excellence, and partners in ministry

And for
Tahlia:
Example of diligence, tenacity, grit, and hard work

You inspire me, and I'm grateful for you!

"Finally, brothers, whatever is true,
whatever is honorable,
whatever is just,
whatever is pure,
whatever is lovely,
whatever is commendable,
if there is any excellence,
if there is anything worthy of praise,
think about these things."
—Philippians 4:8

Contents

List of Abbreviations	11
Preface	13
Introduction: Called to Excellence	17

PART 1: FOUNDATIONS FOR EXCELLENCE

1 The Excellence of God	33
2 The Pursuit of Excellence	43
3 Holiness	55
4 Spirituality	67

PART 2: VOCATIONAL EXCELLENCE

5 Diligence	87
6 Courage	103
7 Passion	117
8 Restraint	127
9 Creativity	137
10 Eloquence	147

PART 3: MORAL EXCELLENCE

11 Integrity	159
12 Fidelity	167
13 Wisdom	177

PART 4: RELATIONAL EXCELLENCE

14	Grace	189
15	Humility	199
16	Interdependence	209
17	Love	223
	Conclusion: Pursuing Excellence	231
	Selected Annotated Bibliography	233
	Notes	239
	General Index	260
	Scripture Index	267

List of Abbreviations

BBR	*Bulletin for Biblical Research*
BECNT	Baker Exegetical Commentary on the New Testament
Bib	*Biblica*
BTNT	Biblical Theology of the New Testament Commentary series
CTJ	*Calvin Theological Journal*
EvJ	*Evangelical Journal*
EvQ	*Evangelical Quarterly*
ExpTim	*Expository Times*
JETS	*Journal of the Evangelical Theological Society*
JSNTSup	Journal for the Study of the New Testament: Supplement Series
LNTS	Library of New Testament Studies
Neot	*Neotestamentica*
NIB	*The New Interpreter's Bible*
NovTSup	Novum Testamentum Supplements
NSBT	New Studies in Biblical Theology
PNTC	Pillar New Testament Commentary
SJT	*Scottish Journal of Theology*
Them	*Themelios*
TJ	*Trinity Journal*
TNTC	Tyndale New Testament Commentaries
TynBul	*Tyndale Bulletin*
VT	*Vetus Testamentum*
WBC	Word Biblical Commentary
WUNT	Wissenschaftliche Untersuchungen zum Neuen Testament

Preface

"It happens, moreover, that the application of Christian principle to the various departments of social intercourse, in all their interesting and delicate details; in other words, the code of what may be called Christian morals, has been less happily illustrated and enforced by books than any other part of Christian truth or duty. In its leading outlines, indeed, it has been often and well exhibited: but the task of minutely filling up what the scriptures have so divinely sketched, has never yet, unless I greatly mistake, been satisfactorily performed. And yet, perhaps, there is no subject, which, on a variety of accounts, requires to be exhibited in more minute detail, or urged with more constant reiteration than this. Still no popular, adequate treatise on this subject, so far as I know, is to be found. And, of course, those who desire to attain excellence in this department of duty, have the greater need to study it carefully for themselves, and to embrace every opportunity of becoming more and more at home in its requisitions." —Samuel Miller (1769–1850), *Letters on Clerical Manners and Habits Addressed to a Student of the Theological Seminary at Princeton, NJ, Letter 1*[1]

Excellence—what do you think of when you hear the word *excellence*? And how do you tackle a subject that many would agree is vital yet has often proven elusive? In my research, I have come across several collections of quotes on the topic, whether in the personal, relational, or vocational realm.[2] I have seen far fewer thoughtful, sustained treatments of excellence from a biblical and theological perspective. How does one go about writing such a book? Most would agree that there is little virtue in mediocrity. Many also aspire to excel in one thing or another, though people often don't know how to achieve mastery in a given field or are prepared to pay the price for attaining excellence. So excellence, however conceived or difficult to attain, is worth sustained reflection.

What is the essence of excellence? What are its component parts, and how do you and I know what these are? Those pondering the subject choose different approaches in tackling this fascinating topic. Some, as mentioned, will simply turn to others who have achieved some kind of notoriety, whether philosophers, poets, statesmen, or various celebrities, and hope to find out what excellence is by compiling an anthology of quotes on the subject. The business world also prizes excellence, and companies regularly aspire to move "from good to great."[3]

When you write a book on excellence, you must, therefore, determine at the very outset which approach you will take. In this volume, I opt to start with God and his character and works. God is excellent in everything he is and does. For this reason, as we pursue excellence, we must first contemplate the excellence of God. Second, we must come to terms with the biblical and theological foundation for our pursuit of excellence. We must wrestle with the fact that any such effort, in keeping with the gospel message, must be undergirded by God's grace while also entailing a vital volitional dimension.[4] In other words, excellence does not fall into anyone's lap; it is the result of sustained, deliberate effort.

This means that believers, once saved by grace and through faith, must exert themselves in pursuit of a series of Christian virtues. Peter's exhortation in 2 Peter 1:3–11 is an excellent place to begin.[5] In this volume, I will, therefore, engage in a close study of this portion of Scripture and its contribution to a biblical theology of excellence. The vital issues of sanctification and spirituality, in turn, are closely tied to the pursuit of Christian virtue. The scholar who would be excellent must be both sanctified and spiritual. For this reason, I will attempt to sketch the contours of a biblical theology of sanctification and to articulate a Christian understanding of spirituality.

On the basis of this foundation, I will then proceed to discuss the most important virtues aspiring scholars ought to pursue in their quest for personal and academic excellence. For convenience's sake, I will group these qualities into three major categories: vocational, moral, and relational excellence. The bulk of the book will engage in a close study of some of the most relevant major virtues and seek to apply these insights to the scholarly task: diligence, courage, passion, restraint, creativity, eloquence, integrity, fidelity, wisdom, grace, humility, interdependence, and love.

Writing this book was challenging but also rewarding because it provided me with the occasion to reflect on my own pilgrimage as a scholar. I could not have written this book without the capable assistance of my research fellow, Alex Stewart, who was a congenial partner and co-laborer in this project. As always, thanks are also due my dear wife, Marny, a capable scholar herself, who has stood by me for over twenty years, always encouraging me to pursue the task of serious scholarship in the service of God and of the church and urging me to do so with integrity, courage, fidelity, humility, love, and excellence.

Last but not least, I thank my God who saved me and called me into his service—and thus to excellence—through my knowledge of the Lord Jesus Christ. It is by his grace that I am who I am (1 Cor. 15:10). Apart from being an incredible honor, serving him has also been a lot of fun! Let no one tell you that the Christian life, and Christian ministry, are dull and dreary drudgery; far from it. *Soli Deo gloria.*

INTRODUCTION

Called to Excellence

No compromise.

Most of my other books, in keeping with proper academic etiquette, keep my personal pilgrimage at arm's length. After all, the academy trains scholars to pursue their work on the basis of a judicious assessment of the available evidence, and, if anything, a scholar's personal background and presuppositions—including, and especially, his or her faith—are to remain unobtrusively in the background. But this is a different kind of book, more personal in nature, which is why I would like to start out by telling you about my spiritual conversion and religious pilgrimage to date. Too often today, pressures mount to drive a wedge between faith and scholarship—as if it were possible to separate these two areas of life—and those of us who pursue our scholarly calling as believers are frequently embarrassed by our faith, concealing it beneath an objective, critical, scholarly veneer. For me, at least, my faith and my scholarship are utterly inseparable.

My Life before and after Christ

Conversion

"For what does it profit a man to gain the whole world and forfeit his soul? For what can a man give in return for his soul? For whoever is ashamed of me and of my words in this adulterous and sinful generation, of him will the Son of Man also be ashamed when he comes in the glory of his Father with the holy angels" (Mark 8:36–38).When I first heard this verse with an open heart in the spring of 1983, I was a freshly minted Christian listening to a sermon in the pews of the Vienna International Chapel, an English-speaking congregation in Vienna, Austria, the city where I grew up. The verse pricked my heart, and I knew there would be no turning back. I would get baptized and publicly identify with Christ. The prospect of Jesus's being ashamed of me at his return terrified me and convicted me not to hold back on identifying with the Crucified One. Compromise was not an option.

This Spirit-induced resolve compelled me to forsake my past, and, as Paul reminisced, "whatever gain I had, I counted as loss for the sake of Christ. Indeed, I count everything as loss because of the surpassing worth of knowing Christ Jesus my Lord. For his sake I have suffered the loss of all things and count them as rubbish, in order that I may gain Christ and be found in him" (Phil. 3:7–9). As an economics major, I could certainly appreciate the financial accounting language Paul used in this passage.

One of the books that made a deep impact on me as a young Christian was Dietrich Bonhoeffer's *Cost of Discipleship*. In his inimitable, uncompromising style, this German theologian and leader in the Hitler-resistance movement penned the following memorable words:

> The cross is laid on every Christian. The first Christ-suffering which every man must experience is the call to abandon the attachments of this world. It is that dying of the old man which is the result of his encounter with Christ. As we embark upon discipleship we surrender ourselves to Christ in union with his death—we give over our lives to death. Thus it begins; the cross is not the terrible end to an otherwise god-fearing and happy life, but it meets us at the beginning of our communion with Christ. When Christ calls a man, he bids him come and die. It may be a death like that of the first disciples who had to leave home and work to follow him, or it may be a death like Luther's, who had to leave the monastery and go out into the world. But it is the same death every time—death in Jesus Christ, the death of the old man at his call.[1]

In my case, it was death to my family. My father, Hannes Köstenberger, upon hearing that I had turned my back on a lucrative career in management consulting and chosen to follow Christ—I had already signed a contract with a firm and was to start September 1 after graduating from university—rejected me. It would be ten years before I would see him again. When I came home for lunch after attending the Vienna International Chapel on Sundays, my mother and sister met me with icy silence, and we often ate almost the entire meal without uttering a single word. As far as my family was concerned, for all practical purposes I *had* died—died as the person they knew. Not that the person they had known didn't *deserve* to die; far to the contrary.

Though the realization was slow and painful, my life had been sinful, and I had strayed far from God. Yet he sought me and found me. It happened one cold winter day on a night train from Vienna to Venice, where I traveled to enjoy the scenic beauty of this unique northern Italian city. A young lady by the name of Joan Zimmerman, an American opera student from Rockford, Illinois—who had herself become a believer only a year prior to our encounter through the witness of a fellow American, Madeline Pfister, while taking a German language course at the Vienna Goethe Institute—shared with me her newfound faith in Christ. "All those old people sitting on park benches in Vienna," she queried. "What are they waiting for? Hasn't Jesus already done everything that must be done for them to be saved?" Somehow, her words penetrated into my innermost being, and I wondered what *I* was waiting for when Jesus had already done everything that needed to be done *for me*.

Joan also read a portion of Galatians 5 that night, the verses listing the fruits of the Spirit (vv. 19–21), and these attributes—love, joy, peace—too, struck a profound chord in my longing, lonely, desperate heart. My parents' marriage had ended in divorce, and my own relationships were fragile and, more often than not, broken. I deeply longed for love, joy, and peace—as well as for freedom, about which the Galatians passage also spoke (even though I was still unaware that it was freedom *from sin* that I needed the most)—and here God was reaching out his hand to me and inviting me to enter into his love, his joy, and his peace in the Lord Jesus Christ. Over the course of the months that followed, his invitation proved irresistible.

Once back in Vienna, I eagerly bought an English Bible, devouring it as a man close to starvation might ravenously gulp down a meal. My pent-up spiritual hunger for truth and for a word from God was overwhelming, almost unbearable. In six months' time, I read through the entire Bible twice, gradually realizing that I was not merely in need of moral reform but desperately needed a Savior. This realization did not come easily, however. Between what you might call my spiritual "conception" on that night train from Vienna to Venice and my spiritual new birth were agonizing months of trying to reform myself. I went back to church, the Roman Catholic Church where I had grown up. But what I learned during these distressing times is that you never know how sinful you are until you try really hard to be good. As a result, I temporarily sank into a serious depression during which I desperately struggled to come to terms with my own sinfulness and need for Christ.

At one point during this process, I had some sort of vision while eating my lunch during a break from work, sitting at the side of the Danube channel (I was completing my "civil service," a substitute for military service, by working at the Lutheran Hospital located in Vienna's 9th district). At that moment, I felt immobilized on one side of a vast, unbridgeable gulf, desperately wanting to cross over to the other side yet being completely unable to do so. Who would take me across the river? I knew I couldn't do it on my own; it took me several months before I realized that it must be Jesus. Finally, I gave up all resistance, intellectual and otherwise, and abandoned myself completely to my Lord, who took me and brought me safely to the other side by virtue of what he had done for me on the cross.

One of the issues that caused me particular agony was the notion of God's sovereignty. How could God allow me to grow up in a family of parents whose marriage ended up in divorce? How could God conceivably redeem not just my future but also my past which, I increasingly came to realize, I had wasted in empty, godless pursuits? Only gradually did God's Spirit fix my spiritual gaze on the cross of Christ where God's sovereignty had turned evil into good, allowing his Son to be subjected to brutal, excruciating torture in order to accomplish our—my—salvation. I also had a very hard time conceiving of a personal relationship with God through Christ apart from any human mediation, whether through a Roman Catholic priest or someone else.

Then, one night, in the presence of a friend named Jerry Pfister, a trumpet player and American missionary to Vienna, all my defenses broke down, my intellectual resistance melted, and my persistent objections vanished. The floodgates opened, and God's bright light of salvation entered my soul as I prayed, asking him to forgive my sins and pleading with Christ to be my Savior. And so I gave my life to Christ, to paraphrase one of my favorite authors, C. S. Lewis, "the most dejected convert in all of Austria."[2] A few Sundays later, sitting in the pews of the Vienna International Chapel, I suddenly felt almost physically as if an enormous load had been lifted from my shoulders—my sins, which I no longer needed to bear on my own but which my Savior had borne for me. And as I wept uncontrollably in my seat, the congregation sang the familiar hymn:

> And can it be that I should gain
> An interest in the Savior's blood?
> Died He for me, who caused His pain—
> For me, who Him to death pursued?
>
> Amazing love! How can it be,
> That Thou, my God, shouldst die for me?
> He left His Father's throne above
> So free, so infinite His grace—
> Emptied Himself of all but love,
> And bled for Adam's helpless race:
> 'Tis mercy all, immense and free,
> For O my God, it found out me!
>
> Long my imprisoned spirit lay,
> Fast bound in sin and nature's night;
> Thine eye diffused a quickening ray—
> I woke, the dungeon flamed with light;
> My chains fell off, my heart was free,
> I rose, went forth, and followed Thee.
>
> No condemnation now I dread;
> Jesus, and all in Him, is mine;
> Alive in Him, my living Head,
> And clothed in righteousness divine,
> Bold I approach th'eternal throne,
> And claim the crown, through Christ my own.[3]

By the time the congregational singing had reached the line "No condemnation now I dread," an overwhelming peace had come over me, and I knew that God's judgment for sin had fallen on Christ. Even though I had sinned against God in many ways, his judicial verdict regarding me was "not guilty" because of what Christ had done for me. I had blessed assurance of salvation, and though I had no idea of what God might have in store for me, at that moment it did not matter. Having been justified with God, I had peace with him in the Lord Jesus Christ (Rom. 5:1).

My New Life in Christ

Then, quickly, like a series of falling dominoes, the Spirit did his convicting work in me. I gradually examined and severed several relationships with members of the opposite sex that I came to see did not honor God. I gave away most of my books and records (including some cherished Genesis, Supertramp, and Jethro Tull albums), and even my beloved ARP synthesizer on which I had played in a band (called "Stonehenge") during my college years. I completed my doctoral studies in economics and social sciences at the University of Vienna (with a major in nonprofit management) and sought advice from some of the men at the Chapel (including my mentor, Hans Finzel) on pursuing theological training. Fearing the theological liberalism at many German universities, and feeling inadequate at my young spiritual age to judge which schools were theologically solid, I decided to attend seminary in the United States. In order to pay for my education, I sold an apartment (near the university) I had been given by my grandfather Hans, providing me with the funds needed to enter the United States as a foreign student (what at the time seemed to be a whopping amount—about $25,000). I wept most of the way when my sister Dorice took me to the Vienna airport as I left my native country of Austria, knowing I would never return to live there. Eight hours later, I arrived, close to midnight, at the Columbia (South Carolina) International Airport, with two suitcases carrying all of my earthly possessions. I was ready to start over and to begin my new life in Christ in earnest pursuit of "knowing Him and making Him known," per the school motto of Columbia Bible College and Graduate School of Missions where I had enrolled. I was twenty-seven years old.

In the three years that followed, I studied Greek and Hebrew with men such as Drs. Paul Fowler, Paul Wright, William Larkin, Paul Ferris, and Alex Luc. I took courses in systematic theology and church history with Igou Hodges and Bill Davidson, among others. I received instruction in hermeneutics and ethics (Robertson McQuilkin), Old and New Testament survey (Terry Hulbert), and a variety of other subjects. Above all, during my third and final year of MDiv study, I met my future wife, Marny. The first time we talked was one Sunday afternoon while I was working at the seminary switchboard for the then-minimum wage of $3.35 an hour. Later, we reconnected at an open women's dorm, followed by a Valentine's Day date (my level of interest in Marny can be gauged by the fact that I asked her to go out with me six weeks in advance; fortunately, that didn't scare her off!).

After a year of courtship, we were engaged in the spring of 1989, and less than nine months later, we married in Scarborough, Canada, a suburb of Toronto, Ontario, where Marny had grown up. Hans Finzel, who had discipled me in Vienna during the two years following my conversion prior to my move to the United States, officiated at the wedding. Half a year later, it was off to Trinity Evangelical Divinity School in Deerfield, Illinois, where I felt irresistibly drawn to study under the tutelage of the accomplished scholar D. A. Carson. Having read his book *Exegetical Fallacies* during my seminary years in Columbia, I knew I wanted to pursue doctoral work with him, and God graciously made it possible for me to do so.

My years at Trinity (1990–1993) were among the best years of my life. While Marny selflessly and sacrificially worked as a nurse so I could go to school and earn my doctoral degree full-time, I devoured the New Testament scholarly literature with a voracity comparable to my thirst for Scripture in the early days of my faith. I had always been on a quest for learning, and now this craving zeroed in like a laser on this particular object of spiritual and scholarly interest. D. A. Carson, Douglas Moo, Grant Osborne, and Scot McKnight provided me with tremendous role models of serious scholarship, and Nigel Cameron, the program director, exhibited an uncanny ability to administer, care for students, and nurture a community of learners in pursuit of academic excellence. In addition, I benefited from the wisdom of Kenneth Kantzer (who taught the Integrative Seminar), Thomas McComiskey, and Carl F. H. Henry (from a distance). I also developed a friendship with Harold O. J. ("Joe") Brown, whose impeccable grasp of German and whose jovial nature, coupled with his intellectual rigor, made a deep impact on me.[4]

Part of me wished my time at Trinity and in the doctoral program would never come to an end. But after a little over three years, I had completed my dissertation (on the mission motif in John), and it was time to secure a position teaching the New Testament. I spent the next two years at Briercrest Bible College, a surprisingly large school in the Saskatchewan prairies. Those were years of preparing lecture notes on

New Testament survey, hermeneutics, and various Bible classes, as well as initial forays into publishing. Then, the opportunity presented itself to take D. A. Carson's place at Trinity Evangelical Divinity School during one of his sabbaticals in Cambridge during the 1995–1996 academic year. So it was back to Trinity for another wonderful year, this time teaching the classes of my esteemed mentor. Knowing that I had but a one-year appointment, I actively looked for another position and was hired by Dr. Paige Patterson to teach New Testament at Southeastern Baptist Theological Seminary in Wake Forest, North Carolina, a Southern Baptist school that had only recently taken a conservative turn. With two young children in tow, we packed the moving van and made the long trek from Saskatchewan to Wake Forest, hoping for a measure of permanence that had eluded us in the years up to that point during which we had moved close to ten times in as many years.

Our Wake Forest years (which continue to this day) have been years of personal growth and ministry. About four years into my tenure at Southeastern, the position of director of PhD studies opened up when the director, Dr. David Puckett, decided to devote himself to serving as the full-time founding principal of Trinity Academy, a Christian school in Raleigh, North Carolina (he later became the PhD director at Southern Seminary in Louisville, Kentucky, a position he still holds). In short order, I was appointed associate director and then director of these programs, a post I have now occupied for over ten years. My wife, Marny, besides giving birth to two more children and seeing to her many other duties, also managed to complete a ThD (doctor of theology) in systematic theology at UNISA (with a dissertation topic on feminist hermeneutics).[5] Apart from homeschooling our children, she is teaching adjunctively as professor of women's studies at Southeastern and serving in the women's ministry at our local church.

The Plan and Purpose for This Book

Why This Book?

Why did I want to write this book?[6] Essentially, it was to discharge a burden: pleading with zealous young theological students not to sacrifice their scholarly integrity for the sake of attaining academic respectability. My message to these individuals is that believing scholarship is not only possible but in fact is more virtuous than critical, unbelieving, or supposedly objective academic work.[7] To this end, I urge all of us who sense

God's call to scholarly labor to pursue earnestly, and with God's help, the scholarly virtues discussed in this book. Again, Jesus's words come to mind: "For what does it profit a man to gain the whole world and forfeit his soul? For what can a man give in return for his soul? For whoever is ashamed of me and of my words in this adulterous and sinful generation, of him will the Son of Man also be ashamed when he comes in the glory of his Father with the holy angels."

Yet, I fear that some have already strayed from the narrow path of a scholarship of integrity—dedicated to the glory of God and undergirded by a love and respect for his inspired Scriptures—having instead veered off onto the broad road of seeking to win the approval of their academic peers, or at least avoiding their disapproval. Some may, chameleon-like, have chosen "safe" topics that do not require them to reveal their true spiritual colors. Others may have caved in to prevailing paradigms that are *en vogue* among the current scholarly elite—though they may be here today and be replaced by another, new paradigm tomorrow. Yet others have moved from conservative to liberal to agnostic or have slid at least part of the way on this slippery slope.[8]

Academic and social approval is not worth the loss of integrity. To be sure, some detractors may contend that "evangelical scholarship" is an oxymoron and that the truly enlightened scholar will cast off all constraints of doctrine and pursue his or her scholarship once freed from such confessionalism. Other detractors may be disturbed by the exclusivity of the gospel and succumb to the pressures of religious pluralism in a religiously diverse culture. To both sets of detractors, I say that "evangelical" and "scholarship" can in fact be wonderfully wedded together.[9]

Similar to the realm of science, where faith in God may fuel a joy of wonder and discovery of the world God made, the biblical scholar, once liberated from his or her unbelief and skeptical mindset and grounded in the fear of God and his Word, will be open to explore God's revelation in history as recorded in Scripture. In this, he or she will gladly follow Anselm of Canterbury's famous *dicta*, *credo ut intellegam* ("I believe so that I may understand," based on a saying by Augustine of Hippo) and *fides quaerens intellectum* ("faith seeking understanding"). As the apostle Paul wrote in his first letter to the Corinthians almost two millennia ago,

> For who knows a person's thoughts except the spirit of that person, which is in him? So also no one comprehends the thoughts of God except the Spirit of God. Now we have received not the spirit of the world, but the

> Spirit who is from God, that we might understand the things freely given us by God. And we impart this in words not taught by human wisdom but taught by the Spirit, interpreting spiritual truths to those who are spiritual. The natural person does not accept the things of the Spirit of God, for they are folly to him, and he is not able to understand them because they are spiritually discerned. The spiritual person judges all things, but is himself to be judged by no one. "For who has understood the mind of the Lord so as to instruct him?" But we have the mind of Christ. (1 Cor. 2:11–16)

In this passage, Paul bears telling testimony to the fact that it is only by the Spirit that the person interpreting Scripture is able to understand the thoughts of God. Far from being a hindrance, faith is thus an essential prerequisite for the interpretation of Scripture.

The Plan for This Book

In the following pages, I will take you on a journey in the pursuit of personal and academic excellence. In the opening chapter, I will first raise the question, "Why excellence?" As we will see, the answer is bound up with the nature and character of God. In chapter 2, I will present 2 Peter 1:3–11 as the inspiration, model, and scriptural foundation for the pursuit of excellence discussed throughout this book. On the basis of God's excellence and grace, and employing a rhetorical zeugma, Peter exhorts believers to add various godly virtues to their faith.[10] The presence and increase of these godly virtues, in turn, will result in effective ministry.

In addition, chapter 2 discusses two important concepts: virtue and vocation. In recent years, evangelicals have at times neglected discussions of virtue, perhaps because we have been too busy with pragmatic activism to take the time to ponder the deeper aspects and implications of our faith. Yet this neglect of virtue has been to our detriment, because growth in godly virtues is central to our pursuit of excellence. In the same vein, we must recapture a proper understanding of vocation. As Christians, we do not merely have jobs or careers but rather vocations. Each Christian has been called by God to serve in a particular way. God's calling invests our day-by-day duties with transcendent significance and provides the motivation necessary to pursue excellence in whatever task we find ourselves engaged.

Chapter 3 takes up the relationship between holiness and excellence, engages in a brief biblical-theological analysis of holiness and sanctification, and discusses what it means for a scholar to be holy. Both Testaments bear witness to the fact that God's people *are* holy because they are the special people of the holy God and yet must *pursue* holiness because God is characteristically and eternally holy. As Christians, and as Christian scholars, we are therefore *already* holy as God's set-apart people yet must still continually pursue holiness, striving to grow in conformity to our holy God in our thoughts, words, and actions, and in our research, writing, and teaching. Being set apart unto God as a scholar also entails a rejection of the false modernist dichotomy between faith and scholarship, a wholehearted pursuit of truth, complete dependence on the guidance and empowerment of the Holy Spirit, a balanced life that does not turn our scholarship into an idol, an awareness that the primary orientation of our work is to be missional, and an engagement in spiritual warfare through faithful witness to the truth.

In chapter 4 I will explore genuine, biblical spirituality. The necessity of spirituality for our pursuit of excellence becomes abundantly clear as we begin to put the insights discussed in the previous chapters into practice and pursue holiness and growth in godly virtues in our day-to-day living. The presence, activity, and work of the Spirit are presented in Scripture as necessary for both sanctification and growth in virtue. Without the Spirit's empowerment, our pursuit of holiness and excellence through growth in godly virtues will devolve into mere human self-effort that invariably results in pride and failure.

Biblical spirituality, at its core, entails the presence, activity, and work of the Holy Spirit in a believer's life, beginning at conversion with regeneration and continuing throughout the entire process of sanctification. What is more, Scripture ties spirituality closely to active obedience and an engagement of the world in one's mission for God. Biblical spirituality does not consist primarily of mystical, emotional experience, inward impressions and feelings, introspective meditation, or a monastic withdrawal from the world. The primary spiritual disciplines advocated by Scripture are prayer and the obedient study of God's Word.

These four initial chapters in part 1 lay the foundation for the discussion of the particular virtues necessary for academic excellence in parts 2 through 4. Each chapter in these latter three sections is structured in a similar manner so you can easily follow the discussion and refer back to relevant sections at a later time (though some variation is unavoidable due to the uniqueness of each virtue). Typically, each chapter begins with an initial discussion or definition of the respective virtue, followed by a more or less thorough biblical-theological investigation (depending on factors such as the availability of material and the required degree of detail). After this, I make specific application of the respective virtue to the vocation of the Christian scholar.

While I take my cue from the list of virtues in 2 Peter 1:3–11, the specific virtues selected for discussion are not identical to that list but specific to the scholarly calling. Though these distinctions are not hard and fast, part 2 focuses on virtues more related to vocational excellence (diligence, courage, passion, restraint, creativity, eloquence); part 3 is concerned with moral excellence (integrity, fidelity, wisdom); and part 4 is devoted to a discussion of relational excellence (grace, humility, interdependence, and love). Undergirded by the grace of God, we will make progress in our pursuit of excellence as we add to our faith the various virtues discussed throughout this book. To adapt 2 Peter 1:5–7, therefore, "Make every effort to add to your faith excellence, diligence, courage, passion, restraint, creativity, eloquence, integrity, fidelity, wisdom, grace, humility, interdependence, and love."

How to Read This Book

This is a book you will want to read with both your head and your heart. Come ready to evaluate the path you have taken and, if needed, reassess the direction in which you are headed. Be open to see how God might use some of the Scripture passages and personal examples cited in this book to urge you on to greater fidelity and integrity as a person and as a scholar. Be impressed by the fact that your identity and vocation are rooted in God's calling and commission, and be prepared to affirm, embrace, and act on the realization that vocational, moral, and relational excellence are inextricably wedded together.

Be impressed also by the fact that God's call to scholarship, like any divine calling, entails a call to die to self—which, in the case of scholars, might particularly manifest itself in the form of aspirations to fame and fortune, which, as mentioned, might lead to sacrificing doctrinal fidelity for the sake of academic respectability. God's call to scholarship also involves dying to self-seeking arrogance and forsaking the allure of power, position, and prestige, as well as steadfastly and resolutely resisting temptations to sexual immorality and moral compromise.

You won't want to be a fine scholar but a terrible, or even mediocre, husband and father. You won't want to excel in scholarship but fail as a wife and mother. Neither should your calling as mother or father, and wife or husband, necessarily induce you to engage in mediocre scholarship if you are called to an academic career. If God is excellent—which he is—and if he has called you to pursue excellence in everything you do, then you should strive to excel *both* as a husband and father, or wife and mother, *and* as a scholar. Join me, then, on a journey of discovering some of the virtues that, if pursued diligently and consistently, will make you both a better person *and* a better scholar—without needing to sacrifice your faith at the altar of academic respectability.

Part One

FOUNDATIONS FOR EXCELLENCE

1

The Excellence of God

The character of God is the grounds of all human excellence.

Why pursue excellence? Many young seminarians or doctoral students who are considering a career in the academic world find themselves pulled in a thousand different directions. They must find a way to support their spouse and children while still having enough money for tuition and books. They have exams for which to study, papers to research and write, sermons to prepare, and the yard to mow. Wouldn't a book on simply surviving the process of becoming a scholar be more appropriate? Why focus on excellence when it is nearly impossible to keep your head above water from one assignment and deadline to the next?

Why Excellence?
Excellence is particularly important in such a context where the pressures toward sheer survival and mediocrity are particularly intense. Why? The primary reason for this is bound up with the nature and character of God.[1] *God is the grounds of all true excellence.* He is the one who

fills any definition of excellence with meaning, and he is the reason why we cannot be content with lackluster mediocrity, halfhearted effort, or substandard scholarship. Excellence starts and ends with God and is first and foremost a hallmark and attribute of God. Without God as our starting point and continual frame of reference, our discussion of excellence would be hopelessly inadequate.

Systematic theologies generally do not list "excellence" as one of God's attributes. For this reason it may appear at first glance that excellence is not all that important.[2] This conclusion would be premature, however, for excellence can be viewed as an overarching divine attribute that encompasses all the others. *Everything God is and does is marked by excellence.* Wayne Grudem discusses God's summary attributes of perfection, blessedness, beauty, and glory as "attributes that summarize his excellence."[3] Perfection indicates that "God lacks nothing in his excellence."[4] Blessedness points to the fact that "God takes pleasure in everything in creation that mirrors his own excellence."[5] Beauty is a reflection of God's excellence, and "God's glory is something that belongs to him alone and is the appropriate outward expression of his own excellence."[6] Understanding excellence as an all-encompassing attribute of God also means that the concept is not exhausted by the word "excellence." Other descriptions of the uniqueness, greatness, glory, or perfection of God are pertinent as well.

To the greater glory of God: stained glass window of the calling of John and Andrew

On a basic level, we may think of excellence as the quality of standing out or towering above the rest, being eminent or superior (though not *feeling* superior, which is the essence of pride), and distinguishing oneself in some extraordinary or special way.[7] As mentioned, God's excellence is the ultimate point of reference for all true human excellence. Perhaps God's attribute of perfection is most closely related to his excellence. God excels and is so far superior to all other beings in every way that *perfection* becomes the appropriate word to describe his excellence.[8] In the book of Isaiah, God declares his own excellence, superiority, and preeminence as follows:

> Thus says the LORD, the King of Israel
> and his Redeemer, the LORD of hosts:
> "I am the first and I am the last;
> besides me there is no god.
> Who is like me? Let him proclaim it.
> Let him declare and set it before me,
> since I appointed an ancient people.
> Let them declare what is to come, and what will happen.
> Fear not, nor be afraid;
> have I not told you from of old and declared it?
> And you are my witnesses!
> Is there a God besides me?
> There is no Rock; I know not any." (Isa. 44:6–8)

God lodges a similar claim concerning himself in the book of Jeremiah: "I will appoint over her whomever I choose. For who is like me? Who will summon me? What shepherd can stand before me?" (Jer. 49:19). God embodies true, unmatched excellence.

God's perfect excellence, then, sets his communicable attributes apart from humanity's possession and exercise of them. Humans, in their character and dealings with one another, may be marked by holiness, justice, love, mercy, and goodness to varying degrees, but God alone excels in all of these and does so to a perfect degree. Complete excellence characterizes everything God is and does. He is holiness, justice, and love, and he is holy, just, and loving in all that he does. This excellence of God rightly and frequently becomes the grounds of praise for God in Scripture.[9] Peter, in his first epistle, notes how our change in status—the fact that we are now God's own people—should result in praise, "that you may proclaim the excellencies of him who called you out of darkness into his marvelous light" (1 Pet. 2:9). We praise God, in part, because he is excellent, and the declaration of his excellent characteristics forms the content of our praise.

Apart from offering God praise, how should we respond to God's excellence? In short, we should seek to imitate and emulate it. In his letter to the Ephesians, the apostle Paul issues a simple command that encapsulates the logic undergirding much of the exhortation found in Scripture: "Therefore be imitators of God, as beloved children" (Eph. 5:1). As God's redeemed children, we are to strive to be like God. This, it appears, includes striving for excellence. As Millard Erickson writes:

> God's perfection is the standard for our moral character and the motivation for religious practice. The whole moral code follows from his holiness.... Because of God's flawlessness, a similar quality is expected of those objects or persons set apart unto him.[10]

Also, many of the exhortations in the Sermon on the Mount are built on Jesus's statement, "You therefore must be perfect, as your heavenly Father is perfect" (Matt. 5:48). We are called to emulate our perfect heavenly Father. In no way am I trying to blur the line between the divine and the human elements here. There is a clear sense in which God is God and we are not. We are not called to emulate what scholars call God's "incommunicable attributes"—yet we are to strive to emulate those qualities that are communicable.[11] To be sure, we will never become completely like God in his eternal, infinite excellence and perfection, but we must make every effort to grow in the virtues we are called to share. In the following pages, we will look at several of these attributes one by one and ponder how we can pursue various dimensions of excellence in our lives and especially in our scholarly pursuits for him.

Created in God's Image

Not only should we strive for excellence because God himself is excellent, but also we ought to pursue excellence because we were each *created in God's image*. What does it mean for humanity, both male and female, to have been made in the image of God? As I have written elsewhere:

> Popular notions of what it means to be created in God's image have often been unduly influenced by Greek concepts of personality. Thus, God's image in the man and the woman has frequently been identified in terms of their possession of intelligence, a will, or emotions. While this may be

presupposed or implied to some extent in Genesis 1:27, the immediate context develops the notion of the divine image in the man and the woman in terms of *representative rule* (cf. Ps. 8:6–8). . . . While *substantive* elements of the divine image in man (that is, an analogy between the nature of God and characteristics of humans) cannot be ruled out, a *functional* understanding (humans exercising the function of ruling the earth for God) seems to reflect most accurately the emphasis in the biblical record.[12]

Our creation in God's image, therefore, primarily relates to the fact that God placed humanity on the earth to rule it as his representatives.[13] How can we best fulfill this role? It stands to reason that as beings created in God's image, creatures who are called to exercise representative rule over his creation, we must do so with excellence. This is true even more so in a world that is fallen and because of sin falls short of God's glory (Rom. 3:23). The world desperately needs to see a display of what God is like. This extends to everything we are and do—our own personal lives, our marriages and families, our moral and ethical standards, and the pursuit of our calling, including scholarship.

As we have seen, God truly excels in the sense that he stands out from all the rest. His excellence is evident in his unmatched superiority to everyone and everything else. Because God is the proper standard of excellence, we should not measure our achievements by comparing ourselves with others. Our pursuit of excellence should not take place in the kind of competitive spirit according to which only few can participate and where in the end there is only one winner. Since we are *all* created in God's image, *everyone* can be truly excellent.[14] God is unique, and we are made uniquely in his image as distinct creatures. *We can each achieve excellence as we are increasingly fulfilling the potential God has built into us.*

The New Testament discussion of spiritual gifts emphasizes this uniqueness. We are not all the same; if we were, what would become of the body of Christ, the church (1 Cor. 12:19)? While this truth can liberate us from a sense of inferiority caused by improper comparison with others, it must not turn into an excuse for mediocrity and for failing to pursue the excellence for which God has created us. As God's children made in his image, we should live our lives grounded in the conviction that excellence, while requiring considerable and consistent effort, is nonetheless within our reach. This includes the vocational, moral, and relational realms, all of which we will explore in some detail later on in this volume.

Since excellence, then, is an all-encompassing attribute of God, and since we are exhorted in Scripture to imitate God, having been made in his likeness, excellence should mark our lives as his children, extending both to who we are (our character and our relationships) and what we do (our work or vocation). Excellence should characterize every thought we have, every paper we write, every relationship we pursue, every assignment we undertake, and every word we speak (see, e.g., Matt. 12:36–37; Eph. 4:29; James 3:1–12). *Excellence should describe our lives in their totality and encompass every area of our lives, no matter how large or small.*

At this point, the difference between ideal and reality becomes glaringly obvious. Far too often, we evangelicals are *not* characterized by excellence in our character and pursuits. On a moral level, the divorce rate of Christian marriages differs little from that of non-Christian ones. When others think of Christianity, they frequently think of scandals in the lives of religious leaders, whether financial or sexual (no doubt influenced to some degree by media attention). When it comes to evangelical scholarship, the situation is not all that different. Although the past few decades have witnessed a remarkable rise in the quality of evangelical scholarship,[15] we are still not at a place where scholars in the field would readily associate "evangelical" with "excellence," especially when scholarship is defined as advancing knowledge in a given field.[16]

Rest

One (perhaps surprising) way to increase excellence in our work is to imitate God in his "rest." In the creation narrative, we learn that God, after creating the universe, set aside a special day of rest (Gen. 2:2–3). Subsequently, God's people were to keep the Sabbath as a day on which they refrained from work (Ex. 20:8–11). The same principle is also operative in the Sabbath year and the year of Jubilee (Lev. 25:1–22). Later, it was made clear that the Israelites' entry into the Promised Land serves as a symbol of the rest God's people can look forward to enjoying one day in heaven (Heb. 3:7–4:13). Therefore, as the writer of Hebrews states, "So then, there remains a Sabbath rest for the people of God, for whoever has entered God's rest has also rested from his works as God did from his" (Heb. 4:9–10).

In the meantime, the psalmist calls God's people to "be still, and know that I am God" (Ps. 46:10). We are to rest in the peaceful assurance that we have a God who loves us and provides for us and who will never let us down. Even in our spiritual battles, we can know that the battle is won "not by might, nor by power, but by my Spirit" (Zech. 4:6). Make no mistake about it: we will still have to fight the battles; but as we do so, it will not be our strength (or lack thereof) that carries the day, but God's power working for us, in us, and through us. In our work, therefore, we should rest in God and rely on his power in us. As the apostle Paul wrote regarding his goal of presenting everyone mature in Christ, "For this I toil, struggling with all his energy that he powerfully works within me" (Col. 1:28–29).

In the midst of our busy lives, we need to learn to look to the Lord in faith and to wait for him to act on our behalf, accomplishing his good purposes in and through us. In other words, we must learn to value God's grace and live by it—relying on it each and every day. As scholars, likewise, we need to be still before God and await his direction. What are the topics he wants us to research? What is the contribution he wants us to make to the academy and to the church in light of the natural and spiritual gifts and abilities he has bestowed on us?

Scripture teaches that God cares intimately for every detail of our lives. Can we not also expect him to guide us in specific steps of research and in the writing process? Too often, we are overworked and frantically try to meet deadlines and juggle family and work responsibilities while leaving God out of the picture. We need to cultivate the discipline of rest, of regular time set aside for reflection, planning, and relaxation. In the long run, this will ensure that we will be at our most productive. I often find that after a week or two away from the office, I return invigorated, sharper, and more focused and alert.

This is true even more in the case of that most wonderful of all academic privileges—the sabbatical leave. Inevitably, we will get worn down if not burnt out after teaching Sunday school or preaching in the pulpit Sunday after Sunday. We give out week after week, only to find that we end up depleted and in desperate need of a tune-up. That's where a sabbatical can work wonders. Not only can we catch up on those pent-up writing projects, and perhaps engage in various other professional development activities, but we can also recharge our batteries by traveling to other places, spending extra time with family and friends, and engaging in stimulating conversations with colleagues or other scholarly peers.

Well-planned and profitably spent sabbaticals are truly in the best interest of the institution where we serve, of the students we teach, and of our own personal and professional pilgrimage. Blessed are those schools and faculty members—and churches and pastors!—who have a sabbatical policy. The principle, then, is this: rest in God's grace, look to him for guidance, and then do the work (in that order!). Don't put self-effort and striving ahead of listening to God. And balance hard work with regular rest and relaxation (which means don't forget to take a vacation once in a while, or take a day off on your son's or daughter's birthday or on your anniversary).[17]

In Pursuit of Excellence

In this spirit, therefore, let us pursue excellence. As we have seen, far from being optional, excellence is in fact a divine mandate that applies to every aspect of our lives, for God himself is characterized by excellence. Mediocrity, sloppy workmanship, and a half-hearted effort do not bring glory to God or advance his kingdom.[18] How do we move from mediocrity to excellence? How do we advance from "good" to "great"? This book represents an attempt to probe the nature of scholarly excellence and to suggest ways in which we can make progress in our quest to achieve it.

Yet this is not another self-help book! The message here is not simply to try harder, to put in more effort, and to make things happen through sheer force of will. Salvation is entirely by God's grace (Eph. 2:8–9), and sanctification is by grace as well (Eph. 2:10). This means that the pursuit of scholarly excellence must be undergirded by a keen sense of God's continual grace in the personal and professional spheres of our lives and that we should pursue scholarly excellence in an environment of grace, not in a spirit of self-effort or unhealthy competition.

In a remarkable and highly pertinent passage in his letter to the Philippians, the apostle Paul holds human striving and divine enablement in proper tension when he writes, "Work out your own salvation with fear and trembling, for it is God who works in you, both to will and to work for his good pleasure" (Phil. 2:12–13; cf. Phil. 1:6). *God is at work within us* to develop excellence for his own glory, and *at the same time we must also make every effort* to pursue the excellence to which God has called us.

In this regard, we will do well to appreciate the vital importance of mentoring. How will we be able to pursue scholarly excellence if we have not been taught how to do so and if we have not seen the pursuit of excellence consistently lived out in the lives of others? Paul and Timothy provide a well-known biblical example of this dynamic: "You, however, have followed my teaching, my conduct, my aim in life, my faith, my patience, my love, my steadfastness, my persecutions and sufferings that happened to me" (2 Tim. 3:10–11). Just as Paul called God's people to be imitators of God as his beloved children (Eph. 5:1), he also wrote, "Be imitators of me, as I am of Christ" (1 Cor. 11:1). The pattern of imitation is thus to proceed from God to Christ to the mentor and to the mentee.

Jesus, likewise, exhibited a similar dynamic in relationship to his Father: "Truly, truly, I say to you, the Son can do nothing of his own accord, but only what he sees the Father doing. For whatever the Father does, that the Son does likewise" (John 5:19).[19] At another occasion, Jesus observed that "everyone when he is fully trained will be like his teacher" (Luke 6:40). Jesus's calling and training of the Twelve constituted a central part of his earthly ministry.[20] This book cannot substitute for a flesh-and-blood mentor, but perhaps it can help you follow the calling of God in your life and inspire you to pursue greater excellence in your fulfillment of that call.

The Pursuit of Excellence

Being precedes doing.

As evangelicals, we have too often, in Franky Schaeffer's words, been "addicted to mediocrity," and this mediocrity has in many cases become a curse—a curse that has kept us from reaching our personal, creative, and academic potential given to us by God, and has prevented us from impacting other believers as well as unbelievers for the glory of God and for his kingdom.[1]

Called to Excellence

Now that we have explored the notion of God's own excellence and the way in which his divine excellence ought to inspire our efforts to pursue excellence in all that we do, we are ready to contemplate God's call to excellence in greater depth and detail. Peter's words in 2 Peter 1:3–11 provide the inspiration, model, and scriptural foundation for our exploration of scholarly excellence.[2] Several important points arise from this passage of Scripture.[3] First, Peter exhorts believers to develop excellence or virtue (*arête*, 2 Pet. 1:5) *because they have been called by (or to) God's own glory and excellence* (*arête*, 2 Pet. 1:3).[4] As we saw in the previous chapter, God is the reason and grounds for our pursuit of excellence. Second, believers must make every effort to add certain virtues to their faith (2 Pet. 1:5–7). In this sense, then, our faith is not enough. The Christian life does not stop at salvation; believers must supplement their faith with a variety of Christian virtues. What is more, in our pursuit of these virtues, we are exhorted and expected to be *deliberate* and *intentional*. Third, the command addressed to believers to add various virtues to their faith is *grounded in God's gracious promises* (2 Pet. 1:3–4) and is therefore not simply a command to strenuous moral self-effort or self-discipline. Fourth, the presence and increase of these virtues *will result in effective Christian service* (2 Pet. 1:8). Growth in godly virtues is not an end in itself, benefiting merely the virtuous individual; it makes that person a channel of blessing to others. Fifth, the *absence* of these virtues provides an *occasion for warning* (2 Pet. 1:9), while its *presence and increase* constitute *grounds for assurance of final salvation* (2 Pet. 1:10–11). Peter links growth in godly virtues with increased assurance of end-time salvation.

These points, drawn from a close reading of the text of 2 Peter 1:3–11, apply not merely to the apostle's first readers but to all Christians. On the basis of God's gracious and precious promises, Peter exhorts believers to make every effort to add to their faith the qualities that will produce effectiveness in their Christian ministry and result in assurance of final salvation. This volume, written as an aid particularly to young or aspiring scholars as well as to all believers who aspire to grow in Christian virtues, seeks to build on the model and foundation of Peter's words by applying the passage specifically to the vocation of a Christian scholar. What does excellence look like in the life of a Bible teacher or pastor-theologian? What virtues are vital to engender effectiveness and fruitfulness in the scholarly realm? This chapter will lay a foundation for the remainder of the book by elaborating in greater detail on each of the points drawn from 2 Peter 1:3–11 in the previous paragraph.

Believers' Pursuit of Excellence Is to Be Grounded in God's Own Glory and Excellence (2 Peter 1:3, 5)

As Daniel Harrington and James Keenan contend, "From an ethical viewpoint, the end is the quintessential point of departure, since strong ethical systems always start with the end. The goal always defines the agenda being pursued. The agenda, from start to finish, is shaped by the end."[5] Machiavelli's classic masterpiece *The Prince* clearly illustrates how the end goal determines an ethical system. If the goal is power, then characteristics that are conventionally viewed in negative terms turn into virtues: whatever is necessary to gain and maintain power is not only expedient but in fact virtuous.

By contrast, the starting point for Christians, as well as the end goal, is God's own glory and excellence (2 Pet. 1:3), as believers seek to be effective and fruitful participants in what God is doing in the world today (2 Pet. 1:4, 8).[6] On the basis of God's call extended to believers to (or by) his own glory and excellence (2 Pet. 1:3), they should respond by adding to their faith a variety of virtues, starting with excellence (2 Pet. 1:5). This casting of God's character as the starting point and the end goal, setting the agenda for what Christians should pursue, pervades all of Scripture. In his first letter, Peter declares, building on Leviticus 11:44, "You shall be holy, for I am holy" (1 Pet. 1:16). Both Paul and Peter exhort believers to imitate Christ (1 Cor. 11:1; Eph. 5:1; 1 Pet. 2:21), and Paul affirms that those whom God "foreknew he also predestined to be conformed to the image of his Son" (Rom. 8:29). The end goal of believers' lives is not power, influence, money, security, or possessions, but becoming once again like their Creator and Savior, in whose image they were originally made. This is the basis on which Peter exhorts believers to "make every effort to supplement your faith" with various virtues (2 Pet. 1:5).

The Greek word *aretē*, translated "excellence" by the ESV in 2 Peter 1:3 but "virtue" in 1:5, has a considerable semantic range, which makes it often difficult to determine the precise meaning of the term in a given context.[7] A basic core component of *aretē* is that of eminence or excellence. With regard to human attributes, *aretē* could convey the notion of valor. In the context of Greek moral philosophy, *aretē* often referred generally to moral virtue. In conjunction with Greek gods, *aretē* could denote power. In other contexts, *aretē* could also refer to fame and be equivalent to glory (cf. 1 Pet. 2:9).[8]

In the context of our study, it seems best to translate *aretē* as "excellence" in both 2 Peter 1:3 and 1:5, primarily for two reasons. First, choosing the same rendering in both instances maintains the lexical and logical connection between the uses of *aretē* in these two verses. It is precisely *because* Christians have been called to or by God's glory and excellence that they are to add excellence to *their* faith. Second, understanding the word as designating a *particular* virtue, "excellence," rather than as encompassing *all* the virtues in the list, seems to make better sense of the location of *aretē* in the list of virtues in 2 Peter 1:5–7.[9]

If these insights are valid, then "excellence" is the first virtue in Peter's list. All of life is to be lived for the glory of God. Undergirded by moral excellence and godly character, all of our work should be performed with distinction and excellence. Mediocrity and sloppy workmanship never glorify God. Christians must strive for excellence—including, and especially, in pursuing their scholarly calling.

Believers Must Be Intentional about Adding Certain Virtues to Their Faith (2 Peter 1:5–7)

There has been a noted revival in discussions of virtue following Alasdair MacIntyre's publication of *After Virtue: A Study in Moral Theory* in 1981.[10] Since that time, many studies have focused on the role of the virtues in moral formation,[11] but to many American Christians, *virtue* remains a missing term in discussions of discipleship, sanctification, and ethics. In part, as Harrington and Keenan point out, this neglect may be due to the fact that in earlier discussions of the subject, "moral theology was shaped predominantly by a concern about the sins one should avoid, and not about the good to be pursued."[12] Virtue ethics, by contrast, focuses on the virtues an individual must develop to become the kind of person who will consistently, and characteristically, choose what is right and reject what is wrong.

Virtues are defined in various ways, but there is a consistent emphasis on the priority of *being* over *doing*. It does little good to emphasize what is right and wrong if people are not developing the inward character that will result in their choice of what is right. As Jay Wood observes:

> Virtues are dispositional properties, along with the concerns and capacities for judgment and action that constitute them. They are properties that we can possess even at times when we are not acting virtuously or overtly displaying them in some way. Rather, various circumstances we encounter trigger our acting out of the virtue.... So virtues are deeply embedded parts of character that readily dispose us to feel, to think and to act in morally appropriate ways as our changing circumstances require.[13]

The excellence to which God calls believers requires the development of Christian virtues. J. P. Moreland directly links ingrained virtue with excellence:

A virtue is a skill, a habit, an ingrained disposition to act, think, or feel in certain ways. Virtues are those good parts of one's character that make a person excellent at life in general. As with any skill (for example, learning to swing a golf club), a virtue becomes ingrained in my personality, and thus a part of my very nature, through repetition, practice, and training.[14]

In the end, of course, being and doing sustain a close relationship. A person's actions reveal his or her character, while character produces actions. Jesus affirms that it is out of the abundance of the heart that the mouth speaks (Matt. 12:34; Luke 6:45).[15] The argument made in the field of virtue ethics is that since character produces actions—and thus being precedes doing—the emphasis of moral formation must be placed on becoming the man or woman a person ought to be in order to achieve a particular goal. In other words, the goal typically defines one's entire ethical system. Harrington and Keenan aptly summarize this way of thinking:

> Virtues are characteristic ways of behaving that make both persons and actions good, and also enable persons to fulfill the purpose of their lives. Virtue ethics focus on the question, Who should we become? Indeed, virtue ethicists expand that basic question into three key, related questions: Who are we? Who ought we to become? and How do we get there?[16]

The above-discussed passage on Christian virtues in Peter's second epistle answers each of these questions. (1) *Who are we?* We are a people of faith who have been given all that we need for living a godly life and have been called to (or by) God's own glory and excellence. In this way, we may participate in what God is doing in the world (2 Pet. 1:1–4). (2) *Who ought we to become?* The persons we ought to become stand in direct continuity with who we already are (discussed above in terms of the end goal that determines the content of the entire system). The goal is progressive transformation into Christlikeness.[17] (3) *How do we get there?*[18] We achieve God's purpose for our lives by making every effort to add to our faith the virtues that will make us more and more completely the people God has called us to be.

Jay Wood registers several helpful observations regarding the development of virtue in answer to this third question, "How do we get there?"

> First, cultivating the virtues is a developmental process extending through a lifetime.... Second, growth in the virtues is not automatic.... Third, we

are not alone in our efforts to become morally and intellectually virtuous persons; our careers as moral and intellectual agents are developed in a community context.... Fourth, we must work to sustain our gains in the moral and intellectual life, since regression is a real possibility.[19]

Wood's emphasis on the importance of community for the formation of virtues would have strongly resonated in the early church, where community involvement was essential for every aspect of life. In our twenty-first-century context, on the other hand, true community is the exception rather than the rule. Because of the rampant individualism in our culture, far too few Christians today are genuinely involved with a Christian community at a level that significantly impacts their moral development.[20]

Wood adds a further point that fits well with Peter's exhortation that believers make every effort to supplement their faith with various virtues. As Wood makes clear, the development of virtue requires intentional, deliberate effort:

> By saying that virtues are voluntary and acquired traits I mean to underscore the fact that whether the virtues or the vices take deep root within a person depends in some measure on the person's deliberative will. No one becomes compassionate or patient or self-controlled accidently. You could not wake up one morning to the serendipitous discovery that you had overnight become habitually wise or prudent or discerning. Rather, we bear varying degrees of responsibility for our moral and intellectual traits insofar as our choices either thwart their development or contribute to it.[21]

The apostle Peter is determined to motivate his readers to action: to exert the moral effort that is both expected and required by their divine calling. In view of his impending death, he is resolved to remind them of their need for these virtues (2 Pet. 1:12–15). The response to God's calling envisioned by Peter is not docile passivity or a happy-go-lucky, laissez-faire attitude, but determined and intentional effort.

In his recent volume, *After You Believe: Why Christian Character Matters*, N. T. Wright draws on the insights of virtue ethics while forging his own path in dealing with the Christian pursuit of virtue. Wright contrasts rules with character and affirms the priority of the latter without denying completely the value of the former as overall guidelines. Defining "virtue" as character transformation and stating that "*virtue* is what happens when wise and courageous choices have become 'second nature,'"[22] Wright espouses his own form of virtue ethics when he posits three elements in the transformation of Christian character: (1) aim at the right goal; (2) figure out steps to get to that goal; and (3) those steps become habitual, or second nature.[23]

At the heart of Wright's ethical presentation is Jesus's proclamation of God's kingdom, especially in the Sermon on the Mount, in contrast to the Greek teaching on virtue epitomized by the fourth-century BC philosopher Aristotle. Wright points out that the pursuit of Christian character is not at heart a self-centered pursuit but proceeds within the larger overall context of the advancement of God's kingdom here on earth, in anticipation of the eternal state. Thus our pursuit of Christian virtues is to be understood within the framework of our worship of God and our stewardship for God.[24]

Wright's effort of grounding the pursuit of Christian virtue in the soil of biblical theology is commendable. He points out that as in the case of Old Testament Israel, Scripture urges believers not to go back to their former slavery and bondage; they must learn to live as God's free people and "take redemptive responsibility for the whole of creation."[25] The goal, according to Wright, is "eschatological authenticity."[26] We must be "people of the goal."[27] As such, we are called not only to be recipients but also agents of forgiveness and to confront and defeat the forces of evil.[28] In this regard, the kingdom and the cross belong together.[29] What is more, humans suffer from a fatal "sickness of heart"—sin—which cannot just be reformed but must effectively be killed. Wright's description of the remedy is worth quoting in full:

> Moreover, since one of the primary telltale signs of that corruption and decay was human pride, there could be no place for the kind of "virtue" which saw itself, in effect, as self-made. The greatest of the pagan moralists could only glimpse the reality of a truly human existence in which the goal of human life was realized step by step through training the heart and life into new habits. That reality shimmered like a mirage on the other side of a deep, fast-flowing river that pagan moralism could neither swim nor bridge. Jesus plunged into the river and, being well and truly drowned, was carried to the farther shore. And he told his disciples to follow him. The way to the kingdom is the way of the cross, and vice versa—as long as you remember that "the kingdom," once again, is not "heaven," but the state of affairs in which God's kingdom has come, and his will is being done, *on earth* as it is in heaven.[30]

What Christians are called to, according to Wright, is "kingdom-in-advance life."[31] While salvation is a work of grace, and virtues, too, must be undergirded by grace (1 Cor. 15:10), their acquisition is not automatic but requires moral effort. In this, Wright contends, the biblical teaching extends, enhances, and transforms Aristotle's ethic. Thus the "goal of human life, the *telos* which the New Testament holds out as the true reality of which Aristotle's *eudaimonia* was a pagan approximation, is given already in Jesus. He is the 'end,' the goal," and the individual's journey proceeds "within an end that has already begun, an eschatology that has already been inaugurated."[32]

The overall eschatological framework for the biblical vision of the pursuit of Christian virtue sketched by Wright is an important ingredient, and in many ways more satisfying than the at times unduly stilted presentation in certain versions of virtue ethics.[33] In any case, what is important for our purposes here is not the explication of a particular ethical system but the application of the biblical teaching on virtues to the vocation of Christian scholarship. In what follows, I will, therefore, take my point of departure from the apostle Peter's presentation on Christian virtue in 2 Peter 1:3–11 as I seek to discover the relevance of this foundational passage for those who aspire to greater excellence in pursuit of their academic calling.

The Command Addressed to Believers to Add Virtues to Their Faith Is Grounded in God's Grace and Promises (2 Peter 1:3–4)

The emphasis in 2 Peter 1:5 on the necessity of human effort to develop the various virtues described, along with the discussion above on the active role of the volitional effort of the human will, may make some of us uncomfortable. Where is God's grace? All this talk of developing virtues sounds like the Christian life is all about human effort and self-righteousness. If salvation is by faith alone, apart from any human works, how can the gospel of "by grace alone, through faith alone" be squared with this emphasis on developing Christian virtues other than in terms of human works?

I cannot address these issues in depth here, but I will register several observations from our passage in 2 Peter.[34] First and foremost, *God's gracious initiative precedes any human response* (2 Pet. 1:1, 3). Second, God's gracious saving initiative *enables and produces the human response*. It is *God's power* that has given believers all they need for living a godly life (2 Pet. 1:3). Third, God has also given us his precious and very great promises so that *"through them"* we may progress in virtue (2 Pet. 1:4). As Ruth Anne Reese astutely observes, "Before there is any challenge to act, there is the reminder at the very beginning of the book (1:3) that by the divine power of Jesus Christ believers have already been supplied with everything that is needed for life and godliness."[35]

How has God's divine power "granted to us all things that pertain to life and godliness" (2 Pet. 1:3)? We have been given all things that pertain to life and godliness "through the knowledge of him who called us to [or by] his own glory and excellence," that is, God in and through Jesus Christ (2 Pet. 1:3; cf. 1:2). Let that sink in for a moment. It is not by reading self-help books, or by meditating on quotes of famous people—whether Confucius, or Buddha, or Mahatma Gandhi—that we are equipped for achieving excellence. God has supplied us with all that we need to attain excellence *through our knowledge of God in our Lord and Savior Jesus Christ*. It is *God in Jesus Christ* who called us by (or to) his own glory and excellence. Thus, not only is God characterized by excellence, but so is Jesus Christ. Our pursuit of excellence must, therefore, not only be theologically oriented and fueled by some vague belief in God; it must be christological in nature, that is, grounded in Christian discipleship, in active, committed followership of the Lord Jesus Christ in every aspect of our lives in this world.

The effort Peter exhorts his readers to exert is thus far removed from the notion of pulling oneself up by one's own bootstraps. Peter does not present human effort as something a person can put forth apart from his or her prior acceptance by, experience of, and dependence on God's gracious gifts and promises. Believers do not apply effort to add various virtues to their faith *in order to earn* God's grace, forgiveness, or salvation, but rather *in response to* the grace, forgiveness, and salvation *already received*. The presence of saving faith is assumed (2 Pet. 1:1) and constitutes the foundation on which believers are told to add a series of virtues (2 Pet. 1:5). If the presence and growth of these virtues does not produce salvation, what does it do, and why is it needed? After listing the various virtues, Peter discusses their significance.

The Presence and Increase of These Virtues Results in Effective Christian Ministry (2 Peter 1:8)

In verse 8 of our present passage, Peter claims that the presence and increase of these virtues in a believer's life will keep him or her "from being ineffective or unfruitful in the knowledge of our Lord Jesus Christ." *Growth in virtue toward excellence results in effectiveness in our knowledge of Jesus Christ.* At this point, the Christian concept of vocation is relevant.[36] The Christian philosopher J. P. Moreland draws some necessary distinctions between a Christian's "job" and his or her "vocation":

> Further, as a disciple of Jesus, I do not have a job, I have a vocation; and if I go to college, I go to find and become excellent in my vocation, not simply to find a job. A job is a means for supporting myself and those for whom I am responsible. For the Christian, a vocation (from the Latin *vocare*, "to call") is an overall calling from God.[37]

Every Christian, regardless of his or her particular job or career, should view that assignment as a special calling from God, a vocation. In that vocation, whether or not it is the job they would most like to have, believers are to pursue excellence in order to fulfill their calling effectively and to bring glory to God. Every duty we have as Christians must be discharged with all our strength, because ultimately we are serving God, not other people (Eph. 6:5–8; Col. 3:23).[38]

If every job or duty with which we are charged as Christians involves a specific call by God, that is, it constitutes a vocation, we must strive for effectiveness and fruitfulness. A genuine Christian will want to please his or her Master and be a servant who effectively discharges every duty in a way that pleases the one to whom he or she must give an account (Matt. 25:21, 23; Luke 19:17). Peter argues that the presence and increase of virtues in a believer's life will accomplish the precious results of effectiveness and fruitfulness.

The Absence of These Virtues Is Grounds for Warning, While Their Presence and Increase Is Grounds for Assurance of Final Salvation (2 Peter 1:9–11)

Peter proceeds to provide further motivation for believers to "make every effort" to add to their faith both excellence and various other virtues. First, he warns that the lack of these virtues will issue in blindness and forgetfulness of salvation. Second, Peter tells his readers that the presence and increase of these virtues, in addition to producing effectiveness, will engender assurance of salvation: they will never fall (2 Pet. 1:10) and in due course will receive entrance into Christ's eternal kingdom (2 Pet. 1:11).

This assurance comes with an exhortation mirroring the earlier injunction found in 2 Peter 1:5: "Therefore, brothers, *be all the more diligent* to make your calling and election sure" (2 Pet. 1:10). Peter's emphasis on the importance of growing in the various Christian virtues he has listed makes it clear that *growth is not optional*. Believers must make every effort to supplement their faith with the development of Christian virtue and growth in Christian character. This will be reflected by a pursuit of excellence resulting in effectiveness in whatever vocation God has called a particular believer. While no one can lay any foundation other than the one already laid, Jesus Christ (1 Cor. 3:11), we must be diligent to build on this foundation by actively pursuing Christian virtues and by growing in Christian character.

The importance of a leader's character, in particular, is stressed throughout the Pastoral Epistles, especially in the lists of qualifications for leadership. Elders and deacons ought to live out their Christian faith, exhibiting the development of godly character (1 Tim. 3:2, 8). Because of this, we should take care not to appoint recent converts (1 Tim. 3:6). Progress in godly character does not happen overnight. James, for his part, warns teachers that they "will be judged with greater strictness" (James 3:1). Those who have been called by God to serve as Bible teachers or pastor-scholars must not neglect their character but devote sustained attention to the development of godly virtues. Paul's words to Timothy come to mind: "Keep a close watch on yourself and on the teaching. Persist in this, for by so doing you will save [i.e., help preserve] both yourself and your hearers" (1 Tim. 4:16).

Conclusion

On the basis of God's grace and excellence, Peter exhorts believers to add various godly virtues to their faith. The presence and increase of these godly virtues, in turn, will result in effectiveness in ministry. Not everyone is called by God to the particular vocation of academic work and Christian scholarship, but a few believers are called by God to serve in this way. As mentioned, a sense of calling ought to undergird a Christian's specific activities, priorities, and pursuits.

Calling, for its part, is not necessarily, or even primarily, a mystical experience but rather a function of creation and gifting, both natural and supernatural. It is my hope and prayer that those who have been called to the particular vocation of Christian scholarship will find in this book helpful guidelines for becoming the kind of person who can effectively pursue scholarly excellence for the glory of God.

The central goal of this book is to identify, describe, and encourage those virtues that are essential to fulfilling a specific call to glorify God by pursuing excellence in Christian scholarship.[39] The virtues listed in 2 Peter are foundational in this regard, but other vital virtues are highlighted throughout Scripture or called for by the particular demands of the academic world. In all of our efforts, the glory of God should be our ultimate goal.

3

Holiness

Become what you are.

The notion of excellence which I have been exploring in the past couple of chapters is closely related to the biblical concept of holiness. In the first chapter, I characterized excellence as "the quality of standing out or towering above the rest, being eminent or superior, and distinguishing oneself in some extraordinary or special way." Similarly, holiness, as will be seen below, is best understood in terms of uniqueness, otherness, and being set apart. Both holiness and excellence serve as all-encompassing divine attributes that can appropriately be applied to all the other attributes. God is completely holy, set apart from all else.

"Be Holy, for I Am Holy"

Because God Is Holy, We Must Be Holy

Throughout the Bible, Christians are exhorted to be holy. Peter explicitly grounds his command to his readers, to be holy in all their conduct, in God's recurring command to the Israelites in Leviticus, "Be holy, for I am holy" (1 Pet. 1:15–16; cf. Lev. 11:44–45; 19:2; 20:7, 26). God's own holiness is the basis for all biblical teaching concerning holiness and sanctification. Because of God's utter and complete holiness, only those who share his holiness can live in relationship with him and have a part in promoting his kingdom in the world.

The Old Testament Scriptures repeatedly declare God's holiness: "The fundamental truth about the character of God in the Bible is that he is holy."[1] The affirmation that God is holy indicates that he is unique and set apart from all others.[2] God is wholly and completely other (Hos. 11:9). Regarding the implications of this complete separation from the world, David Peterson rightly notes that "an important dimension to God's separateness and distinctness is his *moral purity and perfection*."[3] God is in a league of his own. His complete otherness means that he is untouched and unstained by evil and thus morally pure and perfect (James 1:13).

The repeated refrain throughout Leviticus, "Be holy because I am holy," provides the rationale for the whole Levitical code. The completely set-apart and holy God took the initiative to enter into a special covenant relationship with a chosen group of people. In order for God to dwell with the Israelites, they must share his holiness and be set apart from the world and cultures around them—set apart for God. The entire Levitical code provided the instructions necessary for the people to live in such a set-apart manner that a holy God could dwell in their midst: "You shall be holy to me, for I the LORD am holy and have separated you from the peoples, that you should be mine" (Lev. 20:26). Holiness involved being separated from the other nations, the surrounding world, and belonging exclusively to God.

The Levitical code, therefore, far from involving legalism, is predicated upon grace. God took the initiative to set the Israelites apart for himself as a people by choosing them and delivering them from their bondage in Egypt. They, in turn, must be holy, because the God who saved them and dwelt in their midst is holy. They had already been set apart by God by his decisive salvific intervention in the past; now they must continue to live in a separated manner, pursuing a lifestyle of holiness.

> When they came to Sinai, Moses was told to consecrate them ritually, to prepare for a unique encounter with God (Ex. 19:14). They were already a holy nation because God had drawn them to himself, but now they would discover the awesome implications of being in a special relationship with him. Even the priests were required to "consecrate themselves," lest he "break out against them" (19:22). The point of these instructions was

to teach Israel about God's overpowering holiness. Even a "holy people" could only approach him and relate to him on the terms that he laid down. A system of mediation was necessary to prevent the Israelites from being destroyed by God's holiness (19:22, 24).[4]

The New Testament builds on the Old Testament precedent of the Israelites being set apart by God and making their way into the Promised Land. In his first epistle, Peter presents Christians as strangers and resident aliens here on earth while they embark on their pilgrimage and journey to their heavenly homeland (1 Pet. 1:1, 17).[5] As Moses Chin observes, "It seems that the church, like Israel, could not shed off its . . . identity—as a people on the move, as sojourners in a pilgrimage from their earthly abode to their heavenly home."[6] Peter stresses the fact that because God is holy, we, as God's people—pilgrims, strangers, and resident aliens in this world—must be holy as well (1 Pet. 1:14–16). An unholy Christian is a contradiction in terms.

Paul, similar to Peter, builds on God's command to his people in Leviticus, "Be holy, for I am holy." In 1 Thessalonians, Paul writes, "For this is the will of God, your sanctification: that you abstain from sexual immorality. . . . For God has not called us for impurity, but in holiness. Therefore whoever disregards this, disregards not man but God, who gives his Holy Spirit to you" (4:3, 7–8). In this passage, Paul links sanctification and holiness with sexual purity and singles out these traits explicitly as "the will of God." This connection of holiness with sexual purity is an extension of the root meaning of "set apart" into the moral sphere. Someone set apart from the activities and practices of this fallen world ethically and morally will be sexually pure.

Dealing with Sexual Temptation

Failure in the area of sexual purity has led to the downfall and ineffectiveness and loss of ministry of many Christian leaders over the centuries.[7] The failure of Christian leaders to be holy in this area has done untold harm to the kingdom of God, both in causing confusion and doubt among their followers and in bringing dishonor to God among the unbelieving world.[8] Christian leaders and men of God are particularly vulnerable to sexual temptation and must guard against succumbing to it. For women, temptations may perhaps be more subtle in this regard, but women, too, must guard their heart and strive for utter fidelity to their spouse and family as they pursue their academic calling. In the following chapter, I will discuss the importance of spirituality more fully, including the vital significance of maintaining and growing in a vibrant relationship with God. Later in the book, I will also address the importance of developing the virtue of restraint. At this point, I will limit myself to a few initial remarks on overcoming sexual temptation.[9]

First, confession and accountability to other godly individuals is essential. In our individualistic Western culture, we idolize heroes who singlehandedly save the day, epitomized by the title of the old Western television show *The Lone Ranger*. In real life, what happens to lone rangers? They die. Any soldier out on the battlefield alone will not survive to tell about his exploits. We desperately need genuine community with other believers at a sufficiently deep level where we can help and support one another and bear one another's burdens.[10] James 5:16 commands, "Therefore, confess your sins to one another and pray for one another, that you may be healed. The prayer of a righteous person has great power as it is working." We are all sinners and need to come to God in united, humble prayer and in the recognition that we need one another's support in our struggle against sin. I have one friend, a seasoned veteran in the faith, who prays for me every day, and we are both committed to encouraging each other in the challenges and opportunities we each face. This is a friendship I greatly cherish, and one that I desperately need to stay the course in my Christian pilgrimage.

Second, it is not enough to flee from sexual temptation; the man or woman of God must also pursue a series of godly virtues: "So flee youthful passions *and pursue* righteousness, faith, love, and peace, along with those who call on the Lord from a pure heart" (2 Tim. 2:22). Trying to overcome sexual temptation by renouncing it, avoiding it, and rejecting it is not enough; we must pursue righteousness, faith, love, and peace in genuine community with other Christians. It is not enough simply to renounce worldly vices; we must actively pursue godly virtues.

Third, as I cautioned elsewhere, "*do not overestimate your ability to resist temptation nor underestimate the power of the temptation and the Tempter himself.*"[11] The second half of the first verse of Martin Luther's famous hymn "A Mighty Fortress Is Our God" rightly puts our own strength (or lack thereof) into proper perspective:

> For still our ancient foe
> Doth seek to work us woe;
> His craft and power are great,

> And armed with cruel hate,
> On earth is not his equal.

The second stanza of the same hymn continues the theme of our weakness but proceeds to introduce the great game-changer, the one who is our great hope and strength:

> Did we in our own strength confide,
> Our striving would be losing,
> Were not the right man on our side,
> The man of God's own choosing.
>
> Dost ask who that may be?
> Christ Jesus, it is he;
> Lord Sabaoth, his name,
> From age to age the same,
> And he must win the battle.

Our victory is sure and certain in Jesus Christ, but in our pursuit of holiness, we must not overestimate our ability to withstand temptation or underestimate the power of sin and of our enemy in the process.

So important did Luther regard this area in the life of a theologian that he discussed it under a separate rubric, *tentatio* (German *Anfechtung*). Invoking the example of King David, Luther writes, "For as soon as God's word takes root and grows in you, the devil will harry you, and will make a real doctor of you, and by his assaults will teach you to seek and love God's word."[12] As a result, Luther urges the continual study of Scripture (*meditatio*). Then, according to Luther, "You will not only despise the books written by adversaries, but the longer you write and teach the less you will be pleased with yourself. When you have reached this point, then do not be afraid to hope that you have begun to become a real theologian, who can teach not only the young and imperfect Christians, but also the maturing and perfect ones."[13] In this way, the Devil drives us to Scripture, which teaches us humility. I will have more to say about this in a later chapter.

Holiness: Being and Becoming

We have seen that believers are called to be holy and that this call, in turn, is rooted in the character of God. But how does this work in practice? How do we become holy? It may come as a surprise to some, but *we already are*! Believers are regularly called "saints" (though not in the Roman Catholic sense of canonized individuals characterized by unusual piety) or "holy ones" throughout the New Testament. Paul even calls the Corinthians—who were hardly the epitome of godly virtue in their dealings with one another—"those sanctified in Christ Jesus" (1 Cor. 1:2).

How could Paul call "holy" one of the most troubled, unholy churches featured in the entire New Testament? He can do so because, at conversion, through union with Christ, these believers were genuinely set apart and made holy: "And *because of him you are in Christ Jesus*, who became to us wisdom from God, righteousness and sanctification and redemption" (1 Cor. 1:30). You might call this phenomenon "*definitive* sanctification." On the basis of this accomplished fact of a believer's sanctification at the moment of his or her conversion, Paul proceeds to spend the rest of the letter exhorting these same believers to holiness, urging them to *become what they already are*—holy ones or saints. This process of becoming holy, you may call "*progressive* sanctification." The just-described interplay between definitive and progressive sanctification is not only a New Testament concept; it is firmly grounded in Old Testament teaching as well.

As mentioned above, God's people at Sinai were *already* holy by virtue of their special relationship with him. At the same time, they must still pursue holiness, live set-apart lives, and adopt a holy lifestyle, because the God with whom they have entered into a relationship is holy. There is thus both a *definitive* and a *progressive* aspect to the sanctification of God's people in both Testaments. In the Old Testament, the *definitive* aspect of sanctification involved God's election of a people, deliverance of that people from bondage in Egypt, and giving of the law to that group of people at Sinai. The *progressive* aspect of sanctification involved the same people living in holiness in response to God's saving and sanctifying initiative. The failure of the people to be holy as God was holy eventually led to judgment in exile. In the New Testament, the *definitive* aspect of sanctification involves God's election of a people and deliverance of that set of individuals from sin through the sacrificial death and resurrection of Jesus. The *progressive* aspect of sanctification involves these set-apart people living and growing in holiness in response to God's saving and sanctifying activity.

The interplay between the definitive and the progressive aspects of sanctification is particularly evident in the letter to the Hebrews. In Hebrews 10:10, the author articulates the *definitive* aspect when he writes, "And by that will we have been sanctified through the offering of the body of Jesus Christ once for all" (cf. Heb. 10:14, 29). The blood of Jesus from his once-for-all sacrifice sanctifies believers and provides them with access to God so that they can now draw near to him with confidence (Heb. 10:19–20). This definitive aspect of sanctification makes believers God's children, whom God proceeds to discipline for their good, "that we may share his holiness" (Heb. 12:10). This holiness is the result of a process of discipline and represents the *progressive* aspect of sanctification. The author of Hebrews proceeds to exhort his readers to "strive for peace with everyone, and for the holiness without which no one will see the Lord" (Heb. 12:14). This holiness for which believers must strive makes up the progressive aspect of sanctification.

Believers, as God's set-apart people, find themselves in a somewhat paradoxical situation where they are *at the same time holy and yet still must strive for holiness*. We must *become* what, on the basis of Christ's sacrifice and union with him, we already *are*. Holiness is both an event—an act of God—and a process. What is more, this growth in holiness, on the basis of already having been declared holy and set apart, is not optional but required of every believer, because without holiness "no one will see the Lord" (Heb. 12:14).[14]

Holiness and Scholarly Excellence

So far in this chapter, I have attempted to lay a biblical foundation for discussing our need to pursue holiness. This biblical foundation consists in the understanding that our call to pursue holiness is ultimately grounded in the character of God—specifically, his holiness—in which we are made to share by virtue of our salvation in Christ. As believers, we already possess positional, definitive holiness on the basis of his once-for-all sacrifice and our union with Christ. Because God is holy, we must become what we are. The legitimate question arises: What does all this have to do with excellence as a Christian scholar? What does it look like for me, as a Christian scholar, to be completely set apart for God? How does my holiness, my separation from the world for God, translate into my life as a scholar? Several points deserve reflection.

Believing Scholarship—an Oxymoron?

It would seem self-evident that for those who have been made holy and have been set apart by God and for God, faith and the pursuit of scholarly excellence are of necessity inseparable. Some, however, argue that faith has no place in scholarship (defined as advancing knowledge in a given field). A recent debate between members of the Society of Biblical Literature has called the very legitimacy of faith-based, confessional scholarship into question. Michael Fox, a former president of this organization, has been particularly outspoken in this regard.[15] His argument can be summarized as follows: (1) The presuppositions and premises of genuine scholarship must not be inviolable and must be open to change in light of publicly accessible evidence. (2) The presuppositions and premises of faith-based study are inviolable and are based on faith, not publicly accessible and meaningful evidence. (3) Therefore, faith-based study, by definition, cannot be genuine scholarship.

Space precludes a lengthy rebuttal, but, as R. Albert Mohler Jr. has ably pointed out, nothing could be farther from the truth.[16] For true believers, there are not two realms, one of scholarship and one of faith, but rather there is only one sphere of operation: the totality of life lived as a holy, set-apart believer. Christian scholars are individuals who have been made holy and set apart for God. It is hard to conceive of a scholar who has been set apart for God and who strives to be holy as God is holy and yet approaches his or her academic work as if this status of being set apart for God has no necessary impact on his or her work. The exact opposite is true. The faith and Christian calling of committed Christian scholars must have a determinative influence on their work. Contrary to the claims of Fox and others, however, scholarly work undergirded by faith has the potential of producing better, rather than inferior, scholarship (though, of course, this is not necessarily the case). Who will be more motivated to pursue the truth relentlessly wherever the evidence leads: the scholar who is not even sure that truth exists or matters, or the one who is convinced that God is truth and has created truth and who has been called by that faithful God to a vocation of pursuing his truth?[17]

In any case, since we all are guided in our scholarly work by a set of presuppositions (even people like Fox, whether he is aware of this or not!), the issue is scholarly competence and virtuous practice, not the superiority of unbelieving or value-neutral over believing scholarship. Believing scholarship does not have a monopoly on bad scholarship, Professor Fox—I've seen my share of poorly executed critical scholarship over the years! True, I've also seen shoddy believing scholarship, and for that very reason have written this volume to urge believers to greater excellence in their academic work.

The pursuit of holiness on the part of the Christian scholar, I contend, of necessity ought to result in a pursuit of excellence. As Christians who have been set apart for God's use and called to the vocation of scholarship, we do not engage in our research as disinterested, detached observers but as individuals who have been separated from the world and made holy by a holy God. We passionately pursue the truth wherever it leads because we know that God is truth. Our interest in scholarship lies not simply in exploring a topic academically. It is fueled by a quest for God's truth for the sake of arriving at important insights, clearing up prevailing misconceptions, or both.

For this reason we need not be embarrassed by our faith, nor should our faith commitments be considered a necessary obstacle to our academic work. Instead, our faith should motivate us to pursue academic excellence, attaining to the highest scholarly standards on the basis of publicly accessible evidence. Our status as those who have been set apart by God and our pursuit of excellence in the investigation of truth should result in a level of scholarship that nonconfessional scholars, if they are at all fair-minded, will readily recognize and acknowledge as excellent, even though they do not share some or any of our faith commitments.

Reliance on the Guidance of the Holy Spirit[18]

Second, as Christian scholars who have been set apart by God and who pursue holiness, we should go about our scholarship, research, writing, and teaching in conscious dependence on God and expect the Holy Spirit to guide us in this process. We should not surmise that God is merely tolerating our academic work so that we have to engage in it "behind his back," as it were. Rather, we should have every expectation that God wants to, and will be, actively involved in our research, even delighting in it, and guiding us every step of the way. As we look to him in faith, as his dear children whom he set apart for this very purpose, he will lead us into excellence for the sake of his glory and as a testimony to his grace.

Luke, the third evangelist, stands as a biblical example of a man who devoted himself to extensive, God-glorifying research (Luke 1:1–4). God, for his part, divinely inspired and greatly used the results of Luke's diligent work, in the form of Luke's Gospel and the book of Acts, to promote the Christian gospel and to undergird the mission of the early church. While we cannot legitimately claim inspiration for our work in the way in which the biblical authors were inspired, and while our research will never be infallible or beyond critique, we can legitimately expect the Holy Spirit to direct our scholarly pursuits as we look to him in prayerful dependence.

A genuine attitude of humility will be the inevitable result of such prayerful dependence on the Holy Spirit.[19] Awareness of our desperate and complete need for God to be at work in our lives to guide and direct us and to produce fruit in us is the only true protection we have against arrogance and pride. As Jesus said so well, "I am the vine; you are the branches. Whoever abides in me and I in him, he it is that bears much fruit, *for apart from me you can do nothing*" (John 15:5).

Christian leaders and scholars are particularly vulnerable to the danger of self-reliance. We have spent longer hours poring over God's Word than the average Christian and have published articles and monographs to convey the fruit of our learning to others. While we can be satisfied with a job well done, we should always remember that it is God who enabled us to accomplish our work in the first place and guard against a prideful, arrogant disposition.

As scholars who have been set apart by God for his use, we know that our success is dependent on the indwelling Holy Spirit, who made us holy and who saved us out of this world to serve and glorify him. As we consciously and consistently look to God in prayerful dependence, he will receive the glory, and we will not forget that we are only servants, rendering nothing but our duty toward our Master to whom we must one day give an account (Luke 17:10). This also means that the true measure of our success is not human acclaim but faithfulness to God's calling in our lives.

Balance, Not Neglect: Living Our Lives Holistically

Third, as we pursue our calling as those who are holy and have been set apart by God for him, it is only natural that scholarship will be an integral part of the *entirety* of our lives while at the same time never *becoming* our life. This calls for proper balance with regard to our responsibilities pertaining to family, ministry, and the academic arena. If our scholarship ever becomes so all-encompassing that our families fall apart, or if we have no time to be involved in the local church, we will have failed to maintain proper balance.[20] Because of our pursuit of holiness, there should be a strategic concern not to neglect our personal responsibilities in all the various areas of our lives.

When I was a student, I once noticed that one of my fellow students tended to spend long hours around campus talking with other students, whether over the lunch hour or at other times. I assumed that he was able to do so because he had a very supportive spouse. I also was perhaps just a bit envious because it seemed that he didn't have to study very hard. Maybe he was a lot smarter than my fellow students and I! Little did I know that, as I happened to find out years later, that student's spouse abandoned the marriage. The student went on to earn a PhD degree and published a fair amount of scholarly work—but at what price! No PhD degree is worth ruining a marriage or breaking up a family.

Christian Scholarship as Part of Our Calling to Bear Witness to the Unbelieving World

Fourth, as holy, set-apart Christian scholars, we will be actively involved in bearing witness to the unbelieving world, or even to fellow believers who have gone astray in a particular area of truth. Being set apart for God is not a call to isolation but rather a means to be sent back into the world in order to engage the world with God's message.[21] We should not conceive of our scholarly work exclusively as a means of adding to our own learning or that of others, but also as a means of engaging the unbelieving world with the truth of God's gospel.

This can take several forms. It may involve addressing misconceptions regarding the Christian faith, as Luke and the early apologists did. It may entail articulating the teaching of Scripture with sound, historical methodology in a way that will demand the attention of unbelievers. However this engagement may manifest itself in a given situation, holiness demands that we live our lives and pursue our scholarship in a way that brings glory to God and bears witness to his truth. As I wrote elsewhere, commenting on 1 Peter 1:15–16, "Significantly, this exhortation to holiness, rather than being focused on believers' relationship with God or with one another, is directed towards their responsibility to reflect God's character in the midst of an unbelieving world."[22]

Holiness is inextricably bound up with the mission of God. The Gospel of John, in particular, demonstrates how Jesus, sent by God on his mission, commissioned and called his followers to be a part of and share in his mission to the world (see, e.g., John 17:18; 20:21).[23] Living life as a Christian scholar engaged in witness means, among other things, that we will be involved in scholarly societies outside our immediate evangelical borders and that we will seek to find avenues to disseminate our work more broadly, whether through blogging, television appearances or radio interviews (though not everyone will have this opportunity), or a variety of other means.

Conclusion

As Christian scholars, we are set apart for God and holy, yet we must continually pursue holiness. This pursuit of holiness in the world of scholarship can be conceived as *excellence in pursuit of truth on mission for God in the world*. Being set apart as a scholar entails, among other things, a rejection of the false modernist dichotomy between faith and scholarship, as well as resistance toward the academic and social pressures of pluralism in a culture that celebrates diversity and eschews all notions of absolute, compelling truth.[24]

This countercultural intellectual and spiritual stance will enable us to engage in a wholehearted pursuit of truth as we depend on the guidance and empowerment of the Holy Spirit. In conjunction with this, we should strive to cultivate a balanced life that does not turn our scholarship into an idol, develop an awareness that our primary work is missional, and engage in sustained, committed spiritual warfare as faithful witnesses to the truth. Before turning to a discussion of specific Christian virtues, one more foundational topic remains: spirituality.

4

Spirituality

Christian spirituality is grounded in the work of the Holy Spirit.

How is spirituality a necessary component of moral, personal, and academic excellence? Before exploring the relationship between spirituality and excellence, we must first define spirituality.

Spirituality: What Is It?

Terminological Confusion and the Widespread Search for Spirituality
Spirituality is a word with almost as many definitions as there are people using it. D. A. Carson observes that "spirituality is a person-variable synthetic theological construct."[1] By that he means that "one must always inquire as to what components enter into the particular construct advocated or assumed by a particular writer and what components are being left out."[2] Just as it is often difficult to know what a politician means strictly on the basis of the words he or she uses in a given speech, readers of literature on spirituality are often less than certain as to what a particular writer means by the term. One of the reasons for this, according

to Carson, is that "readers are constantly trying to infer what theological underpinnings are presupposed."[3]

Some of this confusion is caused because *spirituality* is a buzzword that is popular both in Christian circles and in the larger general culture. Many people who reject Christianity are dabbling in some form of Eastern spirituality, whether Buddhism, Hinduism, or the New Age movement. One of the reasons why people are interested in spirituality even if they reject Christianity is that their mere attachment to the material world rarely satisfies. Augustine famously stated near the beginning of his *Confessions*, "You stir man to take pleasure in praising you, because you have made us for yourself, and our heart is restless until it rests in you."[4] Even fallen sinners, as people made in God's image, sense the need to reconnect with God in some way. In most world religions, this is done through various forms of self-effort, such as meditation, yoga, or other spiritual exercises. This proliferation of interest in spirituality makes it "exceedingly difficult to exclude anything—absolutely anything—from the purview of spirituality, provided that there is some sort of experiential component in the mix."[5]

Pointing the way forward, Carson helpfully lists the following necessary component parts of a distinctively Christian spirituality:

> 1) Spirituality must be thought of in connection with the Gospel. . . . (2) Christian reflection on spirituality must work outward from the center [spirituality must not become an end in itself]. . . . (3) At the same time we should be rightly suspicious of forms of theology that place all the emphasis on coherent systems of thought that demand faith, allegiance and obedience but do not engage the affections, let alone foster an active sense of the presence of God. . . . (4) Nevertheless, what God uses to foster this kind of Gospel spirituality must be carefully delineated [Carson emphasizes the spirituality of the Word]. (5) Finally, such Word-centered reflection will bring us back to the fact that spirituality, as we have seen, is a theological construct.[6]

My own discussion of spirituality in this chapter will build on these points. No discussion of Christian or biblical spirituality can legitimately be divorced from the gospel of salvation in Christ alone and the coming of God's kingdom in his person and work. The Christian gospel of salvation in Jesus Christ is far closer to the center of biblical theology than the notion of spirituality. In addition, Carson's recognition that spirituality is a "theological construct" helps us think about this concept from a biblical-theological perspective. Our understanding of spirituality must be based on careful study of the relevant biblical material, from which we can attempt to construct a Christian understanding of spirituality.

Components of Biblical Spirituality

There are at least two foundational components in arriving at a biblical understanding of spirituality. The first such aspect is *union with and abiding in Christ*. The second element is *the presence and activity of the Holy Spirit*. John discusses "spirituality" primarily in terms of "abiding" in Christ, while Paul often speaks of being "in" Christ—united to him in his death and resurrection. The Holy Spirit is presented in John, Paul, and much of the New Testament as the person of the Godhead who indwells, empowers, and works in and through believers.[7]

As mentioned, John presents abiding in Christ as the heart of genuine spirituality.[8] At the beginning of John's Gospel, "abiding" points to the way in which Jesus's first followers spent time with him (John 1:38–39), but the idea of abiding in Jesus is spiritualized as early as John 6:56 where Jesus says, "Whoever feeds on my flesh and drinks my blood abides in me, and I in him." John 8:31 presents true discipleship as continually holding to, that is, abiding in, Jesus's teaching: "If you abide in my word, you are truly my disciples." Chapters 14–15 provide a significant concentration of the spiritual uses of "abiding" language in John:

> Abide in me, and I in you. As the branch cannot bear fruit by itself, unless it abides in the vine, neither can you, unless you abide in me. I am the vine; you are the branches. Whoever abides in me and I in him, he it is that bears much fruit, for apart from me you can do nothing. If anyone does not abide in me he is thrown away like a branch and withers; and the branches are gathered, thrown into the fire, and burned. If you abide in me, and my words abide in you, ask whatever you wish, and it will be done for you. (John 15:4–7)

Abiding in Christ is presented as *the* necessary condition for fruitfulness (effectiveness) and answered prayer. The bearing of fruit through abiding in Jesus demonstrates genuine Christianity and brings glory to God (John 15:8). The disciples must also abide in Jesus's love by obeying his commandments (John 15:9–10; 1 John 3:24), the primary commandments being to believe in him and to love others (John 13:34–35; 15:12–13; 1 John 3:23). Not only are believers exhorted to abide in Christ, but also all three persons of the Godhead indwell and abide in believers to comfort, confirm, teach, and empower them (John 14:16–26; 1 John 3:24).

Paul's "in" and "with Christ" language points to a similar reality of spiritual union with Jesus. Believers have been spiritually united to Christ in his death, resurrection, and ascension (Rom. 6:1–11; Eph. 2:4–6; Col. 2:12–13; 3:1). God unites believers with Christ in order that they might walk in newness of life, no longer be enslaved to sin, and have confident hope in the future resurrection. Romans 6:1–11 makes clear that this spiritual union with Christ entails that believers are dead to sin (union with Christ in his death) and alive to God (resurrection to new life through Christ's resurrection). This statement of Christian spiritual realities provides the basis for Paul's imperative not to let sin reign in our bodies but rather to present the members of our body as instruments of righteousness to God (Rom. 6:12–14).

Both John and Paul integrally connect this spiritual union with Christ to the practical actions and decisions of everyday life. Spiritual union with Christ is expressed in obeying his commandments (John 15:9–10; 1 John 3:24) and living in newness of life, which entails a rejection of sin and a pursuit of righteousness (Rom. 6:1–14). *Biblical spirituality and practical obedience are inseparable.*

While John's discussion of abiding in Christ and Paul's teaching of union or participation in Christ are important components of any biblical understanding of spirituality, in a more technical sense it is *the indwelling and activity of the Holy Spirit* that makes people spiritual. "Spiritual" people are those who have received the Spirit from God. It is this Spirit, in turn, who enables them to impart the wisdom taught by the Spirit, to interpret spiritual truths, to discern spiritually the things of the Spirit of God, and to judge all things (1 Cor. 2:12–16). This filling of the Spirit is inseparably linked to belonging to Christ.[9] As Paul states categorically, "You, however, are controlled not by the sinful nature but by the Spirit, if the Spirit of God lives in you. And if anyone does not have the Spirit of Christ, he does not belong to Christ" (Rom. 8:9 NIV). All genuine Christians have received the Holy Spirit and are thus, biblically speaking, spiritual (though, of course, not all Christians live in this way, and no one lives in the Spirit 100 percent of the time). *Spirituality, for Christians, is therefore grounded objectively in the gospel of Jesus Christ and experienced as a reality in the presence of the Holy Spirit within them rather than merely constituting a subjective mystical experience.*

What is more, the New Testament consistently emphasizes a corporate dimension to the work and activity of the Spirit that is often neglected today.[10] As I wrote previously, "All of the expressions of lives full of the Spirit are in relationships, be it among Christians at worship, in the home, or at the workplace. This corporate dimension to 'being filled with the Spirit' is often inadequately recognized in a theology of a 'Spirit-filled life' that deals primarily with an individual's personal—even private—experience."[11] In the Old Testament, Isaiah 63:10–11 and Ezekiel 36:26–27; 37 show the Holy Spirit as present and active in the covenant community as a whole. The New Testament builds on this foundation and presents the church as God's Spirit-filled temple (1 Cor. 3:16; 6:19–20; 2 Cor. 6:16; Eph. 2:20–21; 1 Pet. 2:4–5).[12] While the corporate dimension of spirituality should continue to be emphasized in our increasingly individualistic age, the fact remains that a given church body is made up of individual members who must each be filled with the Spirit if the church as a whole is to be Spirit-filled. For this reason, we should not dichotomize between the corporate and the individual dimensions of Spirit-filling even as proper attention is due the corporate identity of God's people.

Defining Biblical Spirituality

At this point, it will be helpful to pinpoint the nature of biblical spirituality a bit more precisely. *Spirituality involves the presence, activity, and work of the Holy Spirit in a believer's life, beginning at conversion and regeneration, and continuing on throughout the entire process of sanctification.* The New Testament connects spirituality closely with active obedience and with an engagement of the world as we embark on our mission for God. Spirituality is rarely, if ever, tied to a withdrawal or seclusion from the world as exemplified by the monastic tradition throughout the centuries. A vibrant and full-orbed spirituality, as exhibited by Jesus, involves active engagement with the world on mission for God and as empowered by the Spirit. The New Testament does not define spirituality in terms of solitude or introspection as if a person's spirituality were measured by the amount of time spent in a pursuit of mystical experience of the divine. Times of prayerful solitude must lead to active obedience and service in the world. I will return to this subject in a later section of this chapter.

Spirituality: Why Do We Need It?

In chapter 2 I focused on the need not just to flee from sin and to reject it, but to pursue righteousness through growth in godly virtues. In chapter 3

I drew our attention to our need to pursue holiness. Being a holy scholar who is set apart for God requires, among other things, excellence in pursuit of truth as we embark on our mission for God in the world. The vital necessity of spirituality becomes clear as we begin to attempt to put these insights into practice and to pursue holiness and growth in godly virtues in our day-to-day living. The presence, activity, and work of the Spirit is presented in Scripture as necessary for both sanctification (1 Pet. 1:1–2) and growth in virtue (Gal. 5:16–24). Without the Spirit's empowering presence, our pursuit of holiness and excellence through growth in godly virtues will devolve into mere human self-effort that will invariably fall short of God's purpose and design.[13]

In an important Trinitarian statement concerning salvation, Peter attributes sanctification to the work of the Spirit: "To those who are elect exiles of the dispersion . . . according to the foreknowledge of God the Father, in the sanctification of the Spirit, for obedience to Jesus Christ and for sprinkling with his blood" (1 Pet. 1:1–2).[14] Although not specifically linking the Spirit with sanctification, Romans 8:1–17 makes it unmistakably clear that it is through the Spirit that we put to death the sinful deeds of the body and consequently live. Sanctification depends on spirituality as defined above: the presence, activity, and work of the Holy Spirit in a believer's life beginning at conversion and regeneration and continuing on throughout the course of Christian growth in spiritual maturity.

Likewise, growth in the various Christian virtues requires the presence, activity, and work of the Holy Spirit. In Galatians 5:16–24, Paul contrasts the works of the sinful human nature with the fruit of the Spirit. Although the fruit of the Spirit is not explicitly presented by Paul as virtues, three of the characteristics mentioned by Paul are found in the list in 2 Peter 1:5–7: love (*agapē*), faith (*pistis*), and self-control (*egkrateia*). Apart from these specific parallels, there is a conceptual overlap between Paul's reference to patience, goodness, and gentleness and Peter's mention of steadfastness, excellence, and brotherly love. *A comparison of these two passages leads one to conclude that the growth in godly virtue urged by Peter is described by Paul as the fruit or effect of the activity of the Holy Spirit in a person's life.* Peter urges believers to make every effort to develop and add these virtues to their lives, while Paul draws attention to the fact that such spiritual growth is dependent on the Holy Spirit in whom believers must walk (Gal. 5:16, 25). Spirituality in the true and full biblical sense is thus an indispensable prerequisite for both sanctification and growth in godly virtue.

Spirituality: How Do We Attain It?

If spirituality is so important, how do we attain it? Do we need to spend hours in silent meditation alone with God or fast and pray on a regular basis? How does one become truly spiritual? These questions immediately call to mind the fact that spirituality (the presence and activity of the Holy Spirit in a person's life) shares in the same biblical dynamic as sanctification, which, as mentioned, is presented in Scripture as both *definitive* and *progressive* in nature, that is, as something that believers already possess and yet must continually pursue. I discussed the *definitive* aspect of spirituality in detail above. If anyone is a Christian, a genuine believer in Jesus Christ alone for salvation, that person is spiritual. Such a person belongs to Christ and is therefore indwelt by the Holy Spirit (Rom. 8:9). If anyone does not have the indwelling Spirit of God, that person is not a Christian.

Progressive Spirituality

Along with this definitive, positional spirituality, the New Testament also enjoins all followers of Christ to pursue *progressive* spirituality. John, as mentioned, exhorts believers to abide in Christ (John 15:4–7). Paul commands believers to be filled with the Spirit (Eph. 5:18); to walk, or keep in step with, the Spirit (Gal. 5:16, 25); and not to grieve (Eph. 4:30) or quench the Spirit (1 Thess. 5:19). This implies that it is possible for believers, who are spiritual because they belong to Christ and are indwelt by the Spirit, not to walk in the Spirit and thus to grieve the Spirit and to quench the Spirit's activity in their lives. What can we learn about the pursuit of progressive spirituality from these passages of Scripture?

As mentioned, John equates spiritual growth with obedience to God's command to believe in Jesus and to love others (John 15:10–17; 1 John 3:23–24) and closely connects spiritual growth with the bearing of spiritual fruit (John 15:5), that is, effective participation in Jesus's mission to the world. Spirituality is therefore not an individualistic experience of solitude, defined by the amount of time spent in protracted periods of communion alone with God, but an active obedience to God's commands that practically demonstrates love to others and is integrally involved in Jesus's mission to the world. *Christian spirituality, properly understood, is a spirituality of engagement, not withdrawal*, even though there will be times when Christians, like Jesus, will retreat temporarily from such engagement for the purposes of being reenergized and refocused through prayer, communion with God, and refreshment.

In Galatians, as mentioned, Paul defines walking in, or keeping in step with, the Spirit by contrasting it with the acts of the sinful human nature (5:19–23). The opposite of walking in the Spirit is walking in the flesh, that is, engaging in sexual immorality, impurity, sensuality, and so on (Gal. 5:19–21). The entire discussion is prefaced by a command to serve one another in love (Gal. 5:13–14) and to stop "biting" and "devouring" one another (Gal. 5:15). The section is followed by additional commands directing believers as to how they should interact with one another (Gal. 5:25–6:5). Believers must neither provoke nor envy one another (Gal. 5:26), and those who are spiritual must circumspectly restore those who have fallen into transgression (Gal. 6:1). We are charged to bear each other's burdens and thereby to fulfill the "law of Christ" which is the law of love (Gal. 6:2; cf. 5:14). Two important dimensions of walking in the Spirit are evident from Paul's discussion in Galatians. First, walking in the Spirit primarily manifests itself in concrete actions, in contrast to the deeds of the sinful human nature. Second, walking in the Spirit is lived out in interpersonal relationships: loving each other, restoring each other, and bearing each other's burdens. *As in John's Gospel, growth in spirituality is understood by Paul as active, loving engagement with others for the purpose of advancing God's mission and purposes in the world.*

The commands not to grieve the Spirit and to be filled with the Spirit in Paul's letter to the Ephesians (Eph. 4:30; 5:18) share many similarities with the apostle's just-discussed teaching in Galatians.[15] For our present purposes, it will suffice to quote at some length a summary observation I have registered in a previous publication on Paul's command to be filled with the Spirit in Ephesians 5:18:

> In summary, Paul's use of the expression "Be filled with the Spirit" in Eph. 5:18 in contrast to being drunk with wine enjoins believers to exhibit a wise, maturing lifestyle which is to be expressed in corporate praise and worship as well as in proper Christian relationships. Corporately the Church is to be God's pneumatic community, the body of Christ, the place where God now dwells by his Spirit. Individual believers, as members of this body, are to manifest the Spirit's presence and to avoid anything that might grieve him or hinder his operation.[16]

The command in 1 Thessalonians 5:19 not to quench the Spirit has less contextual information to explain it because it appears in a list of closing commands. The other commands in the context are helpful in that they exhibit what we have seen already, which could be summarized as active, loving engagement with the world. Along with not quenching the Spirit, believers should live at peace with one other (1 Thess. 5:13); warn those who are idle (1 Thess. 5:14); encourage the timid, help the weak, and be patient with everyone (1 Thess. 5:14); not repay evil for evil but rather be kind to everyone (1 Thess. 5:15); always rejoice, pray, and give thanks (1 Thess. 5:16–18); not despise but test prophecies (1 Thess. 5:20–21); and abstain from every form of evil (1 Thess. 5:22).

Throughout this passage, growth in spirituality is evidenced in the form of active obedience, love, mission, and corporate unity and peace. We therefore progress in spirituality as we express love for others in practical and concrete ways, make our day-by-day decisions in obedience to God's commands, involve ourselves in the fulfillment of God's mission in the world, and promote peace and unity within God's church. This is a very different portrait of spirituality than some people might expect or envision, and certainly one that squares less with certain monastic or Eastern versions of spirituality, but one that seems better to represent what the New Testament teaches on the subject.

Spiritual Disciplines

Some may object that I have failed to mention the importance of the spiritual disciplines for an individual's growth in spirituality. What about the disciplines of meditation, prayer, fasting, study, simplicity, solitude, submission, service, confession, worship, guidance, and celebration? The way in which spiritual disciplines are propagated today is often predicated on a withdrawal from the world for regular periods of silence, solitude, meditation, and fasting. This approach is not really borne out by a study of the New Testament itself. While various spiritual disciplines may help believers grow in their relationship with God, the conclusion is unwarranted that this is what biblical spirituality or growth in spirituality in fact *is*. At the heart, New Testament spirituality is characterized by an active engagement with the world in community and in the power of the Spirit as believers embark on their mission for God, not withdrawal or seclusion from the world in pursuit of an inward-focused spirituality.

This is not to say that there is no value in solitude, silence, and withdrawal, as long as the biblical portrait of spirituality is not lost. There is a danger of unduly elevating and importing monastic traditions into the evangelical movement, often represented by the "devotional classics," traditions that are not sufficiently grounded in the active spirituality presented in the biblical texts. Luther converted out of monasticism, got married, and pursued a different form of spirituality. It would seem strange if we, as evangelicals standing in the Reformation tradition, were moving back in a monastic direction. Jesus essentially denounced that type of spirituality in the Sermon on the Mount. The Pharisees paraded their spirituality through their pious faces, their lengthy prayers, and their ostentatious giving to the needy, while Jesus taught his disciples to pray short, concrete, and specific prayers, urging his followers not so much to fast as to rejoice in his presence (Matt. 6:1–15). This represented a marked contrast to the piety practiced by his contemporaries. In Colossians 2:18–23, Paul, likewise, denounced an ascetic spirituality that had the appearance of human wisdom but lacked any real power. When discussing spiritual disciplines, it is important that we do not present growth in spirituality as a series of duties resembling a checklist. This would be to engender a type of legalism, not grace-based, Spirit-filled Christian living.

With those cautions in place, we can now turn to two aspects of believers' relationship with God that are repeatedly stressed in Scripture: prayer and the study of God's Word. A person who sustains a vital relationship with God will pray with and talk to God throughout the day. Just as a healthy marriage requires daily communication, our relationship with God requires daily interaction with God. I can claim all day long that I am close friends with someone, but if I never talk with him or her, then such a relationship is not functional, if it exists at all. We are exhorted by Paul to pray without ceasing (1 Thess. 5:17). I understand this to mean that we are to develop a habit of talking with, praying to, and seeking God throughout the day, cultivating God-consciousness whether or not we engage in actual petition of God.[17] As Leon Morris writes, "It is not possible for us to spend all our time with the words of prayer on our lips, but it is possible for us to be all our days in the spirit of prayer, realizing our dependence on God for all we have and are, being conscious of his presence with us wherever we may be, and yielding ourselves continually to him to do his will."[18]

Scripture reading with meditation is similarly central in the Bible, not just as a command but as a practice regularly assumed. It is a tacit assumption throughout the New Testament that Christians were studying the Old

Testament and the New Testament documents as they became available (2 Pet. 3:15–16). Psalm 119, in particular, expresses our need to read, study, meditate upon, and act in obedience to Scripture. Jesus makes clear that his disciples must abide in his teaching: "If you abide in my word, you are truly my disciples, and you will know the truth, and the truth will set you free" (John 8:31–32). God's Word sanctifies his people (John 17:17). As D. A. Carson rightly notes:

> The heavy stress in Scripture on understanding, absorbing, meditating upon, proclaiming, memorizing ("hiding it in one's heart"), reading, and hearing the word of God is so striking that it will be ignored at our peril. That is why the best of the evangelical heritage has always emphasized what might be called the spirituality of the Word.[19]

This "spirituality of the Word" must be the standard by which any spiritual discipline is measured, because study of, and obedience to, Scripture is the preeminent spiritual discipline taught in Scripture. The spiritual discipline related to Scripture must always include both study and obedience. There is nothing inherently spiritual about the study of Scripture if that study does not lead to obedient, active application.

Both of the spiritual disciplines discussed above are brought together in Luke's account of the apostles' words in the days of the early church: "But we will devote ourselves to *prayer* and to the ministry of the *word*" (Acts 6:4; see also 2:42). All of the other spiritual disciplines in which Christians may engage draw their biblical legitimacy from the foundational disciplines of prayer and Scripture. Solitude, meditation, fasting, community, and so on are not unrelated spiritual disciplines. Solitude and silence become spiritual disciplines only if they foster time to pray and encounter God in the Scriptures. Likewise, meditation is a spiritual discipline only if the object of meditation is God (prayer) or Scripture. Fasting, too, is not a spiritual discipline unless it is joined to prayer and Scripture. Finally, there is nothing inherently spiritual about community if it is divorced from genuine prayer and Scripture. How many churches exist more as a social club than as a place for Christians to gather to seek God together in his Word through prayer and active obedience?

The Spiritual Scholar

Now that we have dealt with spirituality in general, we are ready to ask the more specific question: What does it look like for a scholar to be spiritual? In many ways, there will not be much difference between a spiritual scholar and any other spiritual Christian. The same questions apply to every Christian, regardless of vocation: Is the Holy Spirit present and active in your life? Are you living in obedience to the revealed Word of God and actively involved in God's mission in the world through love and in community? Are you developing habits of prayer and of submission to the teaching of Scripture? Despite the similarity of issues across vocations, it is still possible to make a few observations that are distinctive in relation to the particular calling of the Christian scholar. I will share these points as simple items of reflection without aiming to be comprehensive.

The Call to Scholarship
A genuinely spiritual scholar will be active, not passive, in exploring new opportunities for research and teaching in order to build up the body of Christ and advance God's kingdom. A form of piety with the appearance of spirituality adopts a passive posture, waiting for the Spirit's guidance and direction in every detail. By contrast, the old saying is true: "God can best steer a moving vehicle." Spirituality does not mean that we wait around in prayer until we receive indisputable divine direction through dreams (such as Paul's Macedonian call; Acts 16:9), visions, or strong internal impressions before beginning to work. If God has called you to the vocation of scholarship, the task is set, and you need to get started. God's involvement in our work through the presence and activity of his Holy Spirit does not preclude our active participation.

As spiritual scholars, we are called to put our minds and skills to work with passion, effort, and creativity, always looking for ways in which we can advance the kingdom of God by helping his people better to understand and obey the Scriptures. We can proceed in the confidence that God's Spirit will guide us as we go. We don't need just to sit there and wait for some mystical experience. Neither do we have to live in continual fear that we will veer off course or step out of line, because we have the mind of Christ (1 Cor. 2:16) and are being transformed into his likeness (Rom. 8:29; 12:2). Even if we stray, we can be confident that God will correct and restore and redirect us, as has been the experience of God's people through the ages.

Faith and Reason
Since the time of the Enlightenment, there has been a growing dichotomy between faith and reason among many. Increasingly, scholars have come to view faith as an obstacle to true scholarship. I mentioned this in the

previous chapter with regard to holiness and will note it only briefly here. The model for a spiritual scholar proposed in this chapter is a very different paradigm from that which pits faith against reason or which posits diversity as the only option, a model that cuts against the grain of most contemporary scholarship. By and large, the spirit of the Enlightenment fostered confidence in a scholar's intellectual skills and in objective, neutral analysis, while the Scriptures encourage prayerful dependence on the guidance and power of the indwelling Spirit to lead us into truth (see, e.g., John 16:13; 17:17, 19). Even though people have become increasingly aware that complete objectivity is impossible and that no one is completely free from bias, faith-based or confessional scholarship is regularly viewed with suspicion and looked down upon as less scholarly. However, as mentioned, as spiritual scholars we must not fall into the trap of believing that the separation between faith and scholarship is inevitable.

Piety and Poor Scholarship

If we are not careful, however, a false sense of spirituality or piety can lead to pride and intellectual laziness. Piety, in the negative sense of displaying "a show of godliness," can mask self-righteousness and wrong motives (doing things to please yourself, feeling good about your own spirituality, trying to impress other people). Many can be taken in by an outward form of piety that lacks genuine spiritual depth. This type of piety may serve as a helpful foil for what spirituality is not. Paul warns Timothy to avoid people who have the appearance of godliness but deny its power (2 Tim. 3:5).

In our scholarly work, we must never substitute pious posturing for actual research and engagement with the evidence. It is an ever-present temptation for Christian scholars engaged in a given debate to present themselves and their position as the "spiritual," godly, or Christian interpretation or argument. This manner of framing an issue rarely focuses on the evidence itself and regularly serves to alienate the opposing side, whether nonconfessional or other Christian scholars. Such pious posturing also is guilty of committing the fallacy of engaging in an ad hominem argument. You attack the spirituality of your opponent in a given interchange and imply that anyone holding to such a position cannot be spiritual. Pious posturing must never become a substitute for an appraisal of the evidence, careful research, and logical argumentation.

Also, even if we are genuinely spiritual scholars, this still does not necessarily mean that our work is automatically better than that of others.

For example, you will get your fair share of rejection letters from journal editors and publishers. Instead of indicating a lack of spirituality, or that you somehow mystically stepped out of line or ignored the Spirit's guidance, this may rather suggest that you need to put in more effort, revise your writing, look for further evidence, get more feedback from other scholars, and so on. Spirituality is no substitute for hard, painstaking work.

Luke was inspired as he wrote Scripture, yet he still meticulously researched and investigated every detail (Luke 1:1–4). There is no sense from Luke's preface that the Holy Spirit came to him in a vision or an inward voice and told him what to write. He put in the hard work necessary to deal with the evidence. It is obvious from the end result (Luke-Acts) that the Spirit was at work, but Luke still had to live with the sore feet, weary hands, and tired eyes that would surely have resulted from his tireless labors. Even though we are not producing Scripture, we may expect that the Holy Spirit will similarly illumine us and guide our research today.

Active Obedience to Scripture

We saw that the study of Scripture must always lead to application and obedience. There is no place in the Bible where God's people are enjoined to study solely for the sake of study: the goal is always obedience. Many of the more technical areas of scholarship in which you will be engaged may seem difficult to apply directly, but the point I am arguing here has as much to do with your attitude toward, and your personal response to, Scripture than with the direct topic you are researching, since your stance toward Scripture will be evidenced in your research and writing at many places.

Do you strive to obey and serve God? It would be hard to think of a simpler spiritual diagnostic question. If the technical study of Scripture has caused you to lose sight of its life-changing, convicting, transforming message, you may be headed for trouble. As believers, we sit under the authority of Scripture and must always be attentive to how God would use it to expose sin in our lives, motivate us to obedience, love, and mission, comfort us in times of hardship or loss, and help us remain faithful until the end of our earthly pilgrimage. This posture toward Scripture can be described as an attitude that is seeking to understand and wanting to obey.[20]

There is an intensely personal dimension to this. How can we foster understanding and obedience to Scripture in our readers if we don't personally seek to understand the Scriptures in order to obey them? We cannot lead others where we ourselves have not gone.

A Scholarship of Love

As mentioned, John primarily defines abiding in Christ as obedience to the twin command to believe and to love others (John 13:34–35; 15:12–13; 1 John 3:23). What would it mean to practice a scholarship of love and actually to *love* the people with whom we are debating and arguing? I will discuss this in greater detail in chapter 18 on the virtue of love, but I mention it here because of the connection between biblical spirituality and the practical expression of love to other people. A spiritual scholar will not engage in ad hominem attacks toward opponents or otherwise malign their character. We must surely stand for truth and defend it on the basis of publicly accessible evidence, but we should conduct our critique of others on the basis of the available data without impugning other scholars' motives or casting doubt on their character.

Even if, for argument's sake, it were true that a given opponent in a debate had poor character, had divorced his wife, lived an immoral lifestyle, or committed some other act unworthy of a Christian, we should refrain from using any of these flaws in our argument as if somehow a person's character flaws invalidated his or her argument. Someone may be a bad person and still make a good argument. We show that another person is wrong not by going after that person's personal life and background (as is all too common in politics), but by showing that the evidence supports our conclusions over alternative proposals. Paul's words in 2 Timothy 2:23–26 point the way:

> Have nothing to do with foolish, ignorant controversies; you know that they breed quarrels. And the Lord's servant must not be quarrelsome but kind to everyone, able to teach, patiently enduring evil, correcting his opponents with gentleness. God may perhaps grant them repentance leading to a knowledge of the truth, and they may come to their senses and escape from the snare of the devil, after being captured by him to do his will.

We must not be quarrelsome scholars who try to pick a fight for the sake of winning an argument and thrive on conflict but should rather correct those on the other side with gentleness and love with the goal of persuasion. Even if others will not follow us, we should not grow bitter or develop a siege mentality. If we are convinced that truth is on our side, we should be charitable and kind toward our opponents in a given controversy. We should pray for them and reach out to them on a personal level. Having developed a positive interpersonal relationship with someone on the other side of an issue makes it much more likely that we will eventually gain a hearing for our particular case.

Even if we never persuade anyone of the merits of our position, we are still dealing either with a brother or sister for whom Christ died or with a person made in the image of Christ who is caught in sin and desperately needs to be shown the love of Christ. In the past, I have at times taken minority positions in which others have (so far) not followed me. My view that "saved through childbearing" in 1 Timothy 2:15 refers to women's spiritual preservation from the Devil is one example; my conclusion that the temple clearing in John 2:14–22 is one of the Johannine signs is another.[21] Neither view has been embraced by a majority of scholars, though, as in the case of Paul's preaching in Athens, a few have been persuaded (Acts 17:34).[22]

I continue to hold these views and continue to hold out hope that these views will one day become mainstream positions. In the meantime, I am not resentful, nor do I view those who hold to different views as somehow less spiritual merely because they have not "seen the light" on these fine exegetical points as I believe I have. In those cases, it is not so much a person's spirituality (or lack thereof) but certain interpretive traditions or entrenched arguments that have blinded interpreters to alternative ways of understanding a given passage of Scripture, and it will take time, and patient, careful argument, to help them see that there may be a better way—if I am right, which I well may not be. But that's okay, too, because isn't that what scholarship is all about: propose new hypotheses that are then subjected to public scrutiny by other scholars?

The Quest for Scholarly Significance and the Mission of God

Indeed, discussing what it means to be a spiritual scholar forces the question, Why are we engaging in scholarship in the first place? Is it not because we want to make a difference? Most scholars long for respect and want to stand out in some way—to live a life that counts. What are you hoping to achieve with your life? Write lots of books? Many books are barely read and hardly worth the effort writing. Jesus chose his disciples to bear fruit that would *last* (John 15:16). We want to have a lasting impact. How can we expect to have this kind of effect on the lives of others? It will not happen if we are engaged in scholarship solely for ourselves as an outflow of our quest for significance. Our desires must be submitted to the Spirit and be transformed to become a pursuit of God. Spiritual scholarship is fundamentally a pursuit of God and the things of God.

Because life is short, we must continually evaluate how we can make the most of our time, life, and influence to engage the world and to make an impact (Eph. 5:15–16). How can we be involved in God's mission in the world? The kind of spiritual scholarship that will yield lasting results, even beyond a scholar's own lifetime, and is of true eternal significance will often be missional in thrust. Some of the readers of this book will primarily involve themselves in technical scholarship that will never reach beyond the bounds of a scholarly audience, while others will divide their efforts between scholarly and popular-level writing. Either way, the key to lasting significance is for the scholar to seek to use research, writing, and teaching to advance the kingdom of God. In the end, nothing else will really matter.

Before moving on to discuss various scholarly virtues, I'd like to share with you some reflections I've recently come across on virtue and intelligence.[23] R. R. Reno recalls a query directed to him by a friend: "Great books and good philosophy don't really help us become virtuous, do they?" His answer:

> In the main, reading makes one more articulate, not more wise. It's a good thing to become articulate about the small margin of wisdom one has gained in life, so I commend reading to my students. Furthermore, for certain kinds of people, perhaps you and perhaps me, reading provides a crooked, but useful path to greater wisdom. To express thoughts to oneself in a clear, critical fashion—it's helpful for correcting false truism[s] that have been circulating on your mind.
>
> Though we should beware. Educated folks, especially college professors like me, tend to compliment ourselves with the thought that intelligence gives us an advantage. Hardly. Intelligence only gives us leverage, which like other forms of power mostly magnifies our virtues and vices rather than guides them. Intellectual vanity is more refined than crude arrogance about how much money you make—and it is therefore more difficult to see in oneself and more difficult to dislodge.[24]

Reno concludes with a quotation from St. Bonaventure's *The Journey of the Mind to God* that is worth repeating here. Let us not imagine, he says, "that it suffices to read without unction, speculate without devotion, investigate without wonder, examine without exultation, work without piety, know without love, understand without humility, be zealous without divine grace, see without wisdom divinely inspired."[25] Indeed, spirituality, expressed in a committed pursuit of a series of Christian virtues, is an indispensable prerequisite for achieving true intellectual and academic excellence.

Conclusion

Biblical spirituality is grounded in the presence and work of the Holy Spirit in a believer's life, beginning at conversion in regeneration and continuing throughout the entire process of sanctification. It takes place in community, expresses itself through love, and results in active obedience to God's Word and in conscious engagement with the world as we embark on a mission for God. Biblical spirituality does not consist of mystical, emotional experiences, inward impressions and feelings, introspective meditation, or monastic withdrawal from the world. The primary spiritual disciplines featured in Scripture are prayer and the obedient study of God's Word.

Spiritual scholars will proactively explore opportunities to further their influence in the world as they pursue their mission from God. They will refuse to live by the Enlightenment dichotomy between faith and scholarship and resist the allure of the prevailing pluralism and cult of diversity. They will avoid substituting pious posturing and a show of spirituality for argumentation based on evidence. They will actively seek to apply Scripture to their own lives in Christian obedience, practice a scholarship of love, and find their scholarly significance through participating in God's mission in the world. Genuine spirituality will result in academic excellence.

Part Two

VOCATIONAL EXCELLENCE

5

Diligence

Make every effort to add diligence to your faith.

Building upon the preceding foundational chapters, this chapter shifts our focus to the heart of this book: the various virtues that are necessary for scholarly excellence. In chapter 1 we looked at the need to pursue excellence for God's glory, having been made in his image. In chapter 2 we observed that excellence is achieved through conscious effort exerted to add various virtues to our faith. Chapters 3 and 4 examined the indispensible role of sanctification and the presence and activity of the Holy Spirit in our pursuit of excellence. As Christians, we are already holy and filled with God's Spirit but at the same time must continually pursue holiness and walk in the Spirit. God's grace sovereignly accomplishes and superintends every aspect of our salvation, including sanctification, filling, and empowering by his Spirit. Grace also fuels our pursuit of excellence through growth in godly virtue, the fruit of his indwelling Holy Spirit.

With these foundational concepts in place, we are now in a position to discuss the various godly virtues one at a time that are necessary to achieve excellence in the particular vocation of a Christian scholar. These virtues, of course, are pertinent for all Christians. The following chapters will benefit anyone who is interested in what the Bible has to say about each virtue, but in each case particular application will be made to the vocation of Christian scholarship.

Turning, then, to the subject at hand, in common parlance, we think of diligence as not giving up, sticking with a given task, and keeping on track. In a moment, we will try to dig deeper in Scripture to find out what diligence is according to the teaching of the Bible. As with many of the virtues that we will consider in the following chapters, however, the problem is not so much that we don't know what a given virtue is but rather that we don't apply ourselves sufficiently to its pursuit.

Diligence is hard. It is tough. It is far easier to slack off, take an easier road, follow shortcuts, or simply give up. Diligence is particularly difficult in our fast-food, microwave culture. As Americans, we don't want to have to wait for results or labor and toil for future gain in the absence of immediate gratification. We want the maximum payoff for the smallest possible amount of labor. Modern-day technology, scientific advances, and other modern conveniences often allow us to get by with far less effort than previous generations had to expend, but merely "getting by" will never produce excellence. Excellence requires diligence, perseverance, and plain hard work.

The words *diligence*, *diligent*, and *diligently* only appear thirty-four times in the ESV translation of the Bible, but, as we will see, the broader concept is far more pervasive in Scripture than such a simple search would indicate.[1] To obtain a more complete picture, one would need to study the occurrences of some of the related English words such as *endure*, *endurance*, *persevere*, *perseverance*, or better yet, study the Hebrew and Greek words underlying our English translations. Although space constraints preclude any sort of comprehensive analysis, a broad sketch of the biblical teaching on the virtue of diligence will be useful.

Diligence in the Old Testament

Survey of Relevant Passages

In the Old Testament, the idea of diligence is expressed by a considerable variety of words as well as with the infinitive absolute.[2] The infinitive absolute in Hebrew expresses emphasis by the repetition of the main verb in the infinitive form. For example, Exodus 15:26 reads, "If you will diligently listen to the voice of the LORD your God . . ." No Hebrew word in the verse means "diligently," but the infinitive absolute is employed to indicate how people are to listen. Literally, the expression reads, "If you will *listen listen* to the voice of the LORD your God," that is, really listen or diligently listen.[3]

Several observations can be drawn from a study of Exodus 15 and related passages. God's people are exhorted to listen diligently and to obey his commandments (Ex. 15:26; Deut. 6:17; Ps. 119:4; Isa. 55:2; Zech. 6:15).[4] They must not be slack or slow to keep God's Word. Obedience must be heartfelt and persistent; otherwise, God's people will experience the consequences for covenant violation. They must keep their souls diligently and not forget (Deut. 4:9); be diligent to teach and instruct their children in God's ways (Deut. 6:7); and diligently discipline them (Prov. 13:24).

God's people must obey their leaders with diligence and eagerness (Ezra 6:12, 13; 7:17, 21). Darius learned that the workmen on the temple were working diligently (Ezra 5:8). Moses diligently inquired into the prosecution of the sin offering and was angry at the behavior of Eleazar and Ithamar (Lev. 10:16). God's people should make diligent inquiry before executing justice (Deut. 13:14; 17:4; 19:18). Justice requires diligence in order to know the truth of the matter and act appropriately.

Diligence also serves to describe the thoroughness, completeness, or persistence of an action or activity (Ps. 64:6; 77:6; Prov. 1:28; 11:27; Isa. 21:7). Wisdom must be pursued diligently (Prov. 8:17). The riches that result from diligent labor are contrasted with the poverty that will result from laziness (*rĕmiyyah*, Prov. 10:4; 12:24, 27). The diligent person is further contrasted with the sluggard (Prov. 13:4). The lazy sluggard (*'atsel*) will sleep in (Prov. 6:9; 24:30–34; 26:14); make excuses for not going to work (Prov. 22:13; 26:13); procrastinate (Prov. 20:4); and fail to engage in any meaningful labor (Prov. 21:25).

Summary
Diligence relates to obedience to God and kings, the investigation of truth for the proper execution of justice, and profitable work. The consistent foil for diligence throughout Proverbs, which equally applies to the other occurrences, is laziness or slothfulness. People must not be slothful or lazy in their obedience to God, and judges had better not be lazy in the investigation of the truth of a case. In Proverbs, diligence is presented as a practical necessity for a successful, fruitful, happy life. The lazy person's life will be characterized by lack, poverty, and misery. Failure to be diligent to obey God's commands and to teach one's children to do likewise will

have even more disastrous consequences: judgment and exile from the land, the ultimate curse for covenant violation.

A sculptor's depiction of the vice of sloth

Diligence in the New Testament

Survey of Relevant Passages

Similar to the Old Testament, the New Testament conveys the concept of diligence by a wide variety of terms and expressions.[5] In line with Old Testament usage, *diligence* in the New Testament functions to describe the thoroughness, completeness, or persistence of an action or activity. Herod challenged the wise men to search for the messianic child diligently (Matt. 2:8). The woman who had lost a coin diligently searched until she found it (Luke 15:8). Paul diligently sought to visit the Thessalonians again but was providentially kept from doing so (1 Thess. 2:17; see also 2 Tim. 4:9, 21; Titus 3:12). He exhorted the Ephesians to maintain the unity of the Spirit in the bond of peace with eagerness and diligence (Eph. 4:3).

As noted in chapter 2, diligence is linked with the acquisition of godly virtues (2 Pet. 1:5) and a person's assurance of salvation: "Therefore, brothers, be all the more diligent to make your calling and election sure, for if you practice these qualities you will never fall" (2 Pet. 1:10). Peter closes his second letter with the following exhortation: "Therefore, beloved, since you are waiting for these [the new heavens and the new earth], be diligent to be found by him without spot or blemish, and at peace" (2 Pet. 3:13–14).

The author of the book of Hebrews, likewise, urges his readers to be diligent in the here and now as they progress in working out their salvation: "Let us therefore strive [i.e., be diligent] to enter that rest, so that no one may fall by the same sort of disobedience" (Heb. 4:11). In the same context, Hebrews 6:11–12 specifically contrasts diligence with laziness: "And we desire each one of you to show the same earnestness [diligence] to have the full assurance of hope until the end, so that you may not be sluggish, but imitators of those who through faith and patience inherit the promises."

In Paul's second letter to Timothy, the apostle calls on his foremost disciple to exercise diligence in the context of his pastoral and teaching ministry: "Do your best [i.e., be diligent] to present yourself to God as one approved, a worker who has no need to be ashamed, rightly handling the word of truth" (2 Tim. 2:15). Timothy must do his best, that is, be diligent, and he must be a "worker," that is, work hard and apply himself as he rightly handles God's Word. Such work entails sweat and sustained effort, fueled by a quest for excellence and a desire to get it right no matter what the cost, ultimately in order to please one's heavenly master, the Lord God himself, to whom we will ultimately have to give an account.

Diligence in perseverance and endurance (*hypomenō, hypomonē*) is often linked to trials, persecution, and suffering (Rom. 5:3; 12:12; 2 Cor. 1:6; 6:4; Heb. 10:32; James 1:3–4; 1 Pet. 2:20; Rev. 1:9; 2:2–3, 19; 3:10; 13:10; 14:12) and is presented as necessary for final salvation (Matt. 10:22; 24:13; Mark 13:13; Luke 21:19; Heb. 10:36; James 1:12). Believers *must* persevere to the end through any persecution, difficulty, or suffering they may encounter, and genuine (elect) believers *will* persevere.

Jesus told the parable of the persistent widow and the unrighteous judge in Luke 18:1–8 to teach his disciples that "they ought always to pray and not lose heart" (Luke 18:1). The book of Acts describes the early church as devoted to (i.e., diligent in) the teaching of the apostles and prayer (Acts 1:14; 2:42, 46; 6:4). The believers in Berea diligently and thoroughly studied the Scriptures daily in order to judge the truthfulness of what Paul taught them (Acts 17:11). Paul exhorted the Colossians to "continue steadfastly in prayer, being watchful in it with thanksgiving" (Col. 4:2).

First Timothy 4:13–16 contains three exhortations to diligence in the public reading of Scripture, exhortation, and teaching and links such diligence with assurance of final salvation: "Until I come, devote yourself to [*prosechō*, 'be diligent in'] the public reading of Scripture, to exhortation, to teaching. . . . Practice [*meletaō*, 'continue to do'] these things, immerse yourself in them, so that all may see your progress. Keep a close watch on yourself and on the teaching. Persist [*epimenō*, 'continue, keep on'] in this, for by so doing you will save both yourself and your hearers" (1 Tim. 4:13–16).

One final example comes from the above-mentioned preface to Luke's Gospel, which provides an excellent model for us to follow.[6] Luke writes:

> Inasmuch as many have undertaken to compile a narrative of the things that have been accomplished among us, just as those who from the beginning were eyewitnesses and ministers of the word have delivered them to us, it seemed good to me also, having followed all things closely for some time past, to write an orderly account for you, most excellent Theophilus, that you may have certainty concerning the things you have been taught. (Luke 1:1–4)

First, Luke closely followed the events (v. 3). He engaged in research before writing up his narrative. He built on the very best sources (i.e., eyewitnesses, "those who had seen for themselves," *autoptai*, v. 2) and thoroughly examined all of his material. Note that Luke humbly acknowledged at the very outset that he himself was not an eyewitness. But he turned this possible liability into an asset by diligently applying himself to a careful study of all the available firsthand accounts.

Second, Luke went to the root of the Christian movement, a story he set out to tell "from the beginning" (v. 2). This involved a careful study and presentation of the ministry of Jesus's forerunner, John the Baptist. In this, Luke exemplified the virtue of thoroughness. Rather than merely dealing with surface phenomena, he set out to explore the deeper roots of Jesus's ministry and of the early church's mission. Even though Luke most likely was a Gentile and wrote for a Gentile patron, Theophilus (see further below), he traced the origins of the Christian movement all the way back to its Old Testament moorings. Only in this way could he provide an account of the nature of Christianity that had sufficient explanatory power and did justice to the movement and what drove and motivated it.

Third, Luke did not merely look at evidence that supported his agenda; he looked at everything ("all things," v. 3). He did not commit the fallacy of engaging in a selective use of evidence, using research merely to confirm his own views, but consulted a variety of written and oral material in his quest to present an accurate account of Jesus's mission and of the early Christian movement to his literary patron, Theophilus. In his wide use of sources, Luke displayed a spirit of humility. He was not too proud, nor too lazy, to track down various written sources and likely sought out eyewitnesses who could confirm the accuracy of a given account. In all this, Luke proved to be an earnest seeker for the truth of a given matter, seeking to record things as they actually took place.[7]

Fourth, Luke produced an "orderly account" (v. 3). In his writing, he used logical (though not always chronological) arrangement and gave attention to style and the careful presentation of the material. What is more, Luke wrote with a clear purpose: to reassure Theophilus concerning the fulfillment of salvation in Jesus, not only for Jews but also for Gentiles (v. 4).

The production of Luke's Gospel thus involved diligent research, attention to detail, and an orderly presentation of all the relevant evidence in keeping with Luke's declared purpose for writing his account. In all these respects, Luke provides an example for us to follow in both our research and our writing, especially with regard to the virtue of diligence.

Summary

The concept of diligence in the New Testament maintains the practical dimension noted in the Old Testament concerning the thoroughness, completeness, or persistence of an action or activity. Every day-by-day, practical activity in which a believer engages should be done with all of one's heart as unto God. The well-known exhortation certainly applies here: "Whatever you do, work heartily, as for the Lord and not for men" (Col. 3:23). Believers are to put their best effort into all that they do because ultimately they are not working for a human employer to earn money but for Christ in order to please him.

In addition, the text emphasizes the importance of diligence in two particular ways. First, diligence relates to a person's assurance of salvation and, through perseverance, the attainment of final salvation. Second, diligence characterized the early church's approach to the study of

Scripture and prayer. The diligent study of Scripture took place *daily*, and believers engaged in prayer with diligence. Luke, the second evangelist, provides an excellent case study of one who, albeit inspired, engaged in diligent, committed, and sustained research in a quest for truth and in pursuit of excellence.

Diligent Scholarship

Based on our above study of diligence, especially in the book of Proverbs, we conclude that diligent scholarship will lead to excellence, success, and a good name, while lazy, slothful scholarship will lead to poverty, disdain, and failure. Beyond the goal of earthly success, however, the Christian scholar has an additional motivation: "Do your best to *present yourself to God* as one approved, a worker who has no need to be ashamed, rightly handling the word of truth" (2 Tim. 2:15). Our goal is to please God through excellent scholarship, rightly handling his Word of truth, and diligence is a necessary virtue for the accomplishment of that goal.

Diligence and Hard Work

There is no way to get around the fact that diligence requires large and consistent amounts of sheer hard work.[8] There are no shortcuts. We must embrace the value of hard work. Just because we have been recipients of grace does not mean that excellence comes to us without any effort on our part. Salvation is by grace, and even sanctification is still by grace, but we must cooperate with God's grace as he sanctifies us by his Spirit. There are many aspects of the scholarly task that require diligence, including tracking down sources, ensuring accuracy in citing the contributions of others, following style sheets, and the work of actual writing.[9]

When I was Grant Osborne's research assistant during my three years of doctoral study at Trinity, just before the rise of the Internet (1990–1993), I spent many long hours tracking down sources in obscure places. I could be found on the top floor of a library tower on the North Shore, lying flat on the ground in the basement of some other archive or collection, and crisscrossing town to fill in lacunae left by Professor Osborne as he did his major research for *The Hermeneutical Spiral* on a sabbatical in Tübingen, Germany. I am not asking for sympathy here. My point is that we must learn to apply ourselves diligently to the scholarly task.

Let me illustrate further. If you are teaching at a seminary or other sabbatical-granting institution, you know that sabbaticals are a wonderful thing. You can take care of your pent-up home improvement projects, spend more time with your family, polish your class notes, and just take a long-deserved break, and what is best of all—for pay! Right? At least that's how some may view sabbaticals. The problem is only that none of the above-mentioned tasks comprise the major purpose for sabbaticals. In short, these extended times of study leave are designed for focused research and writing. As such, they require stick-to-itiveness, commitment, and diligence.

In my experience, sabbatical reports often fall roughly into two broad categories. Some report that they actually managed to write the scholarly works they intended to produce, while another group report that, yes, they planned to work on some scholarly project, but things happened in their personal lives or families and they ended up not writing what they had planned to produce. Not just students have difficulty writing; the challenge of making room for scholarly work continues when you are on the faculty or serving a church. Writing never just happens. If you are called to write, you must actively plan for it and doggedly persevere in it.

Diligence requires thoroughness rather than superficiality. Look at several sources on a given issue. It is certainly not possible, nor always necessary, to be exhaustive, but you should be comprehensive in looking at all sides of an issue instead of being selective in your use of the evidence. A colleague told me the following anecdote. "How is your sabbatical going?" he asked another professor, who replied, "It's going great! I'm finding lots of people who agree with me." It occurred to my colleague, and I heartily agree, that whatever this other professor was doing, it can hardly be considered research.

In fact, if all the sources you look at agree with you, this may indicate either that you have not been thorough enough in your research or that you are intentionally consulting sources sympathetic to your point of view. Or everyone already agrees on your subject (which, of course, rarely, if ever, happens) so there is no need for you to write on it! As an editor, incidentally, I occasionally see pieces that are sound but which argue a thesis that has already been sufficiently set forth in a commentary or journal article. Why bother repeating others' work? Scholarship is defined primarily as advancing knowledge in a given field, not as recycling old arguments or information.

If you want to engage in responsible research, you cannot legitimately support and defend a given argument merely by citing those who agree with you. You must interact with those who oppose your position and explain why the evidence supports your conclusion rather than alternative viewpoints. Selective use of evidence may make a position initially look strong but will not survive the careful scrutiny that will surely come if you are arguing for anything significant. People will *know* that not everyone agrees with you. If you omit any reference to opposing viewpoints, your readers will either think that you are disingenuous or unscholarly or surmise that you don't have a satisfactory answer to alternative viewpoints or objections to your position.

Diligence and Deadlines

How are you at meeting deadlines? The longer I work in the scholarly arena, the more I am amazed at how few people are actually taking deadlines seriously. They sign a contract, but then treat it lightly as if they had not given their word (even in a legally binding manner) to produce a certain piece of work. It is almost as if some regard this kind of commitment in a cavalier fashion, not even seriously intending to produce a given item by a certain date at the time at which they commit themselves. It is inconceivable to me how this practice is compatible with being a serious Christian.

Not that life stops short of interfering with scholarship.[10] To the contrary, life happens all the time. People get sick, loved ones need support, we must get a haircut, or go to the dentist, and a multitude of other small (and some not so small) tasks will predictably threaten any meaningful time of sustained research and writing. As the old adage has it, however, if you fail to plan, you plan to fail. Diligence operates in a context of conscious, deliberate planning. Jesus poignantly illustrated this in two of his parables: the story of the king who went to war with an insufficient army, and the story of a builder who started to build but lacked the resources to finish (Luke 14:28–32). Just as believers must count the cost before committing to follow Jesus, students and scholars must count the cost before committing to projects, teaching assignments, or other additional responsibilities.

Of course, parenthetically, there may be yet another problem: a lack of commitment to excellence in the first place. If out of financial considerations we take on a ridiculous amount of commitments, including pastoral responsibilities, additional courses, and miscellaneous other opportunities for extra income, there is absolutely no way that we can fulfill all of these assignments *with excellence*. Unless excellence becomes a core value that governs everything we do, including the amount of responsibilities we shoulder, it is highly unlikely that we will achieve excellence, especially in the scholarly arena.

Count the cost. Do you have what it takes to meet the deadline with excellence? This includes doing your best to anticipate circumstances in your life that may interfere with the successful completion of a research task. Once a student or faculty member makes a commitment and formulates a plan, diligence is the key to the completion of the plan by the deadline. Slow and steady wins the race and meets the deadline. (Of course, fast and steady wins the race faster, as long as quality is not compromised!) The key element, whether fast or slow, is being steady. The danger of going too fast and trying to accomplish too much at one time will likely lead to burnout and low quality of work, with the result that excellence falls by the wayside.

Big projects, in particular, are not written in a night or weekend but require diligence and perseverance. I remember one of my fellow students at Trinity, who happened to be one of the first graduates of its PhD program, tell me that it was his experience and observation that completing one's PhD dissertation was more a test of diligence and perseverance than an indicator of one's actual academic capability. Can a PhD candidate successfully navigate the process, finish the dissertation, and earn the degree? Without diligence, chances are that other assignments will crowd out the larger blocks of time that are vital for doing the kind of quality work a dissertation deserves and requires. Unlike some seminar papers or shorter assignments, you cannot write a dissertation in a day, a week, or even a month.

Diligence also pertains to revising and correcting your work over time.[11] Diligence does not mean that you get everything all right the first time around, but that you are sufficiently committed to improve your writing and research continually until you have accomplished an excellent contribution to scholarship, whether in the form of a book review, an article, a dissertation, or a book. Even if you succeed in finishing, and publishing, your dissertation, I've heard it said that the dissertation is the only book the vast majority of doctoral students ever write. Only diligence will help you succeed past writing the dissertation as you make scholarship—as you should, if God has called you to a scholarly vocation—the pursuit of a lifetime.

We might not think of scholars as a lazy bunch. After all, they are known as spending long hours in the library or in their study. Yet, as D. A. Carson trenchantly observes, "On the other hand [i.e., in contrast to workaholics or perfectionists], biblical studies, strange to say, can become a field where lazy students hide. They never do stellar work, but they get by. If they become pastors, they may put in long hours, but they will be ineffective hours because they diddle away their time in lazy reading, endless visits to blogs, last-minute preparation, and sloppy work habits."[12]

Carson adds, "A seminary education must never be viewed as a ticket to a job. It is the beginning of a lifetime of study and reflection, worked out in the hurly-burly of ministry. Most ministers do not have someone immediately over them to check up on how effectively they have used their time, how honestly they fill their hours. Thus the very posts that may feed the workaholic may be safe-havens for the lazy or ill-disciplined."[13] In these rather stern remarks, Carson sounds an important cautionary note, which leads us to consider, next, some of the downsides of a lack of diligence.

Diligence and Vices

The lack of diligence leads to such vices as plagiarism and laziness. Plagiarism generally becomes a temptation when a student or scholar fails to put in the diligent work necessary and suddenly finds that the deadline is fast approaching. Once there is no time left to do original research, plagiarism can seem like the necessary quick fix, but there is hardly a more deadly ethical violation of the ethos of academic work. If you plagiarize, you are engaging in a form of theft, stealing the intellectual property of others.[14]

What is more, once a scholar's reputation has been marred by plagiarism, it is virtually impossible to regain credibility. Even if those whom you harmed by plagiarism forgive you and you avoid losing your job or being expelled from an academic program or institution, you can never turn back the clock, and your reputation will likely suffer permanent damage. What is more, you bring dishonor to the God whom you serve and with whom you have chosen to publicly identify. Of all students, it is those engaged in biblical and theological studies who should hold to impeccable standards when it comes to respecting and referencing the work of others.

Like other forms of sin, plagiarism may seem appealing when tempted, but it is never worth it. Why would anyone working on a theological degree plagiarize? As mentioned, as a form of intellectual theft, plagiarism is completely at odds with the study of God and of his ways.

Diligence

Ultimately, plagiarism is a selfish act that says, "I want a degree, or recognition, without putting in the work, and I don't care if I hurt or deceive others in the process, as long as I get what I want." This hardly is good character, and even if repented of, still casts doubt on the character of a person who committed this kind of act, especially if repeatedly and egregiously.

All right; you may say that you would never fall into the temptation to plagiarize, and that may indeed be the case, but do you give in to the temptation to laziness? Sin has a way of increasingly desensitizing and deceiving us as to its growth and consequences. Hardly anyone wakes up one morning and suddenly decides to commit adultery and walk out on his or her spouse. Normally, such an act is preceded by a series of "smaller" moral failures and choices. Laziness is just such a "smaller" moral failure that could eventually lead to decisions that destroy your career and damage God's honor.

You may not look at yourself as a lazy person, and you may well not be; many seminary students and scholars are extremely hardworking. But let's make sure we're not blind to our own weaknesses. Laziness may be as innocuous as procrastination and the making of excuses for not actually getting anything done. This indulgent disposition often leads to a last-minute rush of sloppy research with an indiscriminate use of Internet sources, older sources, or primarily devotional and popular rather than academic and more technical scholarly sources. Laziness improperly allows convenience and expediency to control one's research.

Diligence is the surest antidote to these vices. Several specific habits should be developed. First, wake up early. Nothing kills a morning's productivity faster than sleeping in. One of my closest friends gets up at 4:00 or 4:30 every morning, and by the time his colleagues report to work he has already put in several hours of highly productive work. Second, develop a conscious routine of research and writing. In every area of life, effective, well-planned-out routines dramatically increase productivity. The power of good research and writing habits must not be discounted. This includes note-taking habits and other research and writing routines. Third, cut out of your life any unnecessary time wasters by identifying and reducing bad habits. This is a major point to make in our media-saturated, entertainment-driven society.

Examples of diligence-killing time wasters are small talk, television, and video games. There's nothing wrong with small talk as such, but in my experience many spend hours just hanging out, shooting the breeze, and joking around. Not only do these individuals waste much of their own precious time (which is ultimately God's), but they also become a stumbling block to others and cause them to waste time (which, if done at work, also cheats their employer who doesn't pay them just for sitting around talking to other people who show up at their doorstep).

Likewise, watching too many of your favorite television shows or sports teams will surely decimate your available research time. As I am sure you realize, the video game industry is producing increasingly sophisticated and complex games that are designed to be addictive and take up vast amounts of time. These games are not aimed primarily at children but at young adults (including college, master's level, and even PhD students!). Increasingly, even adults, in the middle of their careers, spend large amounts of time playing video games, seeking to escape from the pressures of life into a virtual world.

In other instances, you may find that hunting, golfing, or fishing eat up inordinate amounts of time that compromise your time with family or your pursuit of academic excellence. Be careful in your choice of hobbies, and balance those pursuits with the demands of your familial and vocational commitments. In my case, my family and my writing *are* my major "hobbies."[15] Not everyone will be tempted and distracted from diligent work in the same way, but we all need to know ourselves well enough to realize what particular activities have a tendency to use up unhealthy amounts of our time. Avoid these addictive time wasters at all costs! If they do not kill, they will certainly prolong your dissertation or other major writing projects. We must continually seek to grow in and develop the virtue of diligence.

Conclusion

Both Testaments emphasize the importance of diligence, both for practical, "worldly" success and for working out believers' salvation. True biblical diligence operates not in the arena of self-effort but in the realm of grace-based dependence on the Holy Spirit. It is motivated by gratitude toward God for his salvation and calling.

The virtue of diligence applied to the scholarly vocation does not differ much from the virtue necessary for anyone to do anything well and with excellence. Any successful athlete, musician, or scientist will testify to the necessity of diligence for achieving excellence. Diligence is a vital characteristic for us to cultivate throughout our lives and involves consistent hard work, planning, and follow-through. It is the primary antidote to the vice of laziness.

While important, diligence is by no means the only important virtue for aspiring, and practicing, scholars to pursue. In the following chapters, we will learn more about some of these other essential virtues. Up next for discussion is the virtue of courage.

6

Courage

To your diligence, add courage.

This chapter goes straight to the heart of my reason for writing this book. Generally, when one thinks about courage, the image of a soldier valiantly fighting enemies for the cause of freedom, the firefighter rushing into a burning building in order to save a trapped child, or the explorer boldly venturing to go where no one has gone before comes to mind far faster than the image of a scholar reading a book or typing away on a computer in a stuffy study. The common stereotype notwithstanding, however, the pursuit of excellence in the vocation of a Christian scholar requires a considerable amount of courage.

The Desperate Need for Courage

Simply put, Christians in academia today are often tempted to *sacrifice their integrity for academic respectability*.[1] Pressures abound to go with the flow of scholarly consensus, and the academy often marginalizes those who buck the system. This calls for conviction, commitment, and courage. Will the scholar hide his faith commitments through carefully chosen language in order to gain a wider academic audience for his or her research? Will the doctoral student choose a "safe" topic in order not to sacrifice his or her chances to get a degree? Will the author refrain from speaking out in order not to jeopardize a book contract with a leading publisher? Courage, combined with trust in God, will not choose the path of least resistance.[2]

During my doctoral studies, the Johannine community hypothesis had been elevated to the position of a paradigm that was "virtually established" and was "what students imbibe from standard works, such as commentaries and textbooks, as knowledge generally received and held to be valid."[3] I did not think the evidence required such an interpretation and held to Johannine authorship throughout my dissertation, against the scholarly consensus. Since that time, the Johannine community hypothesis has been gradually weakening and is now considered to be in drastic decline and in radical need of reassessment.[4]

This illustrates several important points. First, the scholarly consensus of today will not necessarily represent the scholarly consensus of tomorrow. Paradigms shift and change in both the physical sciences and in biblical interpretation.[5] Second, the orientation of your major professor and institution is important. I was drawn to D. A. Carson, my mentor, in part because he had the courage to stand against the tide of critical scholarship and possessed the scholarly excellence to earn the respect of his peers at the same time. He served as an important example for me as a scholar who consistently and courageously resisted popular currents and trends that, though adopted by many, did not necessarily square with the best available evidence, and who did so with utmost scholarly excellence.

Conversely, I know of several evangelical PhD students who were accepted into programs in which opposition to the dictates of the reigning critical paradigm meant that they would not get their degree. These students felt forced into neutral topics in literary or linguistic studies—whether characterization of individuals or groups in one of the Gospels or descriptively cataloguing the semantic range of a given biblical term—in order to be able to get through their dissertation without having to express their potentially hazardous faith commitments. Some of these students have written more openly about their faith and have identified with the evangelical community after receiving their degree, but others never have and in fact gradually moved from a high view of Scripture to one that finds frequent errors in Scripture.

As noted in chapter 3, recent arguments have been put forward by certain members of the Society of Biblical Literature questioning the very legitimacy of confessional scholarship.[6] I suspect that this question will continue to be hotly debated in the years ahead. This calls for courage in the pursuit of excellence among evangelical scholars. We must be courageous in standing for what we believe and not back away from divinely revealed truth while at the same time engaging in the highest level of technical and academic scholarship in the investigation and interpretation of the evidence. I, for one, continue to be active in the John, Jesus, and History group of the SBL and other critical academic forums, but people know where I stand and yet still ask me to contribute and participate in scholarly projects and discussions.

Courage in the Old Testament

Courage, one of the four cardinal virtues in Greek philosophy along with justice, prudence, and temperance, represents a pervasive theme throughout Scripture yet despite this has received relatively little scholarly attention.[7] As in the case of *diligence*, many Hebrew and Greek words and phrases could be translated by the English word *courage*.[8] This makes a comprehensive analysis impossible here. Fortunately, such a comprehensive analysis is not necessary for our present purposes, because the broad contours of a biblical theology of courage are readily discernable and fairly consistent across the canon.

The end of the book of Deuteronomy and the beginning of the book of Joshua provide several foundational concepts for a biblical theology of courage on which later biblical authors explicitly or implicitly depend. First, the basis for biblical courage is the nearness and presence of God. Moses, when speaking to the Israelites concerning their entrance into the Promised Land, exhorted the people, "Be strong and courageous. Do not fear or be in dread of them, for it is the LORD your God who goes with you. He will not leave you or forsake you" (Deut. 31:6). Later, God spoke to Joshua: "Have I not commanded you? Be strong and courageous. Do not be frightened, and do not be dismayed, for the LORD your God is with you wherever you go" (Josh. 1:9). In both of these instances, the command to courage is explicitly grounded in God's presence with those he called.

The exercise of courage on the basis of God's presence, in turn, harks back to God's past actions on behalf of his people and is predicated upon God's promises in the present concerning his future intervention. When the

Israelites are on the verge of entering the Promised Land, Moses recounts God's faithfulness to his promises in the past as the basis for courage in the conviction that he will be faithful to his promises in the future (Deut. 31:4). Looking back on God's actions in the past as the basis for faith, courage, praise, and prayer in the present is common throughout the Old Testament (see, e.g., Psalm 135; 136; Nehemiah 9; Habakkuk 3). In Joshua 1:3–5, God does not base the command to Joshua to be courageous on his past actions but on the simple promise of future action. Joshua must act with courage in order to experience the fulfillment of God's promises to him with regard to the future.

Second, since courage is based on the presence and favor of God, the people of God must maintain a right relationship with God through covenant faithfulness and obedience. In Deuteronomy, God's *favorable* presence with his people is closely connected with blessings for covenant faithfulness (Deut. 28:1–14). On the other hand, the curses for covenant infidelity provide no basis for courage but rather indicate God's *judgmental* presence (Deut. 28:15–68) and eventual absence (Ezekiel 10). Lack of obedience will cause fear, not courage (Deut. 28:64–67). Joshua 1:7–9 makes the connection between obedience, God's presence, and courage unmistakably clear:

> Only be strong and very courageous, being careful to do according to all the law that Moses my servant commanded you. Do not turn from it to the right hand or to the left, that you may have good success wherever you go. This Book of the Law shall not depart from your mouth, but you shall meditate on it day and night, so that you may be careful to do according to all that is written in it. For then you will make your way prosperous, and then you will have good success. Have I not commanded you? Be strong and courageous. Do not be frightened, and do not be dismayed, for the LORD your God is with you wherever you go.

Courage derives from God's presence but must be accompanied by obedience. (Of course, it is also true that obedience engenders courage.)

Third, courage relates to the fulfillment of God's particular mission for his people. This is a logical extension from the concept of obedience but distinctive enough to warrant attention. God commands courage and obedience for the accomplishment of his particular purposes. In Deuteronomy and Joshua, this purpose relates to conquering the Promised Land. Joshua and the people stand on the brink of conquest and the fulfillment of God's plan for them, but the future appears daunting, difficult, and dangerous. In light of the unknown, fearful future they must act with courage based on the promise of God's helping presence to fulfill the particular mission to which God had called them.

These three elements, then, provide the basis for understanding courage throughout the canon: (1) Courage is based on the presence of God whom God's people can trust because of his actions on their behalf in the past and his promises of future action. (2) Courage is tied to obedience, because without obedience and faithfulness there can be no confidence that God will act favorably. (3) Courage is necessary to fulfill a particular mission or call from God.

These three points are illustrated in various ways throughout the Old Testament. In Judges 20:22, the people of Israel took courage in their fight against Benjamin, even in the face of incredible losses, because of God's command (Judg. 20:18, 23, 27–28). Joab commanded his troops to be courageous "for our people, and for the cities of our God" (2 Sam. 10:12). David combined the promise of God's presence with the particular task of building a temple for God in his charge to his son Solomon to be courageous (1 Chron. 28:10, 20). Jehoshaphat's command to the judges to be courageous (2 Chron. 19:11) is linked with the particular task of judging the people (2 Chron. 19:8) and of promoting covenant faithfulness (2 Chron. 19:10) and is predicated on God's presence (2 Chron. 19:11). Conversely, courage will fail in the day of God's judgment because of idolatry and disobedience (Jer. 4:9; Ezek. 22:13–14; Amos 2:16). Who can stand against God?

Courage in the New Testament

Christ's life, death, and resurrection take the motif of courage to new heights in the New Testament. God's presence with his people extends to include Jesus (Matt. 14:27; 28:20; John 16:33) and the Holy Spirit (Luke 12:11–12) as the basis for courage in the New Testament. What is more, Jesus's command addressed to his followers to be his witnesses (Matt. 28:18–20; Acts 1:8) provides the standard for obedience and the particular task in which God's people should engage: the proclamation of the gospel of salvation in Jesus Christ throughout the world. In the book of Acts, courage is related to this particular mission given by Jesus to his people.[9]

The connection between courage and the proclamation of the gospel is also evident in the Pauline literature (Eph. 6:19–20; Phil. 1:14; 1 Thess. 2:2). Because of Jesus's high-priestly work, the author of Hebrews can exhort his readers to draw near to God in sacred space with courage (*parr sia*, Heb. 4:16; 10:19). In Revelation 21:8, John begins the list of those whose portion will be the lake of fire with "the cowardly." When it comes to faithfulness to Christ in the face of persecution and possible death, courage can take on soteriological dimensions: "But we are not of those who shrink back and are destroyed, but of those who have faith and preserve their souls" (Heb. 10:39).

Summary

The Bible closely links courage with faith and bases courage on the favorable presence of God. Believers can have courage because God is near, even in the face of an apparently dangerous and uncertain future. He can be trusted on the basis of his past saving actions and his promises to be with his people and to deliver them in the future. God's favorable presence is dependent on faith and obedience. The New Testament ties obedience to the particular task of proclaiming the gospel of salvation in Christ Jesus to the entire world. Believers can have courage as they participate with God in his mission in the world, knowing that God is with them to provide for them, guide them, and protect them.

The Reformation Monument in Geneva Commemorating the Great Reformers

The Courageous Scholar
Seeking God's Approval

Whose approval really matters? This simple diagnostic question will lay bare our motivation. Whom are we really trying to please? Are we trying to gain the approval of our academic peers or the approval of God who saved us and has called us to his eternal kingdom? The apostle Paul found himself in a similar situation and held fast to his commitment. He wrote, "Just as we have been approved by God to be entrusted with the gospel, so we speak, not to please man, but to please God who tests our hearts" (1 Thess. 2:4). Paul could have ended his sermon before the philosophical establishment in Athens without mentioning his belief in Jesus's historical, bodily resurrection (Acts 17:31). Surely Paul knew that his reference to the resurrection would result in ridicule by his educated audience. He did not back down, however, because the historical reality of Jesus's death and resurrection was at the core of the Christian message (1 Cor. 15:17; cf. 15:3–4).

Our answers to the set of questions posed above will determine the orientation of our lives—including our scholarly endeavors—and will either provide us with the courage to stand alone if necessary or induce us to blend into the scholarly consensus. Whose approval matters the most: God's or that of others? Scholarship in the service of God calls for courage. Courage, in turn, requires faith. Are we willing to bear the shame, if necessary, that may be associated with believing in the crucified and risen Savior as we pursue our academic calling? I cannot think of a better statement in this regard than Jesus's words in John 12:25–26:

> Whoever loves his life loses it, and whoever hates his life in this world will keep it for eternal life. If anyone serves me, he must follow me; and where I am, there will my servant be also. If anyone serves me, the Father will honor him.

Similarly, as aspiring and practicing scholars, let us heed the words of the author of the letter to the Hebrews:

> So Jesus also suffered outside the gate in order to sanctify the people through his own blood. Therefore let us go to him outside the camp and bear the reproach he endured. For here we have no lasting city, but we seek the city that is to come. Through him then let us continually offer up a sacrifice of

> praise to God, that is, the fruit of lips that acknowledge his name. (Heb. 13:12–15)

Just like Jesus, who died "outside the camp," and the readers of Hebrews, whom the author enjoined to "go to him outside the camp," we as scholars should be willing to do our scholarship "outside the camp," that is, be willing to endure rejection, even ostracism, by the proponents of the scholarly establishment.

Going against the Grain

The courageous scholar who will successfully swim upstream must be convinced that God's approval is more important than that of other people, including one's scholarly peers. He will never forget that he received his call from the crucified Savior and that following him in this life will rarely be a glorious enterprise. As Jesus and Paul reminded their followers, all believers who courageously hold fast to their Christian commitment will be persecuted (John 15:20; 2 Tim. 3:12). This persecution, in turn, may take on more or less subtle forms. It may involve ostracism from the intellectual establishment, alienation from the cultural mainstream, or other religious, social, political, or economic repercussions. If we have not suffered any of these consequences, perhaps it is because we have not stood up for our Christian beliefs in our surrounding context that denies the gospel either in its powerful ramifications or rejects its truthfulness altogether.

One such courageous scholar was Adolf Schlatter (1852–1938). In his day, the history-of-religions school ruled supreme in scholarly circles, according to which Christianity was largely indebted to Hellenistic or Oriental religions. The Lord's Supper and baptism were considered to be adaptations of sacred meals and initiation rites practiced in Hellenistic mystery religions. John's Gospel, for its part, was construed against the backdrop of Greek philosophy or various strands of Gnosticism. Schlatter, almost singlehandedly, bucked this trend. Courageously, he wrote a commentary on John's Gospel in which he strongly emphasized the Jewishness of the Gospel.[10] In his day Schlatter was largely a scholarly pariah (though he was highly respected by many of his students). A century later, Schlatter stands widely rehabilitated, while most of his contemporaries—including Rudolf Bultmann, a theologian of towering stature in his time—look strangely outdated.[11]

The Role of Faith in Scholarship and Academic Excellence

Above, I have mentioned the dichotomy between faith and scholarship posited by many modernist nonconfessional scholars. Is it true, as these scholars claim, that Christian scholarship is dogmatism in disguise, a charade masking deductive advocacy of faith positions as inductive research? In some, even many, cases, this may in fact be the case, but in principle, faith and scholarship are far from being as incompatible as some critical scholars allege. In fact, their rejection of the role of faith in scholarship is itself based on a prior philosophical commitment to materialism or metaphysical naturalism (the belief that the material is all there is, excluding any possibility of the supernatural). This philosophical presupposition, it should be pointed out, does not derive from all the available evidence but itself serves as the framework within which the evidence is assessed and interpreted. The alternate view that God can, and did, supernaturally intervene in creation and history is just as valid an approach as an anti-supernatural one. The contention by some nonconfessional scholars that confessional scholars invariably distort the evidence because of their faith commitment is therefore invalid. Today, of course, many scholars are postmodern and anti-modern, and it is commonly recognized that pure induction is a modernist illusion and that everyone has faith commitments that guide his or her interpretive choices.

In this context, excellence is particularly important for the Christian scholar because it has the potential of overcoming the prevailing prejudice against confessional scholarship in many circles. Excellence can help transcend such a bias, at least in part, and win a hearing with those who differ with us and reject our faith. An example that comes to mind is a review of an essay I wrote on 1 Timothy 2:12. While agreeing with my exegesis of the passage, the reviewer went on to say that she could not go along with my application because her larger presuppositions suggested otherwise. In the reviewer's own words:

> My theological position is very different from that of Köstenberger. Nevertheless, I often find his analysis of texts and exegetical problems convincing and inspiring, especially if he uses linguistic approaches. . . . Likewise, I agree with Köstenberger's reading of 1 Tim 2. Köstenberger shows that the text demands a hierarchy between men and women and is meant as normative teaching. *But with a different, far more critical view of the Bible, I need not accept it as God's word. (It helps that I do not regard 1 Timothy as written by Paul.)*[12]

The reviewer is to be commended for her remarkable candor and honesty. She shows considerable discernment in distinguishing between exegesis and application and in acknowledging the vital role of hermeneutics and one's view of Scripture on biblical interpretation. In addition, the review helpfully surfaces both the possibilities and limitations of a meaningful dialogue between conservative and critical scholarship. On the one hand, it is at times possible to gain a hearing with scholars who hold different ideological convictions and to meet them on the common ground of the text and the available evidence. On the other hand, it is on the whole unlikely that those who differ with us in their presuppositions will agree with our conclusions or change their mind in response to our research (though in some cases this may actually happen).

One thing is fairly certain, however. If you or I, as evangelicals, produce mediocre scholarship, we will have only minimal influence on those outside our own circles of influence. Our only hope for gaining a hearing outside our immediate sphere, if we remain true to our convictions, is scholarship that is characterized by excellence. The reigning paradigms certainly don't need any additional support from evangelicals, but these paradigms are often far from unassailable when held up to the available evidence. Evangelicals are in a unique position to provide such a critique, provided it is accompanied by excellent scholarship.

Conversely, Christian scholars who attempt to play to both sides, claiming to be evangelical while seeking to gain the approval of the critical establishment by diluting their evangelical beliefs, will likely get caught in the middle and won't fit in well with either group. They will be neither truly accepted by the critical establishment nor trusted by conservative evangelicals. How much better it is to show courage and backbone and to stand up for what you believe in your scholarly work. The principle affirmed by Jesus, "No one can serve two masters" (Matt. 6:24), pertains also to the academic realm. A Christian scholar who tries to retain his or her conservative credentials and yet equivocates in order to gain the approval of the critical scholarly establishment will most likely fail to gain the approval of either side.

Christian Scholars: Set Apart for Spiritual Warfare

Last but not least, let's remember that we conduct our scholarship not merely on a horizontal plane; there is also a vital vertical dimension. As Christian scholars, God has set us apart for spiritual warfare. Divine warfare is a pervasive theme throughout Scripture.[13] Because the Israelites were set apart for God, he gave them particular instructions as to how they were to wage war (Deuteronomy 7; 20), and, as their God, fought for Israel against her enemies (Ex. 15:1–3; Deut. 28:7). God also fought against his own people in judgment for covenant violation (Lam. 2:4–5). The Hebrew prophets pictured God as coming in future judgment as a divine warrior (Zech. 14:3), and Jesus is pictured as the divine warrior both in his earthly ministry (Matt. 3:11–12; Eph. 4:7–8; Col. 2:15) and at the second coming (Rev. 19:11–16).

In his death and resurrection, Jesus redefines how God's people are to wage war. No longer are they to engage in physical warfare as in the Old Testament; they are to wage warfare by bearing witness to a hostile world.[14] The apostle Paul puts the issue well: "For though we walk in the flesh, we are not waging war according to the flesh. For the weapons of our warfare are not of the flesh but have divine power to destroy strongholds. We destroy arguments and every lofty opinion raised against the knowledge of God, and take every thought captive to obey Christ" (2 Cor. 10:3–5). Jesus provides the supreme example of how this warfare by witness to a hostile world must be conducted: by faithful obedience unto death.[15] The lion of the tribe of Judah—the divine warrior—is a lamb, having been slain (Rev. 5:5–6). The book of Revelation pictures believers as God's soldiers involved in holy warfare (Rev. 7:4–14) who gain the victory and overcome through faithful witness unto death (Rev. 12:11).[16]

Although our scholarly work of witness will not necessarily result in literal martyrdom, we should expect spiritual opposition from those who resist the proclamation of biblical truth. Satan can hardly be expected to stand idly by when God's people seek to pull unbelievers from the clutches of hell into the domain of God's kingdom. Paul makes it clear that "we do not wrestle against flesh and blood, but against the rulers, against the authorities, against the cosmic powers over this present darkness, against the spiritual forces of evil in the heavenly places" (Eph. 6:12).

We have a real adversary who is opposed to the establishment of God's kingdom and who wages war against God's people (James 4:7; 1 Pet. 5:8–9; Rev. 12:17). As scholars who are set apart for God, we engage in spiritual warfare by bearing witness to God's truth in order to encourage believers and to win over those who are opposed to God's kingdom. The decisive battle was won by Jesus at the cross (Eph. 4:7–8; Col. 2:15); the eschatological battle will bring the final consummation of God's kingdom.

In the present, we are called to engage in spiritual warfare as we seek to advance God's kingdom here on earth. This takes courage.

Conclusion

In light of the biblical-theological material on courage presented above, we, as evangelical scholars, have a strong reservoir from which to draw courage. We can have confidence in God's favorable presence with us to help and sustain us on a daily basis. God has not called us to this vocation in order to abandon us to struggle on our own! He is with us. In addition, we can draw courage from the fact that we are engaged in the particular task and mission to which God has called his people: the proclamation of his truth to the entire world. We have immense grounds for courage to the extent that we are pursuing our mission from God in the world in obedience to his command and with integrity and courage.

Compromise, retreat, and cowardice will accomplish nothing. God has called us to research, write, and teach his truth with courage and conviction. We can have every confidence that God is with us. We need not fear where the evidence might lead us, because we are assured of God's utter truthfulness and faithfulness. Therefore don't be afraid to stand up for what you believe, even in the face of what at times may seem to be an intimidating or even overwhelming critical scholarly consensus. Never let the need for courage become an excuse for ignoring or distorting the evidence but rather develop the virtue of courage, so that you will be able to engage the evidence judiciously and competently and follow it wherever it may lead.

What is more, courage sustains an interesting relationship with obedience and integrity. One can be courageous only to the point that one has been obedient to engage in responsible scholarly work and has committed oneself to a high standard of academic excellence. Before one courageously proclaims a certain position or interpretation, one must do good scholarly research. Otherwise, courage quickly turns to folly. Likewise, by calling us to courage, I am not suggesting that we be unduly confrontational or abrasive. Courage must be balanced both with wisdom—so that we will know when to be silent and when to speak up (Eccl. 3:7)—and with humility, so that when we speak up, we do so in the right way and for the right reasons.

The scholarly virtue of courage, in turn, pertains directly to the virtue I will discuss next: passion. How could one be genuinely convinced of the truth of God's Word, be profoundly moved by the reality of his call to join him on his mission, and be wholly gripped by the realization of his immediate presence with us, and yet fail to live, research, write, and teach with passion? Courage will inexorably lead to passion as we live out the reality of our convictions before a watching world.

7

Passion

To your courage, add passion.

Passion flows from courage. Courage enables us to deal with rejection and take up unpopular positions in defense of truth, while passion deals with the broader motivation and the tone in which we write. How much do you care about what you are doing? Is it simply a job or career, or does it, in the words of the famous hymn "When I Survey the Wondrous Cross," "demand your soul, your life, your all"? We are not just pursuing scholarship, writing, and teaching because these are jobs that pay the bills and gain us some respect, but because we feel inwardly compelled to pursue truth. This inward compulsion—passion—will be evident in your writing and teaching. It normally does not take a student long to determine if a particular professor is passionate about the subject matter or bored with it. Both passion and boredom are contagious: they pass from teacher to student. Passion for the subject matter in a teacher communicates more than mere words are capable of conveying.

In developing passion, our faith commitment, which may result in rejection or dismissal by some scholars, can become one of our greatest assets, because it enables us to be passionate about what we believe. Passion is certainly no substitute for truth or the soundness of an argument. That said, however, we should be passionate about what we believe. If we are not passionate about a conviction we hold, why are we seeking to communicate it to others, and why should we expect others to care?

A Biblical Theology of Passion

The word *passion* carries a broad range of connotations, not all of them good. In 1993, P. T. O'Brien published a short book on Paul and missions in Australia entitled *Consumed by Passion: Paul and the Dynamic of the Gospel*.[1] In it, he stressed how Paul was "consumed by passion for the lost, for these needy Gentiles who did not know that the Servant's vicarious work of redemption was for them."[2] The American publisher of the same book in 1995 changed the title to the more mundane *Gospel and Mission in the Writings of Paul: An Exegetical and Theological Analysis*, apparently in order to remove any confusion that might arise in an American readership by the title *Consumed by Passion*![3] Rightly understood, of course, passion is good, necessary, and biblical. God is the one who created us with the capacity for passion, and he is pleased with the living out of genuine passion in his service. He is not particularly interested in followers who are ho-hum, cavalier, and disinterested in his mission to the world.

In the biblical texts, "passion" often carries negative connotations with regard to sexual, idolatrous, or worldly desires that are directly antithetical to God's will.[4] In his letter to the Galatians, Paul writes, "And those who belong to Christ Jesus have crucified the flesh with its passions and desires" (Gal. 5:24). The Roman believers he enjoins, "Let not sin therefore reign in your mortal body, to make you obey its passions" (Rom. 6:12). This negative kind of passion is linked with the flesh, sin, and the world.[5] The positive form of passion, on the other hand, is often described by the word "zeal."[6] Both God and humans are described in Scripture as zealous.

God's Passion

According to Isaiah, God is passionate and zealous about his plan and his people: "For out of Jerusalem shall go a remnant, and out of Mount Zion a band of survivors. The zeal of the Lord will do this" (2 Kings 19:31). God's zeal is repeatedly invoked as a guarantee that God will fulfill his promises to his people. Twice more Isaiah declares: "The zeal of the Lord of hosts will do this" (Isa. 9:7; 37:32; cf. 26:11; 42:13; 59:17;

63:15). God's passion in judgment is often described as jealousy (Deut. 29:20; Ezek. 5:13; 36:5; 38:19).

In the New Testament, John 2:17 describes how the disciples connected Jesus's passion in clearing the temple with Psalm 69:9: "For zeal for your house has consumed me, and the reproaches of those who reproach you have fallen on me." Jesus was passionate about the house of God, the temple—so passionate that he was "consumed" by zeal for it and in the end gave his life for his people. In this way, the temple—Jesus's body—was destroyed and raised up in three days, and he became the new temple, the new place of worship for God's people (John 2:19–22; cf. 4:21–24).[7]

Human Passion
Human zeal can be both positive and negative. It is negative when it lacks knowledge or is linked with a goal other than God's plan but positive when it is directed toward obedience to God. Saul acted wickedly toward the Gibeonites when he "sought to strike them down in his zeal for the people of Israel and Judah" (2 Sam. 21:2), because in his zeal he was acting against Israel's earlier treaty with the Gibeonites. Jehu's zeal for God was ambiguous at best (2 Kings 10:16). Although he slaughtered Ahab's descendants and the prophets of Baal, he went too far in killing Ahaziah (2 Kings 9:27) and Ahaziah's relatives (2 Kings 10:13–14) and did not renounce the sin of Jeroboam—the golden calves at Bethel and Dan (2 Kings 10:29, 31).

Phinehas represents godly passion in the Old Testament. After Phinehas had intervened to stop the sexual immorality leading to idolatry in the camp, God affirmed that Phinehas's passion reflected his own (translated in the ESV as "jealousy"): "Phinehas the son of Eleazar, son of Aaron the priest, has turned back my wrath from the people of Israel, in that he was jealous with my jealousy among them, so that I did not consume the people of Israel in my jealousy" (Num. 25:11). The psalmist affirmed that this zealous action was credited to Phinehas as righteousness (Ps. 106:31).

Paul testified that the Jews in his day who failed to recognize Christ had a zeal for God but lamented that their zeal lacked knowledge (Rom. 10:2). Elsewhere, Paul acknowledged that he, too, had at one time possessed such misguided religious zeal, when he had persecuted Christians before his encounter with the risen Christ on the road to Damascus (Phil. 3:6; cf. Acts 22:3; Gal. 1:14). The believers in Jerusalem explained to Paul how many Jews had believed and were zealous for the law (Acts 21:20). Later on in his letter to the Romans, Paul exhorted church leaders to lead with zeal (Rom. 12:8) and called on all believers to serve the Lord zealously (Rom. 12:11). Writing to the Corinthians, Paul commended the zeal that godly grief had produced in that congregation (2 Cor. 7:11). The Corinthians' zeal had also stirred others to give to the needy in Jerusalem (2 Cor. 9:2).

One of the purposes of Christ's redeeming death was to "purify for himself a people for his own possession who are zealous for good works" (Titus 2:14; cf. 1 Pet. 3:13). God's people are to be characterized by a passion to perform good works. Finally, in John's vision, Jesus commands the Laodicean church to "be zealous and repent" (Rev. 3:19). Genuine repentance must not be lackluster or half-hearted. It should be accompanied by zeal and passion for doing what is right.

Biblical Examples of Passion

In addition to the lexical evidence, the kind of passion that pleases God is embodied by the example of various individuals throughout Scripture. In two particular instances, noted above, the passion of Phinehas and Jesus is described both by their example and by specific words denoting their strong affective advocacy of, and attachment to, the cause of God (*qin'ah* and *zēlos*, respectively). A case could easily be made for the godly passion exhibited by biblical characters such as Moses, David, Josiah, the Hebrew prophets, Peter, Stephen, and others. Because of space constraints, however, I will limit my discussion to the apostle Paul.

Paul repeatedly attributed zeal to himself in his pre-Christian life (Acts 22:3 [reported by Luke]; Gal. 1:14; Phil. 3:6).[8] His zeal for the law and the traditions of his forefathers led him to persecute the early Christians. After his conversion and calling on the road to Damascus, Paul continued to exhibit unmatched passion, only now in accordance with the knowledge he had gained in his encounter with Christ and subsequent study of the Scriptures. Paul's post-conversion passion is epitomized in his heartfelt cry in 1 Corinthians 9:16: "Woe to me if I do not preach the gospel!" He was under compulsion and inwardly driven to proclaim the good news of salvation in Jesus. His passion for the salvation of his own people was such that he wished he himself were cut off if this could bring about their repentance (Rom. 9:3).

Summary

God is a passionate and jealous God. His passion moves him to keep his promises to rescue his people and to bring judgment on sin and disobedience. Phinehas demonstrates that it is possible for God's people to share in this passion and to reflect it in their actions. This pleases God. Christians in the New Testament are exhorted to be passionate about doing good works and, with Paul as the prime example, to be passionate about proclaiming the gospel.

P. T. O'Brien helpfully elaborates on the function of Paul's example:

> Paul is not suggesting that they should engage in the same wide-ranging, apostolic ministry in which he has been involved; but each *in his or her own way and according to their personal gifts* was to have the same orientation and ambitions as Paul himself, that is, of seeking by all possible means to save some. They were to be consumed by passion as he was!⁹

The Passionate Scholar
Passion and Self-Knowledge

What motivates you? What are you driven by? Do you have genuine passion for God? After I had published my first article,¹⁰ a fellow student at Trinity approached me and asked me what he should do to get an article put in a journal. I asked him on what topic he wanted to write, and he said he didn't know—he just wanted to publish an article because he thought that's what was expected of him as a theology student. He wanted to write for publication, but he lacked a burden to communicate anything in particular. Rather than being driven by passion to persuade others about a particular truth, or to warn them about a possible error, he simply sought to conform to a set of academic expectations. Needless to say, this is a rather inadequate reason why any of us should want to publish our material.

Ask yourself the following diagnostic questions. What do you feel passionate about? What doctrine would you like to explore in greater detail? What error or misunderstanding concerns you deeply and makes you long for a genuinely biblical response? What specific holy compulsion is part of God's unique calling to you and no one else? God has uniquely positioned you with your background, gifts, skill sets, insights, and passions to research and write on a particular range of topics and issues.

One way to develop the virtue of passion is to get in touch with who you are and what God has called you to do. This will affect your selection of topics for your papers, your dissertation, and your writing projects. This is also why my mentor, D. A. Carson, steadfastly refused to hand me my dissertation topic on a silver platter, as it were, limiting himself instead to responding to ideas I brought to him. I still remember sitting despondently in Dr. Carson's office after having been turned down for perhaps the third or fourth time when suggesting a dissertation topic, quietly mumbling, "I still think there may be a dissertation topic here somewhere." (I believe at the time I was contemplating writing my dissertation on discipleship in John.) "That may be so," Dr. Carson replied stoically, "but, if so, you haven't found it yet!" Feeling rather sorry for myself, I meekly retreated, continuing my search for that elusive dissertation topic. At the time, being left to my own devices in identifying a topic for my dissertation was painful, but with the benefit of hindsight I can see how Dr. Carson was exactly right: only when the idea for a given topic originates from within you can you be sure that you have the passion that will sustain you during the long process of writing a dissertation. After all, it's *your* dissertation, not that of your supervisor.

Passion and Purpose

Passion also extends to our purpose for writing. As Christian scholars, we should be writing to persuade. Passion for truth should therefore motivate our scholarship. This passionate pursuit of truth in our academic work, in turn, will be based on a conviction concerning the strategic importance of scholarship and scholarly writing. In order to thrive as a scholar, you must be convinced that you are engaged in a vitally important task. Your passion will help motivate you to discipline yourself in order to learn the trade of a scholar, to document sources, and to interact with scholarship on a given topic. Most of us are not in scholarship because we love footnoting! It is a means to an end. We need to engage scholarship in order to understand the topic as accurately as possible and to have credibility and influence as we argue for a particular interpretation or application.

My own vision for the strategic importance of writing was initially inspired by reading the book *Dedication and Leadership* by Douglas Hyde.[11] Hyde is a former member of the Communist party who converted to Christianity. In his book he talks about Communist techniques of instilling dedication and the willingness to sacrifice. He also talks about the importance of propaganda for spreading Communism. Reading Hyde's book instilled in me a conviction regarding the strategic importance of writing and literature in spreading and promoting a movement, in our case the infinitely more noble and worthy cause of Christianity.

Another important influence was my experience of working on my doctoral degree under D. A. Carson. When it comes to publishing, Carson has the Midas touch; everything he touches turns into gold. There is virtually nothing he writes that does not make it into publication, and everything he writes is publishable. As his student, I learned invaluable lessons from Carson concerning how he goes about academic writing, how he orders his lifestyle and ministry to accommodate an effective writing ministry, how he uses his research assistants, and so on.

Once I had the privilege of renting the house in Cambridge where the Carson family normally stayed during Dr. Carson's sabbaticals there. Upon arrival, I discovered that Carson had written up an entire manual for taking care of the house, not failing to mention even the most mundane details. If you needed to know anything about taking care of 4 Lexington Close, it was in that manual! I wouldn't be surprised if one day that manual were to make it into publication. On a more serious note, with scholars such as Don Carson, or Wayne Grudem (another one of my professors at Trinity), it may appear to those on the outside that they are primarily driven by academic interests, publishing yet another book with their name on it.

Nothing could be further from the truth. What I learned was that both of these men, and many other noted scholars such as Peter O'Brien and Robert Yarbrough, are motivated by a deep passion for the church and by a love for God's truth and his people. In fact, many of these men's publications were given first in a ministry setting and were printed only later at the initiative of those who benefited from their ministries. I remember Don Carson encouraging me once to get more deeply involved in local church ministry, in particular in student evangelism or university ministry, as he perceived that I was focusing too unilaterally on seminary teaching and scholarly writing.

Indeed, what you will find is that being involved in ministry will deepen your passion for writing and research. Your students will supply you with some burning questions that are being asked in the general culture and need to be addressed with biblical fidelity. Your church members will help you frame an issue in a way that is accessible to the nonspecialist. God will reward your love for others and your commitment to his church by strengthening and improving your writing ministry. In fact, this is exactly what writing ought to be—ministry, service to others, and not merely, or even predominantly, an exercise in self-gratification or an outlet of one's own selfish ambition.

Publications are not an end in themselves; they are the means to an end, a tool for ministry. Have you and I learned this lesson yet? Remember that, as far as we know, Jesus didn't write a single book. And yet look how deep an impact he had! Paul, of course, *did* write quite a bit, but note how all of his extant writings were penned in the context of ministry. Upon reading Paul's letters, one cannot help but be struck by his deep concern for the churches, and individuals in them, that pervades every single one of his epistles. The evangelical celebrity culture in North America today is a far cry from these humble servants of God.[12]

Passion and Communication

In scholarly writing, passion relates to the way in which we communicate on a given issue, but it will not substitute for the strength of the argument itself. In the academic realm, style never trumps substance. Passion should not be used to gloss over a weak argument. If we do have the truth on our side and solid evidence at our disposal, then we should communicate passionately. As mentioned, if we don't strongly believe in our case, why would we expect anyone else to do so?

Many scholarly works are mundane, pedestrian, and boring. They may be accurate, but they do not grab you. As a journal editor, I have received my fair share of articles that start out matter-of-factly, without any effort to give the reader a "hook" on which to hang a given contribution. Even though it is better to be accurate and boring than inaccurate and passionate, it is best to be both accurate *and* passionate in your writing. Scholarly excellence calls for both.

There is a fine line here. Those with a preaching instinct must be careful not to get carried away when writing a scholarly piece, because academic discourse ought to rest primarily on the strength of the evidence, not on the forcefulness of presentation or flowery language used. Be careful not to wear your passion on your sleeve. Be understated in expressing your passion and focus primarily on making a compelling case and presenting it as eloquently as you can.[13]

Passion and Truth

While passion can be a great asset, it can also be fraught with peril. The danger of passion, if not coupled with truth, is that your followers will be misled when they are attracted to or compelled by your passion. Again: do not use passion, pathos, or piety as a manipulative device to get people to agree with you. You've heard it said that you can tell when a preacher's points are getting weaker: he is gradually raising his voice. Passion must not be confused with charisma or oratory, nor does volume substitute for truth. This applies especially to preachers who may be tempted to resort to emotional appeals in the place of careful interpretation and application.

Jesus, as mentioned, had great passion. Yet he never attempted to manipulate people into believing in him (to the contrary, he discouraged people from following him for the wrong reasons!). His passion was for God, and for his kingdom, and he pursued his calling relentlessly and yet with appropriate restraint.[14] Paul did the same. He resolved to put aside oratory where it stood in the way of the simple gospel message. He knew that the gospel was in truth the gospel *of God* (Rom. 1:1) and would do nothing to empty the gospel of its power. When your passion gets in the way of the gospel, you need to exercise restraint. The message is more important than the messenger.

Conclusion

I hope this chapter serves as a call to serious self-examination. What are you passionate about? What drives you? God has given each of us a message, a calling, and this unique calling from God is worth being passionate about. If we are not passionate about a subject, we cannot expect our audience to catch our vision.

Too often students do not finish their degree because of a lack of passion. They don't have the inward motivation and compulsion to persevere to the final defense of the dissertation. I've known students who took numerous seminars, wrote countless papers, and passed several exams up through the comprehensive exam at the end of their program. Then, when it came time to write the dissertation, which was supposed to be the crowning achievement of their degree, they quit. Why? They had lost their passion. Don't lose yours (cf. Rev. 2:4; 3:16).

A particular danger accompanies passion: the temptation to overstate your argument. Because of this, passion must be joined by the accompanying virtue that I will discuss in the following chapter. Restraint protects us from the potential dangers of unbridled or uncontrolled passion and keeps us from going beyond the evidence when we issue and defend our claims.

8

Restraint

To your passion, add restraint.

"Restraint" may seem like an unlikely title for a chapter on scholarly virtue (though, as mentioned above, temperance was one of the four cardinal virtues in Greek philosophy). To be sure, there may be more obvious virtues which I could have legitimately included. What is more, restraint is different from some of the other positive virtues such as love or passion, because it is more about *not* doing things. Yet even though restraint may not be as conspicuous, it constitutes a genuine mark of maturity and a necessary virtue in the pursuit of scholarly excellence. This is especially true for people in leadership: self-control is not optional but required.[1] If anyone lacks restraint, there will be serious negative repercussions in the form of broken relationships, defective scholarship, and the dishonoring of Christ's name.

Some students approach scholarly exchanges as if they were viewing a boxing match and want to see someone's nose bloodied. They wait with anticipation for each new publication of a set of scholars on opposing sides of a given issue to see who can throw the knockout punch. Despite the genuine charity of each of the men involved, I'm afraid some have been following the debate over justification between John Piper and N. T. Wright with this type of attitude.[2] Christian scholarship is not a spectator sport where the audience watches with glee until someone delivers the fatal blow. This calls for restraint in our reading, interpretation, and writing.

Passion for truth is certainly a good and necessary thing, but unbridled passion without restraint can be dangerous, because it will tend to offend or antagonize those with whom you are in dialogue and can pressure you to overstate your case or misrepresent others. It is certainly appropriate for us to hold firmly to our convictions, but we should argue for these with proper restraint. As is our custom, we will first look at some of the biblical material on the virtue of restraint to build a proper framework for our application of restraint to the scholarly calling and community.

A Biblical Theology of Restraint

Many different biblical virtues relate to restraint. These include self-control, meekness, patience, and gentleness, among others.[3] The biblical material often connects self-control to the control of one's temper (Prov. 14:17, 29; 15:18). The following proverb is representative: "A man without self-control is like a city broken into and left without walls" (Prov. 25:28). Paul makes it clear that an overseer must be "self-controlled" (1 Tim. 3:2) and not be "quarrelsome" (1 Tim. 3:3) or "quick-tempered" (Titus 1:7). The Bible also links self-control with sexual purity (1 Cor. 7:5, 9).

In addition to focusing on controlling one's temper and sexual desire, many biblical admonitions present restraint as a virtue that should characterize every aspect of life. Self-control is one of the fruits that the Spirit produces in the lives of Christians (Gal. 5:23). The Pastoral Epistles, in particular, focus on the importance of self-control (e.g., 1 Tim. 2:9, 15; 3:3; 2 Tim. 3:3; Titus 2:2, 5; cf. Acts 24:25; 2 Pet. 1:6). Paul writes, "For this reason I remind you to fan into flame the gift of God, which is in you through the laying on of my hands, for God gave us a spirit not of fear but of power and love and self-control" (2 Tim. 1:6–7). Believers have only one master, Jesus Christ, and therefore must not let themselves be mastered by worldly impulses, fleshly desires, or sensual temptations.[4]

Meekness, gentleness, and humility are related virtues. Jesus pronounced a special blessing on the meek (Matt. 5:5). A person who possesses restraint will not be vindictive or retaliate (Rom. 12:19; 1 Thess. 4:6) but treat others with gentleness and compassion. Meekness should characterize our relationships with others (Col. 3:12; James 3:13). We are to restore each other with gentleness (Gal. 6:1). According to 2 Timothy 2:24–26, kindness and gentleness should characterize even the way in which we interact with those who oppose us:

> And the Lord's servant must not be quarrelsome but kind to everyone, able to teach, patiently enduring evil, correcting his opponents with gentleness. God may perhaps grant them repentance leading to a knowledge of the truth, and they may come to their senses and escape from the snare of the devil, after being captured by him to do his will.

The section below on restraint in the academic world will build on the way in which Paul instructs Timothy to relate with kindness and gentleness to those who oppose him. This requires restraint.

I would be remiss if I failed to discuss the restraint Jesus exhibited throughout his ministry. In dealing with his disciples, he continually exhibited patience, self-control, and gentleness in the face of his followers' perpetual ignorance, hard-heartedness, and impetuousness (Mark 9:28–35; 10:35–40; Luke 9:54–55). When accused of demon possession, Jesus did not lose his temper but was measured in his response, calmly observing that his opponents dishonored both him and his Father (John 8:48–54). Later, Thomas demanded that Jesus reveal himself to him, and Jesus graciously acceded to Thomas's demand, even though he didn't have to (John 20:24–29).

When he was slapped in the face at his trial, Jesus likewise did not lash out in anger or strike back and retaliate (Matt. 26:67). By contrast, Paul, in a similar situation in Acts, hurled verbal abuse at his opponents and completely lost his temper when he was struck in the face (Acts 23:2–3). On the cross, in fulfillment of Isaiah's prophecy, Jesus did not retaliate. Jesus's exercise of restraint calls to mind Isaiah's words concerning the Messiah: "A bruised reed he will not break, and a faintly burning wick he will not quench" (Isa. 42:3; see Matt. 12:20). The Messiah was characterized by restraint.

At other times, it appears, Jesus chose to forego restraint, such as when he cleansed the temple as a symbol of God's impending judgment on the Jewish nation (e.g., John 2:14–22). Yet even at this occasion, Jesus displayed restraint and expressed his zeal for God in a very measured and deliberate manner. In other instances, Jesus forcefully denounced his opponents, such as when he called the Pharisees children of the Devil (John 8:44) and pronounced the Jewish leaders as "hypocrites" or worse (Matthew 23). Keep in mind, however, that Jesus was the Messiah who had come to call the Jewish nation and its leaders to account for breaking faith with God and subverting their God-given role as his chosen people. Rather than imitate Jesus in this unique salvation-historical role, we should take care not to be culpable of similar hypocrisy.

Finally, in many ways, it can be said that God himself embodies the characteristic of restraint. God is all-powerful, but he exercises restraint in patience. He does not use the full strength of his might to annihilate those who oppose his rule. He remembers that we are but dust, and delays his judgment in order for people to come to repentance and salvation (Rom. 2:4; 2 Pet. 3:9; cf. 1 Tim. 2:4). God's salvific restraint will eventually give way to final salvation and decisive judgment at the eschatological day of the Lord. This future judgment, as mentioned, was foreshadowed to some degree in Jesus's clearing of the temple, an incident where restraint yielded to righteous indignation and judgment (John 2:13–17).

Scholarship and Restraint

Whereas with some of the virtues we have been discussing there has not been too much of a difference in the exercise of the virtue between different vocations, restraint in the world of academia leads to some clear vocation-specific applications. In the following section, I want to issue several simple exhortations related to restraint based on my experience and observations. Although the biblical material focuses primarily on self-control in relation to losing one's temper and sexual purity, I want to build on the admonitions to self-control in all of one's life to explore the role of restraint in scholarly writing and teaching.

Keep in Mind the People behind the Books

As mentioned in the previous chapter, the task of scholarship is different from preaching. This may seem obvious, but you may be surprised at how the distinction is not always heeded. Scholarship is a form of dialogue, while preaching is generally practiced as a one-sided conversation or monologue. Because it takes the form of genuine dialogue, scholarship needs to be more understated and focused on the issue and the evidence. The goal in scholarship is not to destroy a person or to discredit his or her reputation but to arrive at the conclusion on a given matter that accounts best for the available evidence.

You may have to keep reminding yourself of the dialogical character of your research and writing, especially when you have been studying and typing alone in your office for hours. It is easy to forget that each book or article with which you interact was written by an author just like you. The scholarly task has a profoundly personal dimension; it is not merely, or even primarily, abstract. Opposing arguments are not just found in books; they represent people who hold them. Your interaction with them should be viewed in relational terms. Since you would not want to be rude, abrasive, or rash to someone's face in your church or community, why would you engage in this kind of behavior in a scholarly publication? If the scholar with whom you are disagreeing were to read your work, he or she should not feel personally attacked, maligned, or misrepresented.

Godly scholarship should not engage in arguments against people who are not there to defend themselves (avoid cheap shots!) but in a dialogue in the hope of winning other people over to our position on the basis of the evidence. If we blast another scholar with a barrage of antagonistic and arrogant rhetoric, we are rarely going to convince him or her of the validity of our position. You never want to caricature the opposing position through lack of restraint. This could lead to damaged relationships with people whom in some cases you will actually meet at some point in your life, whether at a professional meeting or at some other occasion (if not in heaven).

Even if you were never to meet individuals with whom you are sparring academically, you should have the integrity, and restraint, to treat them as brothers or sisters in Christ (if they are believers) or as people created in God's image for whom Christ died (unbelievers). Our opponents may be wrong, but they are still people whom God loves and for whom Christ died. Why not learn to look at them as God's instruments to teach you proper restraint, love, and Christlike character?

Let the Evidence Do the Talking
The relational and dialogical character of scholarship should lead us to focus on the evidence rather than on the person. Restraint will reflect itself in our attitude. I remember one oral dissertation defense in which I sat where the committee had a serious concern with the attitude the student conveyed in his dissertation. There were no major problems with the dissertation as such, but the student's words communicated an arrogant

and disrespectful attitude toward several older, more established scholars. It was evident to the committee that the student had an ax to grind and was uncharitable toward those with whom he disagreed—in some cases his own teachers—and this had a rather negative effect on the way in which the dissertation was evaluated. Attitude makes all the difference when we are disagreeing with someone.

The way you say something can often be as important as what you are saying. There are ways to discuss criticisms in a judicious manner by qualifying or hedging your language ("It seems that something is the case," "So-and-so appears to do something," etc.). You want to avoid inflammatory language that deliberately provokes. Your choice of words matters. For instance, the word *failure* is more negatively charged than the expression "neglect." Likewise, to say someone "completely missed" a piece of evidence is more negative than noting that he or she "overlooked" or "did not sufficiently consider" some data. There are ways to communicate the same conclusion without overstating your case with an arrogant attitude. Give others the benefit of the doubt; remember the Golden Rule. It is often easy to tell by the tone of a publication whether a given student or scholar is contemptuous of others and their work.

The virtue of restraint will help you keep the focus on the evidence and avoid overstating your case. This will affect your choice of language and help you steer clear of logical fallacies. We can be so motivated to prove our point that we commit fallacies such as ad hominem attacks or engage in selective use of evidence. Never attribute to other people sinister motives or otherwise speculate about their motives. Even if you think you know what motivated another scholar to lodge a particular

"Facts, Not Opinions"
sign in London, England

argument, rarely can you be sure what is driving him or her to take a particular position. Despite the well-known example of Martin Luther, who in various publications took aim at the pope and the Roman Catholic Church, name-calling is never a good strategy. Calling your opponent the antichrist, or a blasphemer and heretic, will not win him or her over to your position.[5]

Restraint is a supportive virtue because it allows your scholarship to shine through.

One positive example comes readily to mind, Gary Burge's favorable review of my student (now colleague) Scott Kellum's revised dissertation *The Unity of the Farewell Discourse*.[6] Burge's positive stance is remarkable because this scholar previously argued for a different position than Kellum's, and yet he conceded that Kellum had made a strong argument. This example demonstrates the virtue of restraint in both Burge and Kellum. Kellum presented his arguments in such a way that he did not alienate or malign those with whom he disagreed, and Burge demonstrated a commitment to the evidence and resisted the urge to criticize Kellum for drawing different conclusions than he had done. The virtue of restraint will strengthen your scholarship, whether you are advocating or defending a given position.

Be Aware of Your Limitations

Restraint must be tied to genuine humility. We must consider the possibility that we could be wrong. One main reason why we are committed to our position is that we see things with our own set of eyes, and our conclusions make sense to *us*. However, this does not mean that someone else may not legitimately feel the same way about his or her own position. As the book of Proverbs says, "The one who states his case first seems right, until the other comes and examines him" (Prov. 18:17). Restraint is a mark of maturity in a scholar. Lack of restraint is often what you find in younger, aspiring scholars such as students writing and defending their dissertation.

Not everyone will be a world-renown scholar. What makes you think you are going to be the next D. A. Carson or N. T. Wright? (Perhaps you should abbreviate your first name and go by your initials as those two individuals have done; that may help. Then again, maybe not!)[7] Brilliance is always going to be in short supply. Even diligence and courage are no substitutes for exceptional gifting and ability. So, know your limitations. That doesn't mean you have to opt out of scholarship, but you should avoid adopting unrealistic expectations for yourself, lest you set yourself up for a big disappointment. Don't think too highly of yourself (Rom. 12:3).

Grow toward Maturity

Restraint is just one facet of mature Christian character. I briefly mentioned the Australian scholar Peter O'Brien in the previous chapter. He has written five very fine commentaries along with various other books. I want to invite you to read any of those commentaries. You will notice that he always writes with restraint when he presents his arguments. He does set forth what he believes, but he says it in a measured and careful manner. You would find it very hard to be offended by anything he writes, even if you disagree with him.[8] Conversely, one other scholar comes to mind who seems to have a chip on his shoulder. He often appears to be rather consumed with being right and getting back at those with whom he has a running argument. (All right, I am talking about myself.) But scholarship is not about settling scores. Conduct yourself in a courteous and gracious manner toward all, especially your scholarly opponents, and you will fulfill the royal law of love (James 2:8).

The virtue of restraint does not grow in an instant; it must be deliberately cultivated over a period of time. Exercising restraint is a matter of self-mastery. Lack of restraint is often associated with youthful, immature scholars, but this is not always the case. There are also older scholars who lack restraint, presumably because they have never made a conscious effort to develop this virtue.

On a related note, some scholars habitually argue both sides of a case and rarely take a clear position on a disputed exegetical or theological matter. I do not believe this demonstrates restraint but rather is a case of indecisiveness. On the whole, it is appropriate for the reader to expect a commentator to take a considered position on an issue unless, of course, the commentator feels in some cases that the evidence is equally weighted on both sides.[9] But this should be the exception rather than the norm. In the end, you'll usually want to tell the reader what you think and only rarely leave a matter entirely open. The key is to strike a balance between being overly dogmatic and never coming down on any side of the argument.

Conclusion

Restraint is not being wishy-washy, boring, or unsure of yourself. It is about strengthening your argument by using careful language, refusing to overstate your case, and focusing on the evidence. An author can hurt his or her case by coming off too strongly. Just as people shout louder when their argument is weak, overblown rhetoric may indicate a weak scholarly argument. It is both distracting and unpleasant to read an author who lacks restraint. If for no other reason, you should develop this virtue to increase the strength of your scholarship.

Beyond this, the greater motive should be love for God and others. Love for God will be reflected in careful, controlled writing and argumentation. Even if you have the preponderance of the evidence on your side, you will want to exercise restraint because of charity.[10] There are two possibilities: if the scholar you are opposing is a Christian, he is a brother in Christ. If he is not a Christian, we have a mandate from Christ to love him and reach out to him in the hope he might come to Christ. In both cases, we do not want to antagonize our dialogue partners by lack of restraint in presenting our argument.

In this chapter, I have primarily focused on the way in which restraint works in written scholarly discourse. The following chapter focuses on an additional virtue that should characterize both our writing and our verbal discourse: creativity. The virtue of restraint will limit us from going too far in defending our arguments through logical fallacies by engaging in abrasive and arrogant rhetoric. Restraint, however, does not require that we be boring. This is where creativity comes in.

9

Creativity

To your restraint, add creativity.

Most people do not immediately connect creativity with scholarly excellence or scholarly theological writing. Scholarly writing is generally perceived as dry and boring, just the kind of literature you should read to help put yourself to sleep at night. This lack of attention to creativity is surprising because writing is at heart a creative enterprise. Creativity not only allows a writer to communicate ideas in an engaging manner but at a deeper level enables him or her to perceive connections in the data that other scholars miss, perhaps aided by adopting a new perspective, methodology, or approach. A creative mind is able to visualize the relationship and interaction of different pieces of evidence that others view as unrelated. Almost every significant methodological advance in biblical studies (not to mention other fields of research) has been conceived in a creative mind.

Creativity stretches the notion of virtue because it is more of a quality or gift that some people possess to a greater extent than others. Having said this, creativity can also be cultivated to some extent.[1] Some will find it easier to be creative and possess more creative potential than others, but everyone is capable of becoming more creative if he or she is willing to put in the effort required. One reason for including a chapter on creativity in this volume is to increase awareness that scholarly writing should be interesting, even captivating, to the extent the subject matter allows.

On a practical note, this means that you will have to work hard at enlarging your vocabulary and applying yourself consciously to areas such as style, presentation, and the organization of material.[2] At most of our seminaries, formal instruction in writing is either lacking or conspicuously absent altogether.[3] This is particularly curious because professors give writing assignments all the time. Even though I wrote numerous papers during the course of my seminary and doctoral education, I don't remember anyone teaching me how to write well. Instead, I was taught how to acquire information: just the facts and only the facts. As the director of the PhD program at Southeastern, I have come to realize that my experience was not an isolated phenomenon. Many, if not most, of our students have never had any formal education in writing.

I tend to be a fairly creative person. This may explain why I wanted to devote an entire chapter to the topic. I was admitted to the Vienna Academy of Fine Arts at age ten, then became a full university student at age fifteen, and was a concert piano major until I turned eighteen. At that time, I switched to a business administration track because my father and grandfather thought it would be a better avenue to support a family. I still greatly enjoy music and the arts, and my family is rather musical and enjoys being creative in various ways.[4] As an extension of this history, I approach scholarly writing as a creative enterprise. This chapter will first look at the theological foundation for creativity and then proceed to discuss what it means to be a creative scholar.

A Biblical Theology of Creativity

God's activity in creation and existence as creator provide the theological foundation for all human creativity. Even though the creation of human beings in the image of God primarily relates to representing God's lordship through the functions of ruling and subduing the earth, our ability to employ creativity in the exercise of these functions must not be separated from our reflection of God's image. God has created each of us as unique individuals with the power and ability to create, not *ex nihilo* but through the manipulation of preexisting materials.[5] God's unique position as the eternal creator of all that exists is affirmed and celebrated throughout

Creativity

the canon.[6] The diversity and complexity of life testify to God's creativity as the creator.

The book of Revelation celebrates God's role as creator (Rev. 4:11; 10:6), not least because God's activity as creator ensures that he is able to re-create and make all things new (Rev. 21:5). Our conviction of God's past creative acts (Genesis 1–2) grounds our eschatological hope in God's future creation of a new heaven and a new earth (Rev. 21:1; cf. Isa. 65:17).

The early Christians also wrote about salvation as God's re-creation of individuals: God's future activity of re-creation breaks into the present to make people new, prior to the full and final restoration and consummation of God's creation. Everyone who is in Christ is a new creation (2 Cor. 5:17).[7] According to Paul, "neither circumcision counts for anything, nor uncircumcision, but a new creation" (Gal. 6:15).[8] The church as a unified corporate entity is a new creation of God through the union of Jews and Gentiles (Eph. 2:15). Individual believers are exhorted to "put on the new self, created after the likeness of God in true righteousness and holiness" (Eph. 4:24; cf. Eph. 2:10). The present salvation of sinful people through their union with Jesus Christ represents God's end-time re-creative power at work in the present age.

The early Christians also included Jesus in their affirmations of God's creative activity. The Word made all things (John 1:3). God created the world through his Son (Heb. 1:2). All things were created through and for Jesus (Col. 1:16). Through these affirmations, the New Testament clearly includes Jesus in God's divine identity.[9]

Jesus also demonstrated creativity in his earthly ministry through his humanity. Not only did he teach with authority and power, but he used a variety of didactic tools, including parables, stories, and real-life, hands-on experiences.[10] He taught his disciples by involving them in his day-to-day ministry. When people tried to trap him with difficult questions, he often creatively turned the tables on them by asking a question in return (Matt. 22:17–22; Mark 11:28–33).

The Bible also celebrates human creativity in the service of God. Many of the psalms in the Old Testament testify to David's creativity. He not only prayed and worshiped God but also set his prayers to music for use by the entire community. God particularly empowered Bezalel and Oholiab with the creativity they would need for the construction of the tabernacle:

> Then Moses said to the people of Israel, "See, the LORD has called by name Bezalel the son of Uri, son of Hur, of the tribe of Judah; and he has filled

him with the Spirit of God, with skill, with intelligence, with knowledge, and with all craftsmanship, to devise artistic designs, to work in gold and silver and bronze, in cutting stones for setting, and in carving wood, for work in every skilled craft. And he has inspired him to teach, both him and Oholiab the son of Ahisamach of the tribe of Dan. He has filled them with skill to do every sort of work done by an engraver or by a designer or by an embroiderer in blue and purple and scarlet yarns and fine twined linen, or by a weaver—by any sort of workman or skilled designer." (Ex. 35:30–35)

God's divine inspiration of creativity marks creativity as a trait that has the potential of bringing great glory to God.

Because God is the creator and has created us in his image, we are also able to create. The exercise of our God-given creativity in his service pleases God and brings him glory. Through the exercise of our creative potential, we are better able to fulfill God's divine mandate, given to us when we were first created, to represent God by ruling and subduing the earth.

The Creative Scholar

Creativity and Work

Some people are more creative than others, but any person can develop his or her creativity. Doing so requires time, work, and patience. There are several things you can do to increase your creativity. These suggestions are far from exhaustive.

Read creative authors. N. T. Wright is a very creative writer. This is evident by his writing, the analogies he uses, the words he chooses, and the connections he draws between events. He possesses the ability to conceptualize the big picture and to communicate how the smaller elements fit together.[11] James Dunn's Pauline theology, likewise, demonstrates creativity in the way this scholar conceptualizes and executes his task.[12] Many other creative scholars could be listed. It is important to observe both how such writers communicate their ideas (the choice of words, examples, analogies, and so on) and how they synthesize and present their material.

Read some of the secondary literature on creativity and communication. Joseph Williams's book *Style: Toward Clarity and Grace* is an excellent place to start in order to improve your writing, especially chapter 9, "Elegance."[13] Set aside time to brainstorm. Think through alternative ways to organize your material. Try to think of any elements you might be leaving out or questions you might not be addressing. Spend time considering examples and analogies. Carry a small notebook with you so you can jot down ideas that come to mind throughout the day.

Leave time for revision. One of the main roadblocks to creativity is that we are often so pressed for time, especially when deadlines are looming, that we do not leave ourselves sufficient space to think about creative ways to communicate or present the material. If you wait until the last minute to finish a seminar paper or manuscript, you will have little or no time left to recast sentences or improve the structure or flow of your presentation.

Go the extra mile. After you've done the hard work of research, and crafted your argument in a compelling fashion, go the extra mile: take the time to adorn your writing with elegance and grace. Draw your readers in by recounting a personal anecdote or relevant example, and help them not merely to be informed and educated but to enjoy the journey along the way. A big part of this is writing—this often comes last—a fitting introduction. Here is an example from one of my forthcoming publications, an essay entitled "Who Were the First Disciples of Jesus? An Assessment of the Historicity of the Johannine Call Narrative (John 1:35–51)":

> In the early 1990s, while completing my Ph.D. at Trinity Evangelical Divinity School in Deerfield, Illinois, I experienced a fairly precipitous drop in my ability to see. A typical male, I procrastinated as long as I could before finally going to see a doctor. When, at long last, I got around to visiting an ophthalmologist, my eyesight had gotten so bad I was in desperate need of new glasses (or, as it turned out, special contact lenses).
>
> You might argue that something similar has happened in historical Jesus studies which, for centuries, have heavily tilted toward the Synoptic portrait of Jesus while giving short shrift to the Gospel of John. As long as we wear our Synoptic "glasses" when assessing John's historical value, employing criteria of historicity largely favoring the Synoptics, we are likely to gain a distorted impression of the Johannine record. In order to arrive at a more balanced, and accurate, appraisal of the historicity of John's Gospel, particularly with regard to its portrayal of Jesus, we need nothing more than a new set of glasses.[14]

Then, in the conclusion, I return to my opening illustration to bring closure to the entire piece:

> I'll never forget the day when I left my ophthalmologist's office after receiving my new pair of contact lenses. Especially because I had been diagnosed

with a rare eye disease that required an unusual level of technical expertise to correct, I was deeply grateful to this highly skilled physician for fitting me with a new set of eyes, as it were, enabling me to see better than I had been able to do in a very long time. The criteria employed in the brief present study, I submit, have the potential of having the same effect in assessing the historicity of John's calling narrative relative to the corresponding material in the Synoptics (particularly Mark). Laying aside the customary glasses of assessing the historicity of a Gospel pericope by criteria such as dissimilarity or multiple attestation, and replacing them with more appropriate lenses, we are able to see the historical value of John's presentation (in the present case, his call narrative) in a fresh new light.

My purpose here is not to hold myself up as a shining example of creativity but to provide a concrete example of what creative writing in a scholarly setting might look like. I am sure there are many better examples. Now that you may be more sensitized to the issue of creative writing, perhaps you will be able to spot good examples more readily and be motivated to imitate them in your own writing.

Pursue the other virtues. In addition, any person who is creative must still master and develop other virtues, particularly diligence and hard work. Every musician or athlete knows this. You cannot just ride on your creativity and not practice. Creativity alone, apart from hard work and perseverance, will not produce excellent scholarship. Conversely, a scholar who lacks creativity will tend to produce rather pedestrian, if not boring, scholarship, which will have a negative effect on his or her ability to advance the field in a given discipline.

Creativity and Innovation

Some people think of creativity in the sense of innovation or novelty. I am not advocating innovation in the sense of adding to or subtracting from the gospel—going beyond sound theology and advancing doctrinal novelty.[15] There is a fine line here, but I am speaking of creativity in the sense of presentation, grasping the essence of a topic, and drawing connections. There should be a close connection between creativity and fidelity.[16] The gospel of Jesus Christ is anything but dull and boring, and if we make it appear to be such, this can be due only to our creative lethargy and lack of imagination.

Some might argue that evangelicals can't be creative because of their doctrinal constraints. This is not so! Creativity is something in which we should be able to excel. Sadly, however, evangelicals are not known for their creative writing, and this is definitely an area with considerable potential for growth. Some notable exceptions of scholars who model creativity in their thinking and writing are Ben Witherington, D. A. Carson, Scot McKnight, Robert Yarbrough, and Douglas Moo. Robert Yarbrough, in particular, enjoys a masterful command of the English language and boasts a large vocabulary that he puts to use exceedingly well.

There is intense pressure on young PhD students to push the bounds of orthodoxy in order to gain academic respectability. The pressure is increased by the need for their dissertation to make an original contribution to scholarship. Since the discipline of biblical studies is an inch wide and a mile deep, this can be a daunting task. Creative thinking is the key: drawing connections between the data that others may have overlooked. A creative scholar will not need to cross the bounds of orthodoxy in order to make an original contribution. He or she will balance creativity and fidelity, a trait we will explore in a later chapter.

Creativity and Research

If you are creative, you will be able to break new ground, even on a well-covered subject. It is exceedingly difficult to make a new contribution without creativity. Creativity is a key asset and the factor that makes all the difference between scholarship that simply duplicates other material on the market and academic work that generates something new and unique. Unfortunately, many (if not most) scholarly publications in biblical and theological studies lack creativity. This state of affairs could perhaps be alleviated if publishers were to put a higher value on creativity, but real change will have to come from the ground up—from the scholars themselves.

John Lee's excellent book, *A History of New Testament Lexicography*, compellingly exposes how much thoughtless copying goes on in the scholarly publication of lexicons.[17] The situation is similar in other aspects of biblical studies. We don't start our writing from scratch, nor should we. Secondary literature is good and necessary as long as it doesn't limit our creativity. One of the problems with the way in which scholars tend to copy other scholars is the manner in which we limit ourselves to the questions everyone else is asking. How often have you and I tried to find answers to exegetical quandaries only to find that virtually all the major commentaries fail to address the precise question we or someone in our congregation was asking?

The weight of secondary literature is like a heavy burden that weighs scholars down. You have to absorb a massive amount of literature in order to demonstrate to the academic world that you are a true scholar. I acutely felt this weight in putting together *A Theology of John's Gospel and Letters*. In the preface I wrote the following:

> The prospect of writing a Johannine theology was overwhelming at the outset. Only when I resolved to start with the text of John's Gospel itself rather than with the massive amount of available secondary literature on the subject did the burden lift and the task appear more manageable. Indeed, the decision to work from the gospel and to move outward to incorporate helpful insights from the secondary literature proved critical.[18]

From this experience, I learned the importance of starting with the primary literature. Once you have a firm grasp of the primary data, it becomes a lot easier to add insights from the secondary literature. This practice will foster creativity by forcing you to analyze and understand the primary literature firsthand. It will keep you from some of the ruts scholars get into by primarily addressing time-worn questions and answers. You should also be strategic in interacting with the best secondary literature instead of attempting to read everything written on the subject. In other words, aim to be comprehensive rather than exhaustive. This will free up some of your time to focus on the analysis of the primary material and devote your energies to developing a fresh and innovative mode of presentation.

The organization and presentation of your material is a key place for you to invest your creative energy. The critical juncture at which creativity comes into play is that between research and writing. How much time do students and scholars spend on processing the material? More often than not, there seems to be very little actual processing, and scholarly writing frequently becomes little more than a "research dump" of all the secondary literature that has been consulted. This is where creativity comes in. Creativity allows us to cast issues the way in which we see them rather than how everyone else perceives them. It allows us to ask a different set of questions and to propose different kinds of answers. When I was writing my Johannine theology, for example, I chose to discuss John's eschatology in an early chapter on John's worldview rather than, as is customary, waiting until the very end. This unusual location makes a point by its very placement of the material.

There are, of course, different kinds of projects. With commentaries, scholars are normally bound to comment verse by verse, or unit by unit, and there is consequently less opportunity for creativity. Systematic theologies provide a little more room for creativity. To my mind, we need creative systematic theologians to incorporate missions and eschatology more effectively into the existing systematic categories and modes of presentation. Biblical-theological research provides ample room for the exercise of creativity through the interaction and discussion of various themes across the canon.

Creativity and Uniqueness
Everyone is a unique person with a one-of-a-kind style and background. My contribution is distinguished from others because of my particular upbringing: I grew up in Europe, learned several languages, and was well educated and traveled. Every person's background will be different, and we all bring different things to the table. Your unique background and experiences provide you with what you need to make a unique contribution to scholarship. Creativity will allow you to tap into the strengths that arise from your particular background in order to achieve excellence in your scholarship.

I conclude with some practical advice from one of the most creative Christian writers of the past century, C. S. Lewis.[19] When, in Lewis's last interview on May 7, 1963, Sherwood Wirt asked him how young, aspiring authors could go about developing their distinctive style, Lewis responded: "The way for a person to develop a style is (a) to know exactly what he wants to say, and (b) to be sure he is saying exactly that. The reader, we must remember, does not start by knowing what we mean. If our words are ambiguous, our meaning will escape him. I sometimes think that writing is like driving sheep down a road. If there is any gate open to the left or the right the reader will most certainly go into it." Simple, yet profound advice that is: know exactly what you want to say, and then say exactly that. If it were only that simple! Then again, maybe it is.

At an earlier occasion, in a letter to an American girl named Joan dated June 26, 1956, Lewis fleshed out his proposal in more concrete terms: "(1) Always try to use the language so as to make quite clear what you mean and make sure your sentences couldn't mean anything else. (2) Always prefer the plain direct word to the long, vague one. Don't implement promises, but keep them. (3) Never use abstract nouns when concrete ones will do. If you mean 'More people died' don't say 'Mortality rose.' (4) In writing, don't use adjectives which merely tell us how you want us to *feel* about the things you are describing. I mean, instead of telling us the thing is 'terrible,' describe it so that we'll be terrified. Don't say it was 'delightful'; make us say 'delightful' when we've read the description. You see, all those words (horrifying, wonderful, hideous, exquisite) are only like saying to your readers, 'Please, will you do my job for me.' (5) Don't use words too big for the subject. Don't say 'infinitely' when you mean 'very'; otherwise you'll have no word left when you want to talk about something *really* infinite."[20]

Conclusion

If God has called you to a scholarly vocation, he has called you to creativity. Even though this particular calling is gift- and personality-based to a certain degree, it still can and must be developed. Creativity is often latent, just waiting to be stirred. Writers are called to be creative people, and the exploration of Scripture allows ample room for creativity. There is nothing particularly Christian about dullness or lack of effort in presenting one's message attractively and memorably. Creativity means appreciating God's role as creator and sees creativity as a way to bring glory to God and to bring others to him.

I have spent most of this chapter focusing on creativity as it applies to scholarly writing, but what about oral communication? This is where eloquence enters the picture. It is virtually impossible to be effective as a teacher if students are bored and struggle to stay awake during your classes. As we will develop further in the next chapter, creativity leads to eloquence in effective oral communication and is a necessary and vital ingredient of scholarly excellence.

10

Eloquence

To your creativity, add eloquence.

Eloquence *may be another unexpected entry* in a book on scholarly virtues. At least, I haven't seen that much written on the subject in the context of evangelical scholarship. More commonly, the emphasis seems to lie on setting forth the truth and on refuting error. The manner in which such is to be done, at least in my experience, typically receives comparatively less attention. At times, eloquence may even be viewed as a vice, not a virtue, because it can be seen as detracting from the simple gospel message. For this reason, it will be important to define eloquence and to discuss the question of whether eloquence properly qualifies as a Christian, and in particular a scholarly, virtue.

A perusal of various standard reference works and dictionaries yields the following shared understanding concerning the nature of eloquence. Eloquence is *the skill or ability to engage in persuasive written or oral discourse*. Eloquence in speech or writing involves language that is forceful, vivid, elegant, and compelling, drawing one's audience into a given subject and engaging it in such a way that a powerful connection ensues between the speaker or writer and the listeners or readers of a given piece of communication. Since influence is determined by impact, eloquence is vital for any scholar who seeks to be used by God to persuade others of the truth of the gospel or of the interpretation of the Bible.

How important is eloquence in the life of a scholar? Can a scholar achieve excellence without developing the virtue of eloquence? Some of the virtues I discuss in this book are just as necessary for the non-academician as for the scholar. Every believer should grow in the virtues of love, restraint, and humility, but eloquence is a bit different because it is not directly associated with spiritual growth as such. At the same time, eloquence is inextricably tied to effective communication and for this reason is a necessary virtue for the acquisition of scholarly excellence. What good is knowledge if you cannot communicate it effectively? We are not the first to ask these kinds of questions.[1] Just because someone is a scholar, and even a decent communicator in writing, does not mean he or she is necessarily eloquent. Eloquence requires a different set of skills. It is closely related to creativity, but is more specifically associated with oral communication. In a literate society, of course, all orality is secondary orality, thoroughly conditioned by writing. Eloquence could be simply understood as having a way with words. Some people seem better able to express themselves and are better spoken than others, whether with regard to preaching, teaching, performing in a debate, or carrying on a conversation.

I personally don't feel that I am particularly eloquent. Where I grew up, public speaking was not emphasized. For those who grow up in America, things may be a little different, because people by and large seem to be given more opportunities to speak publicly, whether in interview settings, community gatherings, school meetings, or the classroom. Because of my particular background, I find it much easier to communicate in writing than through public speaking. This does not mean, however, that I can resign myself exclusively to writing and neglect to work on improving my ability to speak with eloquence. An effective scholar must be able both to write and to speak well.

Robert Littlejohn and Charles Evans, two Christian educators, have recently argued that wisdom and eloquence are the two cardinal virtues in education. They express the need for eloquence alongside wisdom in this way:

> But an education for wisdom is only half the formula. Without the ability to communicate effectively and persuasively, wisdom's benefit is singular

to its possessor. Our graduates also require eloquence, especially in a post-Christian, postmodern age when, for many, authority comes not from the Scriptures or from reason but from within. Our wise servant must also be imbued with understanding and compassion for his fellow humans and must be ready to put his wisdom into action by helping "the many" to embrace the greater good that wisdom offers.[2]

Wisdom is important, but in order to be effective it needs to be accompanied by proper, and persuasive, communication. This requires eloquence.

A Biblical Theology of Eloquence

There is no question that eloquence has great potential to enhance the persuasiveness of a given message, including that of the gospel. Many of us who don't feel particularly eloquent would love to be better writers and public speakers. How can we go about developing the virtue of eloquence? I will have more to say about this issue below. But before I do, let us address one important question that arises from the biblical data: Did Paul approve of the quest for eloquence, or did he discourage—or even condemn—it?

In a key passage, the apostle wrote to the Corinthians, "For Christ did not send me to baptize but to preach the gospel, and not with words of eloquent wisdom, lest the cross of Christ be emptied of its power" (1 Cor. 1:17). Later on in the same epistle, Paul elaborated, "I, when I came to you, brothers, did not come proclaiming to you the testimony of God with lofty speech or wisdom. For I decided to know nothing among you except Jesus Christ and him crucified" (1 Cor. 2:1–2). Judging from these passages, Paul seems to have intentionally curtailed his eloquence in order to focus his listeners' attention on the gospel message. Is it legitimate, therefore, to use Paul's example to argue that believers—including preachers—should refrain from cultivating eloquence in presenting the gospel?

As we will see, this conclusion would be premature. An appreciation of the first-century context helps put Paul's words into proper perspective. The Sophists, a group of Hellenistic philosophers, were widely known for their eloquence and rhetorical skill, including in Corinth.[3] By cautioning the Corinthians against unduly relying on human rhetoric, Paul most likely sought to counteract the Sophists' influence, trying to redirect their focus away from human rhetoric to the actual gospel message (see 1 Cor. 2:1–5).[4]

That said, however, Paul's eloquent use of rhetoric elsewhere in his letters—including in 1 Corinthians—makes clear that he did not reject its use altogether. Rather, he cautioned against a misplaced focus on the medium—the human speaker—at the expense of the message: the saving news of salvation and forgiveness of sins in the Lord Jesus Christ. The gospel is powerful, not because of human ingenuity, rhetorical persuasiveness, or oratorical power, but because of the saving work of God. This fact, however, should not lead us to reject eloquence altogether. It is the abuse of rhetoric that Paul opposed, not its proper use in ways that undergird the gospel message.

John Piper helpfully addressed Paul's stance toward eloquence along these lines in a chapter entitled "Is There Christian Eloquence? Clear Words and the Wonder of the Cross."[5] He rightly argued that Paul presented a two-pronged criterion for judging eloquence: does it encourage sinful pride and boastful arrogance, or does it exalt Christ?[6] Eloquence that makes the speaker the center of attention should be rejected, while

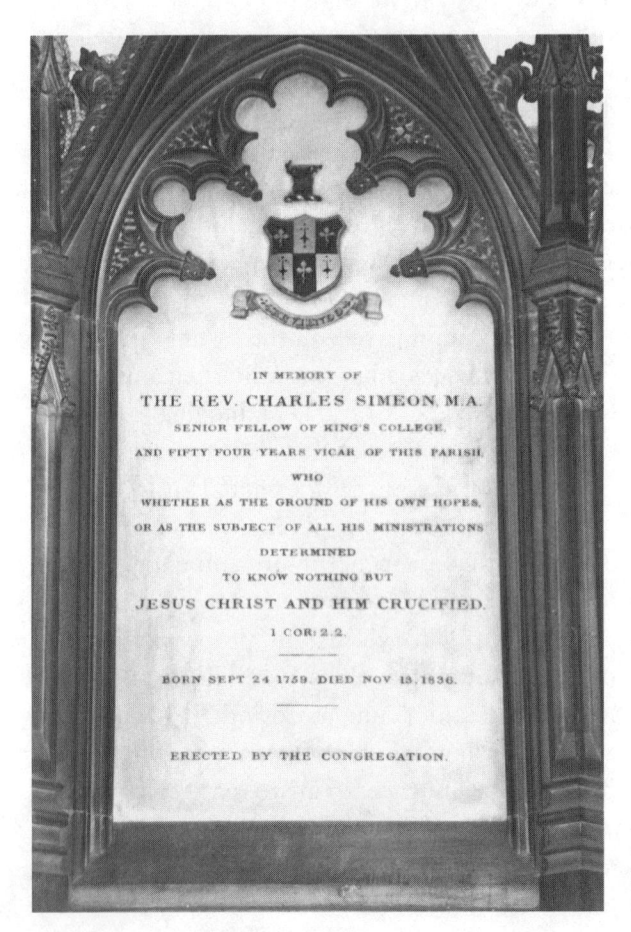

Charles Simeon enjoyed a long, faithful ministry in Cambridge, England

eloquence that draws attention to the crucified Christ and the message of his gospel should be embraced and utilized in preaching and teaching.

Paul's "anti-eloquence" stance in 1 Corinthians should therefore be applied only to situations where rhetoric subverts and obscures the message. It should not be extrapolated to imply a universal prohibition against Christians utilizing eloquence or rhetoric in the persuasive communication of the gospel. This contention is underscored by the pervasive presence of eloquence throughout Scripture. The Bible itself is highly eloquent. It is filled with hymns, poetry, narratives, and letters that display the highest levels of ancient Hebrew and Greek rhetorical achievement.

I could give many examples of this. Psalms 23 and 119, among many other sections of Hebrew poetry, are carefully crafted, artistic masterpieces. When Moses objected that he was not eloquent and lacked rhetorical skill, God provided his brother Aaron to help him communicate God's message (Ex. 4:10–17). The prophet Isaiah employed eloquence throughout his prophecies, so much so that the book of Isaiah later came to be called "The Fifth Gospel."[7] Several of the proverbs extol the virtue of wisdom combined with eloquence. Proverbs 25:11 states, "A word fitly spoken is like apples of gold in a setting of silver."

Even though John's Gospel is simple in vocabulary and style, it displays a high level of eloquence for the purpose of persuading readers to put their trust in Jesus the Messiah (John 20:30–31). Apollos exhibited eloquence in the preaching of the gospel (Acts 18:24; 1 Cor. 16:12; Titus 3:13).[8] The author of the book of Hebrews (Apollos?) felt no need to limit himself rhetorically and utilized every tool at his disposal to make his communication as persuasive as possible.[9] Last but not least, Jesus, especially in his parables and extended discourses, displayed great eloquence and creativity.

John Piper sums up the matter well when he writes,

> The Bible is filled with every manner of literary device to add impact to the language: acrostics, alliteration, analogy, anthropomorphism, assonance, cadence, chiasm, consonance, dialogue, hyperbole, irony, metaphor, meter, onomatopoeia, paradox, parallelism, repetition, rhyme, satire, simile— they're all there, and more.[10]

The Bible is so eloquent because God inspired it, not only to communicate information regarding himself and his plan but also to persuade, convict, and transform its readers.[11]

The Eloquent Scholar

Wisdom and Eloquence

When Paul forcefully spoke against human wisdom and eloquence to the Corinthian church, he was addressing the way in which the church was exalting style at the expense of substance. His caution was well taken, and if I had to make a choice, I would take substance over style every time. Yet, ultimately, such a dichotomy is false. In the Bible, and in Christian proclamation, style and substance are not an either-or proposition, but the manner of presentation has the potential of undergirding the communication of a given message and thus of enhancing its impact and effectiveness.[12]

The cross and the resurrection must be central in our teaching, preaching, and writing. But the very importance of the subject matter requires that it be communicated as effectively as possible—that is, with eloquence. When the medium trumps the message—or becomes the message, let listeners—and communicators—beware. Yet, at the same time, to be fully effective, the message needs the proper medium.[13]

Some additional cautions apply. Those with great oratorical skills need to exercise restraint so that people will remember the points of the lecture or sermon and not simply the illustrations, humor, or style of the speaker.[14] As much as compelling illustrations can aid in persuasive communication, you certainly don't want your illustrative material to overshadow your substantive points.[15]

Also, curb your instincts as an entertainer. We live in an entertainment culture. Everyone wants to be entertained. Just think of the amount of time we spend entertaining our children. I once jokingly remarked that the course evaluations at my school should include a section called "The Teacher as Entertainer," because that's how at least some students seem to measure the success of a given class. Was it entertaining? In this regard, we are at times not all that different from the people in Paul's admonition, "For the time is coming when people will not endure sound teaching, but having itching ears they will accumulate for themselves teachers to suit their own passions" (2 Tim. 4:3). The church is not a theater, nor is it a circus. It is a place where God ought to be worshiped and his Word proclaimed in all dignity and reverence.

On a different note, be aware that some of the elements used with good effect in oral communication may not be equally appropriate in written communication. To give but one example, one of my own students once began his dissertation with an eloquent preamble relating a story about his grandfather's cuckoo clock. I advised the student to remove the story, because in my judgment these types of anecdotal comments and illustrations are not as apropos in scholarly writing as they are in oral communication.[16] Some illustrations and analogies are appropriate for academic genres, but you should choose them with care so they support and clarify your points rather than distract from them.

Eloquence and Integrity

The use of eloquence requires personal integrity. A person of integrity will refuse to use eloquence to manipulate or move an audience in the absence of sound arguments. Adolf Hitler serves as a perennial example of this danger. He doubtless possessed considerable oratorical skills, and could move masses of people to action with his words, but we shudder as we contemplate what he did with his ability. He used his impressive eloquence for shameless self-aggrandizement, brutal military conquest, and a terrible holocaust.

You will not want to use eloquence and rhetorical skills to sway people against their will, their better judgment, or the evidence. I have observed some very eloquent people in the gender-inclusive language debate who have made the use—or nonuse—of gender-inclusive language a standard for doctrinal purity. They engage in populist oratory that effectively persuades their audience but overstates their actual case. This type of popularly effective rhetoric that exceeds the biblical evidence also appears in the debates on the meaning of Genesis 1.

If you are gifted as a communicator, you will need to exercise restraint in your rhetoric, especially if you are involved in biblical studies or theology. In a discipline that promotes the investigation and communication of God's revealed truth, the stakes are high. Many of the topics you debate with others will have an eternal effect on people's lives. Use eloquence effectively to persuade people of the truthfulness of God's message. Wisdom is necessary to discern the line between the two extremes, and restraint is needed not to cross it.

Eloquence and Effectiveness

If eloquence is open to abuse, why is it still so vitally important for scholarly excellence? The reason for this is that we write and teach not merely to convey information but to persuade our audience. Your teaching should not only survey the state of research and present the various views on a given topic. You will also want to influence your students, on the basis of the evidence, helping them realize that some positions are stronger than others and moving them to embrace certain ideas while rejecting others. The evidence, rightly interpreted, has a much better chance of genuinely impacting students if it is communicated effectively.

An eloquent scholar will be able to create interest in students who would not otherwise care about a particular topic. Eloquence helps a professor catch, and keep, the attention of students and stir in them genuine interest, even engagement. Eloquence helps sleepy students stay awake and makes it easier for them to remember the material. Eloquence also has the potential of increasing your effectiveness as a teacher. In the past, I have shown video clips of N. T. Wright or Bart Ehrman (twice) appearing on Comedy Central with good effect, lightening the mood while addressing important subjects. PowerPoint presentations displaying maps, charts, or quotes can also be highly effective in supplementing a lecture.

The Pursuit of Eloquence

Much of this chapter has been concerned to navigate the tension between the proper and improper use of eloquence in the church and in the classroom. In this final section, I want us to focus for a moment on the positive, constructive task ahead: How can we make progress toward eloquence? How can we glorify God by presenting his truth as persuasively and powerfully as possible? Answering these questions could easily take up an entire book, so a few brief suggestions must suffice.

Expand your vocabulary. Read the *New York Times*, or *Time* magazine, or any number of other publications that boast a large vocabulary. As you do, make sure to keep a dictionary close at hand, so you can actually look up the words you don't know and perhaps even put them in a notebook for periodic review. Better still, learn a new word, and then immediately look for a way to use it. That way, you move it from your passive to your active vocabulary, and after a while it will have become part of your regular stock of words.

While still on the topic of building your vocabulary, there are several word-a-day services available that will assist you in building your vocabulary over time.[17] Or go to your local Barnes and Noble bookstore, where you will find a considerable number of books (or calendars) devoted to "word power," whether aimed at high school or college students or at aspiring or practicing writers.[18] Take full advantage of these available resources and build expanding your vocabulary into your daily routine.

Read widely. Expand your horizons. Don't just read in your immediate field (though by all means, do that). Pick up books that interest you and take them with you on trips or read them over Christmas or on summer break. Some books I've read that way are Simon Winchester's *The Professor and the Madman*, Stephen Carlson's *The Gospel Hoax*, Paul Johnson's *The Intellectuals*, and Susannah Heschel's *The Aryan Jesus*.[19] Make reading your passion, and make sure that what you're reading exhibits excellence in writing.

Seize the opportunity. Take advantage of any opportunities to write or speak publicly (within reason, of course; don't overcommit). There is no substitute for putting what you are learning into practice. Write a draft of your talk or sermon and then practice it on your spouse, children, colleagues, or students. Let them give you feedback prior to your speaking engagement. Tape your talk (if you're brave enough), and then watch it afterward. Learn from your mistakes and build on what you did well. There is always a next time when you can do better. In the meantime, remember that God can use even our most feeble efforts to do his work.

Conclusion

So much more could be said, but the bottom line is this: strive for eloquence. Do not prize it over the evidence itself, nor use it to manipulate your audience, but cultivate it in order to increase your effectiveness as a communicator. Excellence in scholarship requires one to be effective in both writing and speaking, and regardless of our strengths and weaknesses, we should all aim to improve in both areas to achieve maximum effectiveness.

I noted above that eloquence should be combined with wisdom and restraint. The right use of eloquence also requires integrity. As mentioned, a man or woman of integrity will not use eloquence to exalt him- or herself, nor employ it to control people and gain power over them. Integrity is the necessary inner strength of character that will enable you to exhibit restraint and use eloquence for the glory of God and for the good of others.

Part Three

MORAL
EXCELLENCE

11

Integrity

To your eloquence, add integrity.

When I was growing up, my dad would always tell me that character is what a person is in the dark, when nobody sees him or her. The truth and power of his words have stuck with me to this day. What do you do when your boss is out of the office, your spouse is away for the weekend, and your Christian friends are not around? What do you do when you are on a business trip and alone in your hotel room after the meetings of the day are over? Are you the same person when people are watching you as when no one is around? What do you do when you think you cannot be caught? All these questions gauge the state of your integrity.

Integrity has to do with genuineness and authenticity of character. The integrity of a foundation or a ship indicates that the structure or hull is sound, firm, and secure, with no cracks or weaknesses threatening to destroy or undermine it. In one sense, integrity represents the embodiment or sum total of all virtues, and it is virtually synonymous with moral excellence as a whole.

People of integrity are those who have committed themselves to biblical principles of morality. They show their commitment to integrity in small as well as big things: how they respond in traffic, tip a waiter or waitress, pay taxes, or treat their family, coworkers, and students. It may be tempting to dismiss some of the smaller issues as inconsequential, but when it comes to integrity, no matters are trivial. Jesus himself makes clear that one's actions pertaining to "small things" determine what one will do in the "big things": "One who is faithful in a very little is also faithful in much, and one who is dishonest in a very little is also dishonest in much" (Luke 16:10). Small things matter and are at the heart of integrity!

John MacArthur defines and describes integrity as follows:

> Integrity essentially means being true to one's ethical standards, in our case, God's standards. Its synonyms are honesty, sincerity, incorruptibility. It describes someone without hypocrisy or duplicity—someone who is completely consistent with his or her stated convictions. A person who lacks integrity—someone who says one thing and does another—is a hypocrite.[1]

Many nonbelievers reject Christianity because they believe the church is filled with hypocrites. They have seen or known Christians who effectively deny Christ and undermine the claims of Christianity by their lifestyle. Conversely, integrity adorns the gospel of Christ and commends it to unbelievers, not least because in the world at large, integrity is in short supply. Too often, people's actions are controlled by what they can get away with, not by doing what is right.

People who eschew the importance of character or downplay the necessity of integrity often stress their independence, refusing to submit to any authority, evading accountability, and viewing themselves as a law unto themselves.[2] A person's integrity manifests itself in the pursuit or neglect of the other virtues discussed in this book. Integrity is a Christian virtue that transcends the scholarly vocation and is therefore a necessary element of any believer's spiritual growth.

A Biblical Theology of Integrity

Psalm 15 celebrates integrity as a necessary virtue for those who want to draw near to God:

> O Lord, who shall sojourn in your tent?
>   Who shall dwell on your holy hill?
> He who walks blamelessly and does what is right
>   and speaks truth in his heart;
> who does not slander with his tongue

> and does no evil to his neighbor,
> nor takes up a reproach against his friend;
> in whose eyes a vile person is despised,
> but who honors those who fear the LORD;
> who swears to his own hurt and does not change;
> who does not put out his money at interest
> and does not take a bribe against the innocent.
> He who does these things shall never be moved.

A person of integrity will live blamelessly, do what is right, speak truth, refuse slander and bribes, and honor God. Integrity means that you will do the right thing even if it is disadvantageous to you personally ("swears to his own hurt and does not change"), and will not change your position or actions simply to make life easier for yourself. A person of integrity will not flippantly cancel an engagement simply because something better has come along. Are you, and am I, a person who keeps your commitments, or do people never know if you are going to follow through with a commitment you've made? If I asked your children, or your spouse, would they affirm that you are a man or woman of your word? Or would they say that you have good intentions but often fall short of keeping your promises? "Many a man proclaims his own steadfast love, but a faithful man who can find?" (Prov. 20:6). Surely, integrity is in short supply. What an opportunity we have as Christians to stand out in this world as persons of integrity!

Several key biblical examples of integrity come immediately to mind. Joseph found himself in a precarious situation. He was in charge of Potiphar's household and was pursued by his master's wife in Potiphar's absence. It would have been easy for Joseph to rationalize acceding to the demands of his master's wife because Potiphar was away and may never have found out about his adulterous indiscretion. In refusing to go along, Joseph revealed the theological rationale underlying his integrity: "How then can I do this great wickedness and sin against God?" (Gen. 39:9). This man of God realized that such actions would be a violation of his earthly master's trust, but even more importantly they would be a sin against God. Joseph knew that nothing is hidden from God's sight and that God is the one to whom we must ultimately give an account.

These truths can also strengthen our hearts in our pursuit of integrity. There are no hidden, trivial sins. Neither are there sins where no one gets hurt. All sin is primarily and ultimately against God, and there is no escaping or hiding from his sight (Psalm 139; Heb. 4:13). Joseph had to pay a price for maintaining his integrity, but God honored his commitment to moral excellence and blessed him beyond his wildest imagination.

Job is another outstanding biblical example of a man who maintained his integrity in the midst of great affliction. Even at the height of Job's trials, when he had lost everything, he held on to his integrity, refusing to curse God:

> Then his wife said to him, "Do you still hold fast your integrity? Curse God and die." But he said to her, "You speak as one of the foolish women would speak. Shall we receive good from God, and shall we not receive evil?" In all this Job did not sin with his lips. (Job 2:9–10)

If anyone ever had a reason to compromise his or her integrity by renouncing, defaming, and cursing God, surely it was Job. He insisted, however, on remaining consistent and trusting God in both prosperity and adversity.

I would be remiss not to mention Daniel's integrity in the face of King Darius's order that all prayers must be directed to the king (Daniel 6). Daniel did what he knew was right, despite the severity of the consequences which ensued, and was rescued by God. Daniel's friends Shadrach, Meshach, and Abednego, likewise chose integrity even though it meant the probable loss of their lives (Daniel 3). Their response expresses confidence and trust in God even though they didn't know whether he would deliver them or not:

> If this be so, our God whom we serve is able to deliver us from the burning fiery furnace, and he will deliver us out of your hand, O king. But if not, be it known to you, O king, that we will not serve your gods or worship the golden image that you have set up. (Dan. 3:17–18)

A person of integrity will do the right thing no matter what the personal cost, whether or not there is any reasonable hope of rescue, help, or personal benefit.

David's failure with regard to Bathsheba and Uriah indicates that God can and does forgive sin and loss of integrity, but consequences remain (2 Samuel 11–12). After Nathan confronted him, David declared, "I have sinned against the LORD" (2 Sam. 12:13). He expressed the same insight Joseph had previously recognized: all sin is ultimately against God, even if it affects other people. David had sinned against Bathsheba and Uriah, but he went right to the heart and confessed his sin as having been first and foremost against God.

In the New Testament, the apostles demonstrated the same integrity that was modeled for them throughout the Old Testament narratives. When they were threatened by their opponents and commanded to stop preaching, they replied, "Whether it is right in the sight of God to listen to you rather than to God, you must judge, for we cannot but speak of what we have seen and heard" (Acts 4:19–20). The apostle Paul was a man of utter integrity. Though his opponents regularly cast aspersions on his credibility, Paul even chose to forego material support from all but one of the churches he established, in large part so that no one could question his motives for ministry (see, e.g., 2 Corinthians 10–13; cf. Phil. 4:15).

Throughout this section, I have attempted to trace the contours of a biblical theology of integrity by looking at how the scriptural narratives present individuals of integrity. Examples could be multiplied, but the basic elements remain the same. A person of integrity will do what is right in the eyes of God no matter what the personal cost or no matter whether other people see his or her actions. It does not ultimately matter if others are aware of what we do, because God sees and knows and will bring every word and action to account (e.g., Matt. 12:36–37; Rom. 14:10–12; 2 Cor. 5:10).

A Scholar of Integrity

A scholar of integrity will excel and bring glory to God by consistently doing what is right. This, of course, does not mean perfection. Jesus Christ was the only perfect human being who ever lived. Those of us who have been united to him are being transformed and conformed to his image by the power and activity of God's indwelling Spirit (Rom. 8:29).[3] Even though we will fall short of perfection, we will guard our integrity with all our might and daily seek to become more like Christ. There are many areas related to integrity that could be discussed, but I want to focus particularly on the following three: financial, sexual, and scholarly integrity.

Financial Integrity

A scholar of integrity will not be motivated by financial gain. We serve God and his kingdom, and our purpose in life must not be to become rich. Some professors try to teach as many courses as they can to make more money. You must certainly do what you need to support your family, but I am thinking more of scholars who overextend themselves to get ahead financially. If you fall into this trap, the quality of your teaching and writing will likely decrease. Even as scholars, we can do only so many things well. We can, of course, always do more things, but if excessive commitments damage the quality of our output, they detract from scholarly excellence.

In my case, I made the decision early on to teach less and focus more time on writing. This meant less money but enabled me to influence a broader audience. People will often ask you to do things for free, and you will need to have a priority scale in order to be able to say no to some opportunities and requests. This will enable you to say yes to the most important opportunities. Seize the moment. Prioritize quality over quantity. Aim to do few things well. You will be no good to anyone if you burn out.

Financial integrity extends also to the many "little things" at work: photocopying, phone calls, or Internet usage. A man or woman of integrity will steadfastly refuse to steal from their employer by using company resources for private purposes in an unauthorized manner. This even extends to engaging in lengthy conversations, whether in person or by phone or over the Internet, during work hours, which effectively takes away from our productivity in our work. After all, our employer doesn't pay us just to socialize (though obviously employees are entitled to breaks and so on).

Integrity also pertains to how we pay our taxes. Even unfair tax laws—one of my pet peeves: why do those without children or families who homeschool need to finance public education with over half of their property taxes?—or the inefficiency of government does not give us the right to find ways to avoid paying the taxes the law requires. Financial integrity demands faithfulness in all the many little things of life, because right is right and wrong is wrong, no matter how small or how big a matter is.

Sexual Integrity

Jerry Jenkins has written a helpful book called *Hedges*.[4] He emphasizes the need for Christian husbands and wives to plant and cultivate protective hedges around their marriages and actively to flee sexual temptation. Some of these hedges include using an Internet filter, developing accountability relationships with mature members of the same sex, and limiting the possibility of time alone with a member of the opposite sex. It is essential to be circumspect in relationships with the opposite sex. Have precautions put in place with administrative assistants, coworkers, and students. Do not be intimate in discussing personal matters, spending time alone, and so on.

I remember one missionary who seemed to think of himself as a very sensible man and apparently beyond the pale of the possibility of temptation but spent long hours in his office talking with a very attractive, young coworker. Years later, I happened to find out from another missionary that this man's marriage had subsequently ended in divorce. What may start out as pleasant conversations based on a similarity of interests may reveal a character flaw that in the end has disastrous results that greatly dishonor the Lord, whom we serve. Small compromises over time may lead to major moral compromise. Sin, even small sin, will always take you farther than you want to go and cost you more than you want to pay. Our families are far too valuable to flirt with compromise in the area of sexual integrity.

Scholarly Integrity

Scholarly integrity will be manifested in several ways. Have respect for others in your research and make every effort not to misrepresent them. Scrupulously cite your sources and acknowledge others' intellectual property. That does not mean that you have to go overboard to the point of being ridiculous. You don't need to give credit for common knowledge. Plagiarism enters in when there is specific wording involved or a specific thought or concept has occurred to you by reading someone else's materials. In this case, you should give credit for both words and ideas. This is not a matter of legalism in which we end up footnoting ad nauseam. In some cases, an initial footnote such as "this section is heavily indebted to . . ." may suffice. Of course, specific quotes must still be cited.

Make sure that you never reach a point in your scholarly life where you primarily cite yourself.[5] Bart Ehrman, in *Jesus Interrupted*, is an example of this practice, because, as even a casual perusal of his footnotes will demonstrate, he primarily cited himself or his students.[6] Being too self-absorbed has the potential of damaging your credibility in the broader world of scholarship. It is certainly appropriate, and can often be convenient, to cite your prior work in order to avoid having to repeat a given argument, but your attitude should convey respect for the work of others, and you should not cite your own work excessively.

Scholarly integrity also extends to the way in which you meet publishing or other deadlines. Do you regularly miss or even ignore deadlines to which you have agreed? There may at times be legitimate reasons why you need a contract extension, and I have occasionally asked for one myself, but this should not turn into a bad habit. Also, as mentioned, when you are in your office, are you doing what you are supposed to be doing, or do you waste your employer's time through laziness? Do you fritter away hours on the Internet through playing games or reading blogs when you should be preparing a lesson or working on a manuscript?

Conclusion

It's the small things that make or break integrity. If you begin cutting corners with regard to small things, this will dull your conscience, and the cumulative negative effect after many years could very easily spell disaster for your work and ministry. Integrity of character is vital both as a mark of personal righteousness and as a matter of credibility with those to whom we minister. Develop the habit of guarding your integrity by rejecting compromise, particularly with the "small sins" that are easy to rationalize. Small sins rarely stay small.

In addition to integrity, scholarly excellence requires fidelity. The world prizes innovation, novelty, and trendiness. Christ prizes fidelity, that is, faithfulness to historic, biblical Christianity. The Christian preacher or scholar will not succumb to the temptation of being original when this means doctrinal compromise. He will see himself as servant, not master; ambassador, not sovereign; representative, not savior. He will "guard the good deposit" (2 Tim. 1:14) as an obedient slave of the Lord Jesus Christ.

12

Fidelity

To your integrity, add fidelity.

While it would be overreaching to demonize the historical-critical method as a whole,[1] many scholars who practice this method manifestly do not value fidelity to Scripture. The doctrines of historic, biblical Christianity are viewed by many as a straitjacket that inhibits or distorts objective scholarly investigation rather than a faithful representation of biblical teaching.[2] There is little reason to remain faithful to Scripture if it is no longer viewed as trustworthy, authoritative, and inerrant. Why be faithful to the Bible if it is only an error-ridden product of evolving human religious consciousness and creative imagination? Evangelical scholars, on the other hand, who believe that God has accurately and sufficiently revealed himself in the Bible, ought to prize fidelity to Scripture and its teachings.[3]

The English word *fidelity* derives from the Latin words *fides* ("faith"), *fidelitas* ("faithfulness"), and *fidelis* ("faithful") and often conveys the related notions of loyalty, devotion, and piety. Evangelical fidelity is centered on a person, the triune God, who has borne witness to himself in the written texts of the canon of Scripture.[4] Evangelicals gladly agree with the apostle Peter when he said, "Lord, to whom shall we go? You have the words of eternal life, and we have believed, and have come to know, that you are the Holy One of God" (John 6:68–69). Since Christian fidelity is centered on a person, it is closely related to loyalty. Evangelicals recognize, however, that this person, who demands our wholehearted and complete allegiance and loyalty, has used written words in particular historical contexts to reveal himself and his plan. Thus, we highly value and defend the need for fidelity to Scripture in the context of faithful interpretation.

Over the past century in America, evangelical fidelity to Scripture has largely centered on the affirmation of biblical inerrancy.[5] This defense of inerrancy has not been an expression of blind fideism. A few years ago I edited a volume entitled *Quo Vadis, Evangelicalism?*, which contains nine presidential addresses from the first fifty years of the *Journal of the Evangelical Theological Society*.[6] These addresses embody fidelity to Scripture, as expressed by the doctrine of inerrancy, alongside methodological and hermeneutical discussions that reflect a high level of academic and philosophical sophistication and excellence. Fidelity to Scripture is not unscholarly and does not involve a rejection of reason.

In his presidential address, for example, Craig Blaising responds to Bart Ehrman's revival of Walter Bauer's thesis that earliest Christianity was primarily characterized by theological diversity with no clear line between heresy and orthodoxy.[7] If there were no original orthodoxy, then fidelity to Scripture and the teaching passed down from Jesus and the original apostles would be a mirage. Blaising, in essence, argues that Ehrman's reconstruction of early Christianity was an exercise in revisionism in support of his own pluralistic beliefs rather than a faithful representation of the historical evidence.[8] Michael Kruger and I recently published a similar, more extensive critique of Ehrman's position in a book called *The Heresy of Orthodoxy*.[9]

The historical evidence points to a clear distinction between orthodoxy and heresy from the earliest times. This means that the faith we confess today, as Christians in the twenty-first century, is essentially that found in the pages of the Bible itself. The New Testament documents represent original orthodoxy, even in the midst of the diversity of contingent historical contexts in the first century, and function as a sure and reliable standard for our faith and practice today. The words of Scripture are God's inspired words, and fidelity to these words is of utmost importance.[10]

A Biblical Theology of Fidelity

The biblical teaching on fidelity is based on God's faithfulness to his creation, in providence and salvation, and to his promises and covenants he established with his people. The Old Testament frequently reiterates that God is faithful to his creation and to his people while God's people are called to be faithful to him. Early in Israel's history, when everyone did what was right in his own eyes (Judg. 17:6; 21:25), Ruth demonstrated amazing fidelity both to Naomi and to Naomi's God (Ruth 1:16–17), and as a result was included in the people of God and in the genealogies of both David and Jesus (Matt. 1:5).

In Hosea, God illustrated the seriousness of Israel's faithlessness by comparing it to marital infidelity (Hosea 1–3), and the prophet Habakkuk noted that because of injustice and oppression "the law is paralyzed, and justice never goes forth" (Hab. 1:4). God described the situation in Hosea's day by declaring, "There is no faithfulness or steadfast love, and no knowledge of God in the land; there is swearing, lying, murder, stealing, and committing adultery; they break all bounds, and bloodshed follows bloodshed" (Hos. 4:1–2). The nations of Israel and Judah were eventually judged by God for their lack of faithfulness, evidenced by idolatry and the rejection of God's laws.

In the garden of Gethsemane, Jesus demonstrated unswerving fidelity to the saving purpose and plan of God when praying, even though he fully knew the cost, "Nevertheless, not my will, but yours, be done" (Luke 22:42; cf. Heb. 5:7). As John makes clear, Jesus is the ultimate demonstration and expression of God's covenant faithfulness (John 1:17).[11] Jesus's followers, for their part, must be faithful emissaries ("sent ones"), representing the gospel with which they were entrusted by their crucified and risen Lord.[12] Because God's character is marked by fidelity to himself, his words, and his purpose, his followers must embody the same kind of faithfulness.

In his exasperated opening remarks to the Galatians, the apostle Paul stressed the importance of fidelity to the gospel message he had proclaimed:

> I am astonished that you are so quickly deserting him who called you in the grace of Christ and are turning to a different gospel—not that there is another one, but there are some who trouble you and want to distort the gospel of Christ. But even if we or an angel from heaven should preach to you a gospel contrary to the one we preached to you, let him be accursed.

> As we have said before, so now I say again: If anyone is preaching to you a gospel contrary to the one you received, let him be accursed. (Gal. 1:6–9)

The apostle described his role and that of his coworkers in terms of faithfulness to God's revealed truth: "This is how one should regard us, as servants of Christ and stewards of the mysteries of God. Moreover, it is required of stewards that they be found trustworthy" (1 Cor. 4:1–2). Timothy must "guard the deposit entrusted to you" (1 Tim. 6:20) and was told, "What you have heard from me in the presence of many witnesses entrust to faithful men who will be able to teach others also" (2 Tim. 2:2).

Several of Paul's companions demonstrated this fidelity. Paul affirmed of Timothy that he had "no one like him, who will be genuinely concerned for your welfare" (Phil. 2:20). Luke demonstrated fidelity through the careful investigation and presentation of the history of both Jesus and the early church (Luke-Acts). Mark, even though he had abandoned Paul on an earlier missionary journey, demonstrated fidelity through continued ministry, and Paul later charged Timothy to bring Mark along because "he is very useful to me for ministry" (2 Tim. 4:11).[13]

Scripture universally affirms that God is utterly reliable; he does not lie (Titus 1:2). His word will not return to him empty but will surely accomplish the purpose for which he sent it (Isa. 55:11; John 1:1, 14). God has fulfilled his promises to the patriarchs and prophets in and through Jesus Christ (Heb. 1:1–2) and will bring history to its final consummation when Christ returns. The author of Hebrews celebrates God's faithfulness and explains how the certainty of the fulfillment of his promises serves as the foundation for our hope:

> For when God made a promise to Abraham, since he had no one greater by whom to swear, he swore by himself, saying, "Surely I will bless you and multiply you." And thus Abraham, having patiently waited, obtained the promise. For people swear by something greater than themselves, and in all their disputes an oath is final for confirmation. So when God desired to show more convincingly to the heirs of the promise the unchangeable character of his purpose, he guaranteed it with an oath, so that by two unchangeable things, in which it is impossible for God to lie, we who have fled for refuge might have strong encouragement to hold fast to the hope set before us. We have this as a sure and steadfast anchor of the soul, a hope that enters into the inner place behind the curtain, where Jesus has gone as a forerunner on our behalf, having become a high priest forever after the order of Melchizedek. (Heb. 6:13–20)

In view of the increase of false teachers and teachings in the church, Jude "found it necessary" to change his original purpose of writing (which was bound up with the salvation he shared with his writers) and instead chose "to write appealing to you to contend for the faith that was once for all delivered to the saints" (Jude 3). This verse illustrates that the early Christians did have a pronounced sense of orthodoxy and heresy. There was a distinct body of teaching, "the faith," that must be defended against competing interpretations. Jude made quite clear that those who deviated from or distorted the faith that had been "once and for all delivered to the saints" were destined for condemnation.

In closing out this brief study of fidelity, I would like to note how closely truth is related to personal faithfulness. The Hebrew word *'emet* includes both faithfulness and truth within its semantic range. John 1:17 affirms that "grace and truth came through Jesus Christ." Truth is a person: Jesus Christ.[14] The ultimate, objective reality of truth, grounded in the person of Jesus Christ, demands our fidelity. If there were no truth, there would be nothing to demand our faithfulness, but the presence of truth in our risen Savior and Lord demands our full allegiance and loyalty.

A Scholarship of Fidelity

Fidelity to God

First and foremost, we, as evangelical scholars, must live out fidelity toward God. Faithfulness to God involves obedience to the teachings found within the Bible, but I want to focus on a more narrow point here: faithfulness to God's calling on our lives. Jesus commissioned his followers to go and make disciples of all the nations, baptizing them and teaching them to obey all of his teachings (Matt. 28:18–20). Are you and I being faithful to God and his calling on our lives by making disciples?

I have often seen the failure to make disciples as a particular danger for mega-churches that employ all sorts of strategies to try to get people to come. Gimmicks will not usually produce faithfulness, and if you get people into a church in a certain way, you will likely have to keep them there by continuing to offer the types of events or programs that attracted them in the first place. Discipleship, not entertainment, produces faithfulness. Having noted the precarious situation in some churches, lack of disciple making is just as much a danger for professional scholars. It is quite possible to teach, research, and publish articles and books without ever exerting any energy on disciple making or intentional mentoring.

This is because mentoring requires time spent with people, and time is the one commodity of which a scholar never seems to have enough. Be faithful to God's call on your life and make sure you are investing energy in mentoring and making disciples. This can be done, in part, through intentional writing and teaching but generally requires personal interaction over time to be effective.

In an academic setting, as mentioned, disciple making takes on the form of intentional, focused mentoring.[15] The aged apostle John wrote, "I have no greater joy than to hear that my children are walking in the truth" (3 John 4). The same is true when applied to academic mentoring. There is little in a teaching and writing career that compares to the satisfaction that comes from seeing a student publish his dissertation or find employment on the faculty of a theological institution. As PhD director, I have the great privilege of focusing most of my energies on mentoring a small group of students. These are my "faithful men" and women who hopefully will be "able to teach others also" when they are fully trained (2 Tim. 2:2; cf. Luke 6:40).

Fidelity to Scripture
Fidelity to Scripture entails a high view of God's written revelation, which is faithful to the Bible's own witness regarding itself as the Word of God. I briefly discussed this point in the introduction to this chapter, but it is so important that I want to revisit it. A high view of Scripture treats the text as inspired, authoritative, trustworthy, and, on a more controversial note, inerrant. In my understanding, you cannot have inspiration, authoritativeness, and trustworthiness without inerrancy. The identification of the words of Scripture with God's words demands that the Bible is free from error.[16]

I am not making a case for blind adherence to a given position that runs counter to the evidence, but I am firmly convinced that the evidence of the biblical texts themselves teaches us right doctrine and action.[17] There is a doctrinal vacuum in scholarship today where most scholars have "freed" themselves from the constraints of systematic theological formulations and creeds. This lack of a doctrinal framework is deplorable and has left an interpretive vacuum in which atomistic interpretation and the neglect of any attempts at a proper synthesis are the rule of the day.[18] Such atomistic interpretation, with little regard to how things fit together scripturally across the canon, leads to a neglect of what really matters: truth and the gospel. The rejection of any form of doctrinal formulation becomes its own form of bondage. Scholarly excellence requires a proper theological framework.

This does not mean that we should allow dogmatics or ecclesiastical tradition to choke the "free investigation of the canon."[19] Thomas Aquinas had his own system, as did post-Reformation scholasticism, and today we have theological systems such as dispensationalism of the classic and the progressive varieties. When J. P. Gabler delivered his address on the distinction between dogmatic and biblical theology at the University of Altdorf in 1787, he certainly had a point, and I, for one, am certainly a very strong advocate of biblical theology, which is devoted to the study of the biblical material in its original historical and terminological setting.[20] Nevertheless, the Enlightenment's rejection of ecclesiastical tradition and its call to study Scripture free from any doctrinal constraints constituted extreme reactions that have left those of us who work in the Protestant tradition without a sufficient doctrinal framework within which to explore the biblical texts.[21]

As evangelical scholars, we must be true to the message of Scripture. This entails fidelity to the mainstream of historic, biblical orthodoxy as defined by Scripture and the early church councils. At the same time, a clear distinction exists between Scripture and tradition. Only Scripture is authoritative, but tradition must not be rejected out of hand. We all bring our interpretive framework, based on tradition, to the text. This is inevitable and can be a good thing, as long as we continually subject our traditions and interpretive framework to the authority of Scripture and are willing to make changes when needed to align our views with biblical teaching. Genuine critique of our own traditions often requires careful and honest interaction with scholarship from other interpretive traditions.

Tombstone of a Scottish minister, Thomas Hog, calling for fidelity.

The gospel, with the central core truths of the substitutionary atonement and salvation by faith in Christ alone, should be our main point of reference. Paul notes, "For I delivered to you as of first importance what I also received: that Christ died for our sins in accordance with the Scriptures, that he was buried, that he was raised on the third day in accordance with the Scriptures" (1 Cor. 15:3–4). Paul received this message and passed it on to others "as of first importance."[22]

Fidelity to Your Institution
Scholarly excellence also requires a degree of fidelity to your colleagues and institution. Some scholars engage in school hopping. Similar to church hoppers, they often move from school to school and position to position. Stay where you are unless the Lord moves you, or as the cliché has it, bloom where you're planted. Many professors and pastors move around from place to place far too easily. The grass is always greener on the other side of the fence, but you don't want to be allured simply by a better title or higher salary. Longevity is important, and most pastors, missionaries, and even scholars can attest to the fact that genuine impact happens only when you stay at a particular place of ministry for a considerable amount of time. This, incidentally, is true for both missionaries and pastors and also applies to seminary professors.[23]

Fidelity to Yourself
Finally, you should be faithful to yourself. What I mean by this is that you cannot dichotomize between vocational and moral excellence. There is no way you can legitimately separate fidelity to your wife and family, on the one hand, from faithfulness to your ministry or teaching, on the other. You can't live this kind of schizophrenic lifestyle and remain true to yourself and to your God.

In some cases, evangelical scholars have some sort of double life in which they are active in their local church but have a totally different persona in their scholarship. It is important to be the same person in your local church as when writing a book or giving a presentation at a professional meeting. We will obviously speak and write on a different level to different audiences, but we must not be different people.

As scholars, we should be authentic and genuine. We must strive to have "a clear conscience" (2 Tim. 1:3). It is possible to be technically faithful on the outside without our fidelity being heartfelt. I am not talking merely about signing a confession of faith, but about living out faithfulness in our work, church, and home. This also requires faithfulness to our roles in our families and in managing our households (1 Tim. 3:2–4, 12; Titus 1:6; 2:3–5).

Conclusion

Our primary purpose as evangelical scholars is to interpret Scripture faithfully and to pass on the message of the Bible rather than to create a message of our own. Let us be faithful to God by being faithful to his revealed Word. Let us never be ashamed of or hide our faith commitments, because the gospel is "the power of God for salvation to everyone who believes" (Rom. 1:16).

Fidelity, in turn, must be accompanied by wisdom. Wisdom looks for application of the biblical message to the contemporary situation without sacrificing biblical truth. Biblical knowledge and truth are ineffectual if they are not applied and lived out by believers. Such living out of the gospel requires wisdom.

13

Wisdom

To your fidelity, add wisdom.

True wisdom, which is rooted in the fear of God, is more than mere knowledge or erudition.[1] Among other things, it entails discernment, prudence (one of the four cardinal virtues in Greek philosophy), and sanctified common sense. The wise scholar will know how to weigh the evidence and will not be impractical or merely theoretical. He will appreciate and draw attention to the real-life value and application of his research. I understand wisdom to indicate the ability to apply knowledge to a concrete situation with which someone is confronted and to choose a biblical, prudent, and advisable course of action.

Knowledge and wisdom are related but distinct. According to 1 Corinthians 8:1, so-called "knowledge," if not coupled with wisdom and charity, "puffs up, but love builds up." Knowledge is good and necessary, but it must be accompanied by love and humility, or it will lead to pride and arrogance. When I was a freshly minted Christian considering seminary training in the United States, an American missionary recounted the story of an aspiring student who was told by a well-meaning counselor,

"God doesn't need your education." To which the young man replied, "God doesn't need your ignorance either."[2]

In the same vein, Aristotle proposed the thesis that a person cannot be or do any good where he is stupid (i.e., ignorant).[3] Ignorance, therefore, must not be put on a pedestal or glorified as somehow more spiritual or pious than lack of formal education. Sadly, this is often the case as churches strangely look down on those with seminary training as if they were somehow handicapped and unfit to cope with real life.

True, seminary sometimes removes students from the real world, and, as one of my former professors never tired of repeating, "must be gotten out of your system," before effective ministry can take place. "Now you know what the answers are," he kept saying. "Go and find out the questions that people are actually asking."[4] To be sure, there are those who are so other-worldly that they are little or no earthly good. But at the same time, there is considerable value in formal training in virtually any profession, and, certainly, education in studying the Bible is no exception.

There is a need to learn the original languages, Greek and Hebrew, in order to interpret the Bible more precisely and to preach it more accurately and authoritatively. There is the benefit of formal instruction in preaching, theology, and church history. If you have a well-educated pastor, or if you *are* a well-educated pastor, don't hang your head—be grateful that God has given you the privilege of receiving proper formal training in studying and proclaiming his Word. Whatever people may say, ignorance is not a virtue. Neither is knowledge, however, unless it is applied and put to proper use. This application of knowledge to real-life situations is called "wisdom."[5]

A Biblical Theology of Wisdom

Proverbs 8:22–31 poetically exalts wisdom by associating it with God in his creative acts at the beginning of time. Wisdom is a divine attribute personified in Proverbs 8 as Lady Wisdom, calling out to people to come to her to gain wisdom, insight, and understanding. "Wisdom" occurs in the Bible often in synonymous parallelism with "knowledge."[6] Proverbs 9:10 declares, "The fear of the LORD is the beginning of wisdom, and the knowledge of the Holy One is insight." True wisdom thus must find its source in the fear of God. As Eugene Merrill observes:

> This [the fear of the LORD] becomes almost the leitmotif of the book (cf. 9:10; 15:33; Ps. 111:10), a thread that ties together its parts but that also

provides the secret to true wisdom. It comes not by education, observation, philosophizing, or introspection but by recognizing and submitting to the sovereignty of God in all areas of life. To fear him is to obey him, and in obeying him one chooses the true path to wisdom.[7]

The source of wisdom in the fear of the Lord connects the Old Testament wisdom literature to broader themes in Old Testament theology.[8] Solomon asked Yahweh to give him wisdom for the particular task of leading the people of God (1 Kings 3:9; 2 Chron. 1:10). God honored his request, and Solomon's reputation for wisdom spread across the world (1 Kings 4:30, 34; 10:1–13). As is well known, however, Solomon's wisdom progressively gave way to foolishness as he multiplied foreign wives and tolerated idolatry.

Wise counselors were highly valued by the kings of Israel and Judah. Proverbs 11:14 declares, "Where there is no guidance, a people falls, but in an abundance of counselors there is safety." David saved his life and defeated Absalom by planting a false counselor, a double agent, in Absalom's court (2 Sam. 15:32–34). Conversely, King Rehoboam made a foolish, irreversible mistake when he rejected the counsel of the old, wiser advisors and heeded the rash council of his young peers (1 Kings 12:6–15).

I have already discussed Paul's instructions in 1 Corinthians 1–2 in the chapter on eloquence above. In addition to contrasting human rhetoric with the power of God, Paul contrasted the wisdom of the world with that of God in the following memorable words:

> For the word of the cross is folly to those who are perishing, but to us who are being saved it is the power of God. For it is written, "I will destroy the wisdom of the wise, and the discernment of the discerning I will thwart." Where is the one who is wise? Where is the scribe? Where is the debater of this age? Has not God made foolish the wisdom of the world? For since, in the wisdom of God, the world did not know God through wisdom, it pleased God through the folly of what we preach to save those who believe. For Jews demand signs and Greeks seek wisdom, but we preach Christ crucified, a stumbling block to Jews and folly to Gentiles, but to those who are called, both Jews and Greeks, Christ the power of God and the wisdom of God. For the foolishness of God is wiser than men, and the weakness of God is stronger than men. (1 Cor. 1:18–25)

Paul, in essence, affirmed the declaration of Isaiah 55:9, "For as the heavens are higher than the earth, so are my ways higher than your ways and my thoughts than your thoughts." God's wisdom, especially as demonstrated in the death and resurrection of Christ, appears counterintuitive and foolish from the standpoint of human, worldly wisdom, but represents the height of God's wisdom and undergirded plan to deliver his creation from the curse of sin and death.

Christ's life, death, and resurrection epitomize the pinnacle of the wisdom of God. Comparing human wisdom to God's wisdom, the apostle Paul declared, "And because of him you are in Christ Jesus, who became to us wisdom from God, righteousness and sanctification and redemption" (1 Cor. 1:30). Elsewhere, Paul referred to Christ as the one "in whom are hidden all the treasures of wisdom and knowledge" (Col. 2:3). Jesus Christ embodies the wisdom of God that was at work from the creation of the world.[9]

Paul prayed repeatedly that God would give believers wisdom (Eph. 1:17; Col. 1:9) and urged them to teach and to live wisely (Col. 3:16; 4:5). The church was commissioned to make God's wisdom known (Eph. 3:10). James closely connected the "wisdom from above" with good conduct, contrasting it with jealousy and selfish ambition and describing it as "first pure, then peaceable, gentle, open to reason, full of mercy and good fruits, impartial and sincere" (James 3:13–17). He focused on the practical outworking of God's wisdom in the lives of believers.

The Wise Scholar

Wisdom and Research

Wisdom is indispensable for excellent scholarship and results in judicious, seasoned, and balanced research. A wise scholar will be able to weigh different sides of an issue and to be sensible in assessing the strengths and weaknesses of an argument. Wisdom is the result of maturity that enables one to weigh and synthesize arguments and to arrive at conclusions that are well reasoned.[10] It can at times be tempting to argue for extreme conclusions in order to get people's attention and stir up discussion. I have often seen scholars make intentionally provocative statements in order to draw attention and to elicit responses to their work. However, this kind of scholarship lacks wisdom and will likely result in controversy and strife.

Impulsiveness is not conducive to sound research. In my experience, students at times have impulses and ideas on a whim that may end up being almost entirely mistaken. Wisdom will keep you from following your unchecked instincts. You may mistake a sudden intuition or idea for the prompting or leading of the Holy Spirit, but keep in mind that this is only a hunch that must be checked out and verified. Nine times out of ten I have had to discard the ideas I got as sudden impulses because they turned out to be invalid on closer scrutiny. The wise scholar will be careful not to go out on a limb with risky, improbable theories.

Wisdom also will move us, whenever possible, to write a draft, set it aside for a while, and come back to it after some reflection. When you work on a given project, try to start writing early enough so that you don't have to hand in your first draft when the deadline has arrived. I do this as often as possible because I know that further reflection of my own and input from others will always make for a better end product. Just recently, I was able to field-test my hermeneutics book in various classes taught by me and others to get feedback from students before it was due at the publisher.[11]

Wisdom and Publishing

Don't rush to publish. Wise scholars are not impulsive or overly quick to publish. They recognize that publishing is not simply about airing their own opinions, but rather involves interacting discerningly with the available literature and advancing the body of knowledge in a given field.[12] Because our culture prizes speed and wants things instantaneously, there is a built-in bias against wisdom that slows things down. Many institutions also stress the urgent need for publishing, and not a few careers depend on the publication of articles and monographs. It's "publish or perish," as the saying goes.

Wisdom, however, will often engender healthy caution and will delay the publication of material in order to gain counsel and feedback. Also, keep in mind that there are more opportunities to publish information than ever before, especially with blogs and other online venues. Blogging will increase your ability to write well, elicit important feedback, and provide you a forum to field-test your arguments and conclusions before submitting your material to a peer-reviewed journal. So will presenting your work at a scholarly conference, such as a regional or national meeting of the Evangelical Theological Society.

Slower publication not only allows you to reflect on your arguments and conclusions, but it also enables you to draw on the wisdom of a multitude of counselors (Prov. 11:14; 24:6). Make yourself accountable to others by showing your work to them before you publish it in order to get feedback. Because it is hard to be objective when a given scholarly contribution is your own work—your "baby"—you need others to critique it (are people objective when they have a real baby of their own?). Students can often provide helpful feedback, especially if they are the target audience of a particular book. Offer to read and critique the work of some of your colleagues before its publication and ask them if they are willing to assess yours. Or promise them a free copy of your book when it comes out.

Perhaps best of all, if you have a spouse who is theologically minded and astute (as I do), have him or her read your work and give you an honest assessment. Even if spouses don't have formal seminary training, they will bring a healthy dose of common sense to bear on the subject, which, sadly, is not always a sufficient ingredient in scholarly writings. Your spouse will raise the "So what?" question that will challenge you to spell out the practical implications of your work. He or she will also tell you where you skipped over a necessary logical step in your argument because you tacitly assumed it. Spouses will tell you when a given argument or assertion simply doesn't make sense, at least the way you worded it. This type of feedback will help keep us from asserting ill-advised claims that exceed what can be established from the evidence and will help us see where our own interpretive framework or background is affecting our interpretation. We all have blind spots; that's where we need the help of others. How much better to surface some of these problems *prior* to publication than to become the target of a bloodthirsty reviewer!

Before I move on, I want to briefly extend this insight to pastors as well. Pastors, too, should make themselves accountable to their elders, deacons, and church members. Many pastors, in my experience, will not allow others to give them real, frank feedback on their preaching or leadership. This feedback might relate to the content of their messages, their mode of presentation, their appearance, mannerisms, or their type of demeanor (some pastors tend to strut around the front of the sanctuary like a peacock).

Similarly, we as scholars need people who will tell us the honest truth. We need objective, critical feedback. Wisdom will seek and embrace such feedback and will move us consciously to take our ego out of the equation as much as possible. Men, in particular, tend to have very big egos that can make it difficult to embrace and learn from the genuine, critical evaluation of others. Humility, which I will discuss below in chapter 15, closely relates to wisdom.

Wisdom will also lead you to stay within your area of expertise. Bart Ehrman, to cite but one example, started out as a textual critic but has been increasingly moving away from his actual area of expertise in which he received formal training and produced his early academic work in order to engage in broader theological and philosophical discussions.[13] The farther you move away from your field of expertise, the less likely you will be to research and write with excellence. It is very important to be mindful of the areas in which you are formally trained and possess technical expertise. Once you have achieved a certain amount of visibility and notoriety, people will try to get you to write and speak on all kinds of things, and if you don't consciously rein yourself in, you will set yourself up for a rough surprise. In this era of increasing specialization, it is becoming more and more difficult to keep up with the scholarly literature in multiple fields, and only the most brilliant are able to contribute to several areas of research.[14] The reviewers will be quick to let you know that you have exceeded your area of competence.

That said, this warning must be balanced by noting the importance of generalists and interdisciplinary research. Many people rightly mourn the deep gulf that separates Old and New Testament studies and biblical and systematic theology.[15] Just yesterday I sat in on a meeting of Old Testament scholars who were discussing the interpretation of Genesis 2 and 3. When in the discussion time after the presentation I raised a question as to Paul's interpretation of Genesis 2 and 3 in 1 Timothy 2, their first reaction was, "That's not in the Old Testament!" If we are evangelicals, whether Old or New Testament scholars, we have two Testaments, and our high view of Scripture demands that we consider both in our interpretive enterprise.

What is more, where the New Testament interprets the Old, the New Testament's interpretation of the Old is authoritative, and we are not at liberty to substitute our own interpretation of the Old Testament for that given in the New Testament, at least not while claiming to be evangelicals with a high view of Scripture. This kind of parochialism, which focuses unilaterally on one's own narrow field of study while neglecting the larger context in which this study ought to proceed, is an example of the type of specialization that skews the results of our research.

It is important and healthy to keep in mind the cross-disciplinary dimensions of our work as long as we are aware of our limited expertise in some of these adjacent fields. For my part, I try to research and write on a variety of topics, even though my primary expertise is in Johannine studies. Just remember to be especially cautious and thorough when you publish in areas outside your primary training and, if at all possible, let an expert in the field you are writing about read your work.

One final warning relates to a phenomenon I have observed several times. Late in people's careers, when they are getting older, they may publish an article or take a position on an issue that mars their career and good name.[16] The end of your career should be the time for you to publish powerful and reflective insights, drawing on a lifetime of scholarship. If you are near or past retirement age, be careful not to use this time to pursue idiosyncratic conclusions. (I hope I remember this when I am close to, or past, retirement myself. If you read this and are so inclined, feel free to remind me about ten or fifteen years from now!)

Wisdom and Commitments

Wisdom means that you will not accept publishing or ministry commitments without praying about it and talking to your spouse. I didn't do this consistently during the first few years of my marriage before children came along, but I eventually realized that every commitment I make affects my family in the form of time away from them to work on a project. Minor commitments are less of an issue, but the bigger a commitment, the more time it takes to complete it. Don't underestimate the amount of effort and time involved in writing a book or commentary. Many commentaries take two or more years to complete.[17]

Also, as mentioned, too many authors do not keep the contractual deadline because of lack of wisdom and foresight when they originally made the commitment.[18] Wisdom enables a scholar to be responsible and to count the cost of future commitments. There have been various times when I have barely made a certain deadline, only to find out that I was the first person to turn in an assignment and one of the few who actually met the deadline.

Your spouse, as mentioned, will often be a great source of wisdom for you, and it is entirely appropriate to run your thesis and various research ideas by him or her. In my case, I have greatly appreciated my wife's help with portions of the *God, Marriage, and Family* volume, especially in the area of parenting (I am no parenting expert!).[19] Even if your spouse is not a scholar, he or she will probably have wisdom from which you can benefit and will be able to help with practical application and general intelligibility.

Wisdom and Application

I am aware that many churches have an unfortunate bias against seminary graduates and professors, as if somehow theological training were a liability that made a person relatively useless and good only for scholarship. The kernel of truth in this prejudicial approach lies in the fact that knowledge, if not properly applied through the exercise of wisdom, can stifle a person's effectiveness. The Bible was not intended by God to be studied scientifically as an antiquarian object of interest but to be applied and obeyed by the community of believers. This application calls for wisdom.

It will generally be more difficult to draw out the significance and applicability of the material in historically oriented research. Likewise, linguistic and semantic studies often primarily serve to supply the building blocks for further research. The distinction between historical research and modern application is often discussed in terms of the dichotomy between what the text meant back then and what it means today. Evangelical scholars are particularly equipped to overcome this dichotomy because we are convinced that, when the text is properly interpreted, what it *meant* forms the basis for what it *means for us today*. We are therefore able to fully engage in historical interpretation with the conviction that, as we develop and formulate our conclusions concerning what the text meant in its historical context, we will be supplying the church with important guidelines as to its significance for us today.

Wisdom and Virtue

Above, I briefly discussed the advantages of knowledge, education, and biblical training over ignorance. I have made the point that contrary to the anti-intellectualism found in some of our churches, lack of knowledge, and Bible knowledge in particular, is in no way more virtuous than having acquired expertise in the Scriptures, whether through diligent study on one's own or through formal training.

I close this section with a thoughtful comment I came across on the Internet recently: "Education reduces the temptation to some vices while, at the same time, increasing the temptation to others. For example, it reduces the desire to engage in thievery, drug use, alcohol abuse, etc., but it increases the temptation to arrogance and intellectual vanity."[20] I believe this comment helpfully balances the respective challenges and opportunities associated with human learning and education.

On the one hand, if any of us feels called to engage in scholarship, we should be deeply grateful that God has extended to us such a significant and wonderful privilege that has great potential for good and for positive influence. At the same time, we will want to be aware of the professional hazards that come with a scholarly calling, in particular those of arrogance and intellectual vanity. Let's beware of being so full of ourselves that we forget that learning is not an end in itself but a means to an end, presenting us with an opportunity for service to other believers and nonbelievers. In many ways, the difference between knowledge that puffs up and knowledge that is put to good and proper use is wisdom—know-how in the application of knowledge to our own life and to the lives of other people.

Conclusion

Wisdom flourishes in the recognition that God is the ultimate source of wisdom. Wisdom is thus founded on reverence for God and the fear of the Lord. If the heart of God's wisdom is Christ and the cross, we should focus on these things in our scholarship. This does not mean that all of our work will dwell exclusively on these issues, but a Christ-centered focus will help us not to write simply on peripheral or relatively unimportant matters but lead us to focus our attention on topics and issues that really matter.

Final accountability for our life and work, of course, comes with God's end-time judgment. We will all have to give an account for the work we have done. Wisdom will lead us to live our lives in the light of the final outcome of all things and will teach us to number our days and to apply ourselves rightly to the task before us. What is more, wisdom will lead us to live a grace-filled life: receiving the fullness of God's grace extended to us in Christ and extending that grace to others.

Part Four

RELATIONAL EXCELLENCE

14

Grace

To your wisdom, add grace.

Everything a Christian does should be characterized by grace. Grace should permeate our thoughts, words, and actions, and make a noticeable impression on those with whom we come in contact, both believers and unbelievers. Unfortunately, I suspect that many unbelievers would not immediately associate graciousness with Christians. More likely, they may think of a church bitterly splitting over petty issues, the bombing of abortion clinics, or how they've heard that Christians hate homosexuals. Such stereotypes cannot be changed overnight, but as scholars it is our responsibility to model graciousness in our interactions with one another and with those with whom we disagree.

I am not talking about grace in a soteriological sense here, but about the way in which we extend grace to others.[1] That said, the grace we show to others is, of course, grounded in our reception of God's grace in Christ. People cannot genuinely extend grace unless they themselves have received grace from God. Showing grace to others means giving people the benefit of the doubt, not pushing them into a corner, and allowing them the opportunity to make their own case for a given position. As an overall disposition reflected in the way we treat others, grace entails forgiveness, love, kindness, and gentleness.

According to John, "Grace and truth came through Jesus Christ" (John 1:17). As people united to Christ in his death and resurrection, we are called to defend truth, but we should also exercise grace. Truth and grace must not be pitted against each other in our lives and witness. Jesus Christ serves as our example in this regard. As Jesus told Pilate, the Roman governor, the purpose for which he came into this world was to bear witness to the truth (John 18:37). At the same time, Jesus was also an exceedingly gracious person who extended grace to everyone he met.

A Biblical Theology of Graciousness

God's grace granted to us in Christ serves as the indispensible foundation for any theology of graciousness. We should be gracious toward others because God has shown great grace toward us. Jesus made this point emphatically in the parable of the unforgiving servant. The king in this parable freely pardoned a man who owed him a very large sum of money. Upon his release, the man found a fellow servant who owed him a very small amount and threatened the man in order to try to extract the money from him.

> Then his master summoned him and said to him, "You wicked servant! I forgave you all that debt because you pleaded with me. And should not you have had mercy on your fellow servant, as I had mercy on you?" And in anger his master delivered him to the jailers, until he should pay all his debt. So also my heavenly Father will do to every one of you, if you do not forgive your brother from your heart. (Matt. 18:32–35)

Because we have been forgiven an infinite debt, we should forgive the small debts others owe us. Jesus made the issue just as clear in Matthew 6:14–15, where he states, "For if you forgive others their trespasses, your heavenly Father will also forgive you, but if you do not forgive others their trespasses, neither will your Father forgive your trespasses."

The apostle Paul used similar logic in his appeal to the Ephesians: "Be kind to one another, tenderhearted, forgiving one another, as God in Christ forgave you" (Eph. 4:32). When writing to the Colossians, Paul expanded on the same theme:

> Put on then, as God's chosen ones, holy and beloved, compassionate hearts, kindness, humility, meekness, and patience, bearing with one another and, if one has a complaint against another, forgiving each other; as the Lord has forgiven you, so you also must forgive. (Col. 3:12–13)

In these verses, Paul closely linked forgiveness of others with kindness, tenderheartedness, compassion, humility, meekness, and patience in a way that I would describe as "graciousness." We should act graciously toward others because God has acted graciously toward us. Our graciousness is not rooted in the goodness of our own hearts—we are all sinners (Rom. 3:23)—it derives from being on the receiving end of God's grace in Christ.

Biblical Examples

In addition to the foundational principle noted above, the Scriptures abound with both positive and negative examples of graciousness in action. David exercised graciousness toward Saul when he could have taken his life on two separate occasions, because David knew that he did not have the right to slay Saul (1 Sam. 24:3–7; 26:7–11). Abigail, in turn, was very gracious to David when she fell at his feet and pleaded for mercy, saving him from acting on his anger toward her husband, Nabal (1 Samuel 25).

The book of Ruth features several examples of graciousness: Ruth's loyal allegiance to Naomi; Boaz's kindness toward Ruth; and Yahweh's faithful provision for his people. In fact, the eminent Old Testament scholar Bruce Waltke contends that *hesed*, a highly significant Hebrew term with a broad semantic range—including the notions of loyal love, unfailing kindness, devotion, and favor—unifies the entire book.[2]

Jesus, as mentioned, the embodiment of grace and truth, consistently exercised graciousness in his dealings with others. He was moved by compassion for those who were poor, oppressed, or in need of healing (Matt. 9:36) and taught and cured their many afflictions. He extended forgiveness to several immoral women (John 4:7–42; 7:53–8:11; Luke 7:36–50) and dined with tax collectors and "sinners" (Matt. 9:10; Mark 2:15; Luke 5:30; 15:1). At the same time, Jesus had little patience for hypocrisy and legalism (Matthew 23). Jesus's graceful disposition stands in marked contrast with the attitude of "the sons of thunder" who wanted to call down fire to consume a Samaritan village that refused to receive them (Luke 9:54). Jesus quickly rebuked them (Luke 9:55).

Paul demonstrated grace when he evangelized his jailor (Acts 16:29–30) and later sought to save the lives of his fellow sailors (Acts 27:10, 31).

Even when dealing with false teachers, he remained fully aware that Christ had appointed him to service even "though formerly I was a blasphemer, persecutor, and insolent opponent. But I received mercy because I had acted ignorantly in unbelief, and the grace of our Lord overflowed for me with the faith and love that are in Christ Jesus" (1 Tim. 1:13–14). As a result, Paul did not denounce false teachers in arrogance but did so in humility, recognizing that he had once been just like them yet God had shown him grace.

Biblical Exhortations

Paul's command to the Colossian believers was this: "Let your speech always be gracious, seasoned with salt, so that you may know how you ought to answer each person" (Col. 4:6). Peter issued the well-known charge, "In your hearts honor Christ the Lord as holy, always being prepared to make a defense to anyone who asks you for a reason for the hope that is in you; yet do it with gentleness and respect, having a good conscience, so that, when you are slandered, those who revile your good behavior in Christ may be put to shame" (1 Pet. 3:15–16). Both Paul and Peter stressed the importance of cultivating speech characterized by gentleness and graciousness. Graciousness is vital in leading others to Christ and in persuading them to be reconciled to God (2 Cor. 5:20). How could Christ's ambassadors be filled with hatred?

James, in elaborating on the importance of using our tongue the way God intended, points out that it is inconceivable for a Christian to curse others:

> With it [the tongue] we bless our Lord and Father, and with it we curse people who are made in the likeness of God. From the same mouth come blessing and cursing. My brothers, these things ought not to be so. Does a spring pour forth from the same opening both fresh and salt water? Can a fig tree, my brothers, bear olives, or a grapevine produce figs? Neither can a salt pond yield fresh water. (James 3:9–12)

A mean-spirited Christian who uses his or her tongue to curse and tear others down is a contradiction in terms. Similarly, going to the root of the matter, Jesus observes that our words are a reflection of what is in our hearts: "For out of the abundance of the heart the mouth speaks" (Matt. 12:34). Unkind words and actions indicate a lack of grace in a person's heart and, in some cases, may indicate lack of salvation.

A Gracious Scholar

Grace in Disagreements

The biblical examples discussed above, particularly Jesus and Paul, demonstrate the ability both to stand firm for truth and yet to extend graciousness to others. In following these examples, we need to learn how to hold strong convictions while differing graciously with the viewpoints of others. Even as I write this at Tyndale House in Cambridge, England, I share a library carrel with Don Hagner, a well-known biblical scholar who for many years taught at Fuller Seminary and is currently working on a major New Testament introduction. While both evangelical, Don and I occupy different parts of the theological spectrum in our views on a variety of issues (such as the authorship of the Gospels, the book of Ephesians, and the Pastoral Epistles, to name but a few), but in treating me in a consistently warm and cordial manner, Don has been an example to me of the graciousness and kindness that should characterize all of our scholarship and demeanor toward others. As a result, we have spent considerable time sharing our positions on a variety of issues over tea, and although I have not always come to see things Don's way, I have certainly benefited from hearing a different view articulated clearly and lucidly—if for no other reason so that I can interact with it and critique it knowledgeably and fairly.[3] It is in any case unrealistic to expect that everyone, or even most other scholars, will agree with you on everything. Not everyone will share all of your views, nor can you force them to do so.

Many people (including scholars) cannot handle disagreements with graciousness. Some feminists I have encountered over the years are like this. Unless you are with them ideologically, they will take on an antagonistic stance. Similarly, many conservative evangelicals (including some complementarians) are not particularly gracious and approach those with opposing viewpoints in an adversarial manner. We are much better known for clinging tenaciously to our convictions, and identifying and opposing falsehood, than for our graciousness. In fact, liberals are often more gracious than those of us who are conservative and hold to a high view of Scripture (though there is, of course, also a very hard-nosed type of liberalism that, while professing tolerance, represents a very intolerant disposition toward opposing viewpoints).[4]

I am not advocating a wishy-washy or spineless brand of scholarship that chooses to conform to the prevailing mood so as not to offend anyone;[5] I am talking about differing with others graciously. I have known more than one scholar who assimilated virtually every idea and proposal he encountered in the scholarly literature in such a way that he blended in with everyone else. Such an approach is unsatisfactory, however, because it does not sufficiently screen the arguments and sift through the available data, exercising discernment in knowing what to embrace and what to reject. The answer is not to check "all of the above" in our scholarship but to test the various positions and to hold on to what we have come to believe is the correct interpretation (following the principle enunciated in 1 Thess. 5:21). In so doing, we need to learn to disagree with others in such a way that they will not feel personally attacked to ensure that the focus remains on the issue, not the person. Who knows but that perhaps occasionally another scholar will even be persuaded by our argument if we lodge it in a gracious and face-saving manner.

What are you and I going to do? Will our scholarship be characterized by a mean-spirited, confrontational, and harsh attitude? The writings of some evangelicals show little love for their scholarly opponents; in fact, one might almost conclude that they despise them. Unfortunately, these brothers in Christ do not seem to realize that the scholars on the other side of a given issue are, ultimately speaking, not the enemy. Satan is our common enemy. As the apostle Paul makes clear, "We do not wrestle against flesh and blood, but against the rulers, against the authorities, against the cosmic powers over this present darkness, against the spiritual forces of evil in the heavenly places" (Eph. 6:12).

You and I will not effectively oppose the spiritual forces of evil in the heavenly places by unleashing ad hominem attacks against those whom we oppose (an insight, incidentally, not always heeded by the great Reformers, Luther and Calvin). Rather, let's make sure our scholarship is characterized by a prayerful, gracious, and persuasive posture toward others in order that "God may perhaps grant them repentance leading to a knowledge of the truth, and they may come to their senses and escape from the snare of the devil, after being captured by him to do his will" (2 Tim. 2:25–26).

Grace When Criticized

How do you and I respond when we are criticized by others? Do we lash out and try to get revenge? Are we holding grudges? Do we keep, and try to settle, scores? As scholars, you and I are certain to face a certain amount of criticism—unless, of course, we never publish anything. In fact, I have known several scholars who were highly reluctant to commit themselves to any position in print, in part, at least, because they feared negative reviews. Do not be hypersensitive when—not if—you are criticized.

I have been on both sides of criticism. As an editor, I have received complaints by those who felt unfairly criticized. I tried to remind them that the reviewer's comments represented only one person's opinion (though they may, of course, be representative of the views and assessments of others as well). At times, a bad review may reflect more on the person writing the review than on the work being reviewed. When one of my own books has been the target of a negative review, my initial impulse usually has been to write a rebuttal of some sort, but, with very rare exceptions, I have resisted such urges. Like always, when something patently unfair happens, it irks you and stirs your innate sense of justice, and you feel like something has to be done to right the wrong. But as a rule we should allow the scholarly review process to run its course.

One time someone wrote a review of one of my books and spent virtually the entire review critiquing a single chapter, almost completely ignoring the other dozen or so chapters in the book. "What about the rest of the book?" I thought. I considered contacting the book review editor in order to protest the review, but better sense quickly prevailed. It is neither possible nor necessary always to have the last word or to appear right or vindicated at all times. Let another plead your case. If your arguments are sound, they will survive the harsh criticism of a particular scholar who disagrees with you.

Scholarly opinion can be fickle, and often different views rise and subside like the ocean tide. This calls for grace under criticism; you and I may very well be vindicated in due course. We may be mocked or ridiculed by scholars holding an opposing view for a season, and our only hope will be that in time the tide will turn in our favor. The Johannine community hypothesis, as mentioned, is a recent example of the gradual change in scholarly opinion. At the time when I was writing my dissertation, there was not much I could do but calmly set forth my reservations concerning the hypothesis—and then wait. Since that time, scholarly support for my position has come, in some cases, from rather unexpected places, and my position is no longer as far removed from the scholarly consensus as was once the case.

Graciousness in response to criticism requires that we take ourselves out of scholarship to some degree and leave the results in God's hands. We cannot chase down, confront, and answer everyone who disagrees with us. The only vindication that ultimately matters will come from God, not from other people. Paul put it well: "But with me it is a very small thing that I should be judged by you or by any human court. In fact, I do not even judge myself. For I am not aware of anything against myself, but I am not thereby acquitted. It is the Lord who judges me" (1 Cor. 4:3–4). Elsewhere, the apostle similarly posed, and answered, the following series of rhetorical questions: "For am I now seeking the approval of man, or of God? Or am I trying to please man? If I were still trying to please man, I would not be a servant of Christ" (Gal. 1:10). On the last day when we will all stand before the judgment seat of Christ, human approval or disapproval will mean nothing. If we keep this reality firmly in mind, we will be able to respond to criticism more readily with a measure of seasoning and grace.

Grace When Criticizing

Just as it is important to respond with graciousness to criticism, it is equally vital to show grace when criticizing others. This graciousness reflects the fact that scholarship constitutes a dialogue. Do you read other authors empathetically? If they fail to present their case perfectly or are awkward in articulating a particular point, are you quick to find fault, pushing your opponents into a corner? Or do you give them the benefit of a doubt and allow them to nuance their argument and clarify their position? Do you criticize others for small errors or graciously interact with them on the basis of what you know they mean?[6]

Millard Erickson proposes that evangelical scholars take the following pledge:

- I will not point out the presuppositions of another's position without acknowledging that I have presuppositions myself.
- I will not contend that another's view is historically conditioned without conceding that mine is also.
- I will be more concerned not to misunderstand or misrepresent others' views than to claim that mine has been misunderstood or misrepresented.
- I will be more concerned that my language be fair and objective than I am that others' language about me may not be.
- I will not caricature my opponent's view to make my own appear more moderate.

- I will not employ ad hominem arguments.
- I will abstain from the use of pejorative language.
- I will not impute motives or emotions to others.
- I will think of intellectual arguments in terms of differences over ideas, not as personal disputes.[7]

This pledge epitomizes the points I am trying to emphasize in this chapter. May we, as evangelical scholars, become as well known for our graciousness as we are known for our defense of biblical inerrancy and our stand on any number of watershed issues that define the nature of biblical authority in our day.

Conclusion

A gracious scholar's speech, both oral and written, will be seasoned with kindness. We have been saved by grace and ought to conduct ourselves with grace toward others. Grace will be evident by the way in which we deal with those who differ with us, whether in the church or in the academic arena. Grace will show itself as a demeanor and disposition that will win over opponents, whereas heavy-handedness fails.

Gracious persuasion will enable us to rightly represent the one whom we serve. In conjunction with grace, we will need humility in order to put the insights of this chapter into practice. Without humility, we will be unable to treat those who differ from us with graciousness, respond well to criticism, and criticize others with graciousness. Graciousness and humility go hand in hand.

15

Humility

To your grace, add humility.

A few years ago, an unexpected envelope appeared on my doorstep with a free book in it. I had no idea what it could be but soon discovered that C. J. Mahaney, a man I had never met, had sent me a copy of his newly published book *Humility: True Greatness*.[1] I asked my wife, "Why did he send me that book? I don't even know him." Without a moment's hesitation, my wife responded matter-of-factly, "He must think you need it." In addition, a friend of mine, whom I had told about my wife's comment, continued to press me to read the book. Let me just say that it can be a little humbling when your wife and friends urge you to read a book on humility!

Humility can be somewhat elusive as a subject of inquiry, because to some extent it relates to something a person is *not*. A humble person is not self-focused or prideful. The fact that most genuinely humble people will fail to recognize that they are humble adds to the elusiveness of the subject. Similarly, when people tell you they are working on being humble, it is easy to think they have not come very far in that quest. By contrast, everyone knows what pride is: arrogance, thinking too highly of oneself, exalting oneself, and overreaching. C. J. Mahaney defines humility as "honestly assessing ourselves in light of God's holiness and our sinfulness."[2] Conversely, he describes pride as "when sinful human beings aspire to the status and position of God and refuse to acknowledge their dependence upon Him."[3]

False humility may fool people, but it will never take in God. What is more, you can count on the fact that if you and I don't humble ourselves, God will humble us. That said, we cannot generate humility through self-effort. Genuine humility starts with an individual acknowledging his or her sin to God and with a broken spirit asking God for forgiveness and salvation. We cannot hold on to our pride when our sin is truly exposed and confessed in the sight of a holy God (see Ps. 10:4).

I was an intellectual European university student like many others, working on my PhD in economics, when, upon hearing God's Word, I was gripped by the realization that I needed salvation. God used this sense of need to drive me to humility before him, to induce in me the desperation that cried out to him for forgiveness, and to engender in me the joy of knowing that my sins had been wholly forgiven.[4] Turning to God for salvation is the first step toward humility. A second step is to acknowledge and submit to the authority of Scripture. A third is to respond appropriately to correction.

A Biblical Theology of Humility

The Bible's teaching on humility can be succinctly summarized as follows: God prizes humility and hates pride. The Scriptures are unequivocal regarding this. The book of Proverbs emphasizes God's hatred of pride by making "haughty eyes" the first item in the list of seven things that God hates (Prov. 6:16–17). Scripture makes it abundantly clear that pride has negative consequences: "Pride goes before destruction, and a haughty spirit before a fall. It is better to be of a lowly spirit with the poor than to divide the spoil with the proud" (Prov. 16:18–19); "One's pride will bring him low, but he who is lowly in spirit will obtain honor" (Prov. 29:23).

Not only will the proud fall, but God will actively oppose them, treat them as enemies, and fight against them (James 4:6; 1 Pet. 5:5; cf. Ps. 147:6; Prov. 3:34): "The LORD preserves the faithful but abundantly repays the one who acts in pride" (Ps. 31:23); "The LORD tears down the house of the proud but maintains the widow's boundaries" (Prov. 15:25).

God lists pride as one of the main reasons for his opposition to various nations in the Old Testament.[5] Pride marred the reigns of Uzziah (2 Chron. 26:16), Hezekiah (2 Chron. 32:25), Amon (2 Chron. 33:23), and Zedekiah (2 Chron. 36:12). After God humbled Nebuchadnezzar, the king declared, "Now I, Nebuchadnezzar, praise and extol and honor the King of heaven, for all his works are right and his ways are just; and those who walk in pride he is able to humble" (Dan. 4:37).

In contrast to his stance toward pride, God looks with favor upon those who are humble: "But this is the one to whom I will look: he who is humble and contrite in spirit and trembles at my word" (Isa. 66:2); "He leads the humble in what is right, and teaches the humble his way" (Ps. 25:9). Throughout the Old Testament, God responds with favor to those who humble themselves before him. This is particularly evident in the reigns of Ahab (1 Kings 21:29), Josiah (2 Kings 22:19), Rehoboam (2 Chron. 12:6–7, 12), and Manasseh (2 Chron. 33:10–13, 19). God promises to give grace to the humble (James 4:6; 1 Pet. 5:5) and vows to exalt them (James 4:10; 1 Pet. 5:6). Humility is to characterize the New Testament community in believers' disposition toward and dealings with one another (Eph. 4:2; Phil. 2:3; Col. 3:12; 1 Pet. 3:8; 5:5).

Scripture's negative evaluation of pride and its exaltation of humility have God's future day of judgment as their ultimate point of reference, envisioning a great eschatological reversal where the last will be first and the first will be last (Matt. 19:30; Mark 10:31). On that final day, God will set all things right. The proud will be irrevocably humbled, and the humble will be permanently exalted:

> The haughty looks of man shall be brought low, and the lofty pride of men shall be humbled, and the LORD alone will be exalted in that day. For the LORD of hosts has a day against all that is proud and lofty, against all that is lifted up—and it shall be brought low. (Isa. 2:11–12)

The prospect of this great future reversal should motivate Christians to persevere with patience even in the midst of suffering, oppression, and pain (James 5:7–11).

Throughout the Scriptures, humility is closely tied to repentance. Second Chronicles 7:14 contains the promise that if "my people who are called by my name humble themselves, and pray and seek my face and turn from their wicked ways, then I will hear from heaven and will forgive their sin and heal their land." James, likewise, closely ties humility to repentance:

> You adulterous people! Do you not know that friendship with the world is enmity with God? Therefore whoever wishes to be a friend of the world makes himself an enemy of God. Or do you suppose it is to no purpose that the Scripture says, "He yearns jealously over the spirit that he has made to dwell in us"? But he gives more grace. Therefore it says, "God opposes the proud, but gives grace to the humble." Submit yourselves therefore to God. Resist the devil, and he will flee from you. Draw near to God, and he will draw near to you. Cleanse your hands, you sinners, and purify your hearts, you double-minded. Be wretched and mourn and weep. Let your laughter be turned to mourning and your joy to gloom. Humble yourselves before the Lord, and he will exalt you. (James 4:4–10)

Remarkably, both James and the author of Chronicles direct this call to humble repentance not to unbelievers but to the people of God. As Todd Penner observes:

> The writer is calling upon the readers to place themselves in the state in which God, when he comes to judge, desires to find his people. God will oppose the proud, and thus the believer must be found humble. The state of "wretchedness" is obviously a metaphor for calling the community back to God in light of the coming judgment. The language is in the style of a call to repentance.... Thus 4.7–12 forms a coherent set of admonitions and warnings to the community members in order to prepare them for the imminent return of the judge.[6]

This means that humility expressed through repentance should characterize a Christian throughout his or her entire life and not be relegated to a one-time salvation event in the past.

Pursuing Humility

There is no question that humility is one of the cardinal virtues in the Christian life and in academic work. Don Carson recalls the words of John Calvin:

> I have always been exceedingly delighted with the words of Chrysostom, "the foundation of our philosophy is humility"; and still more with those of Augustine, "As the orator, when asked, What is the first precept in eloquence? answered, Delivery: What is the second? Delivery: What is the third? Delivery: so, if you ask me in regard to the precepts of the Christian Religion, I will answer, first, second, and third, Humility.[7]

Before discussing the relationship between humility and academic excellence, I want to present and reflect on some of the suggestions that C. J. Mahaney makes concerning the pursuit of humility in his above-mentioned book *Humility: True Greatness*. First and foremost, the pursuit of humility requires that one constantly reflect on the wonder of the cross of Christ.[8] The cross redefines true greatness, exposes sin for what it really is, and reminds us of the great cost God paid to rescue us from our sin.[9]

Next, we should begin each day by acknowledging our dependence and need for God and by expressing our gratitude to God.[10] As a special focus, Mahaney suggests that we study the attributes of God, the doctrine of grace, and the doctrine of sin.[11] Pride will find little opportunity to grow in individuals who continually contemplate God's greatness, holiness, power, and supremacy, their own weakness, sin, failure, and inability, and God's gracious actions in Christ to save, regenerate, transform, sanctify, and glorify them.

In closing, Mahaney notes four practices that will aid a person in the pursuit of humility: identify evidences of grace in others; encourage and serve others each and every day; invite and respond positively to correction; and respond humbly to trials.[12] It is important to foster and engage in thoughts or activities that take our focus off ourselves and redirect it onto God and other people.

The Humble Scholar

Humility and Research

How often do you consider the possibility that you might be wrong? Many people speak and write without any sense that they could be wrong. Some publications are little more than exercises in dogmatism and the airing of personal opinions. One way to guard against this is to make sure that you do not overstate your case. Be modest in your claims. Honestly ask yourself, "What have I really established?"

Novice scholars, in particular, tend to exaggerate their case because they crave respect and recognition. Don't overstate your contribution because more mature scholars will quickly see through your overblown conclusions and dismiss your entire argument. It is far better to be understated and to allow others to draw attention to the significance of your work. As Proverbs 27:2 states, "Let another praise you, and not your own mouth; a stranger, and not your own lips."

Humility and Lasting Significance

You can foster humility in your scholarship by taking a long-term view on your significance. Between my MDiv and PhD studies I engaged in an independent study on the history of hermeneutics. I remember some particular observations I made while reading Stephen Neill and Tom Wright's book *The Interpretation of the New Testament: 1861–1986*, Werner Kümmel's *The New Testament: The History of the Investigation of Its Problems*, and some other books on the subject.[13] These authors would often discuss the entire life of a scholar in a footnote or spend a few pages summarizing the contribution of a given author, only to comment that most of his conclusions were wrong. The fact that our entire scholarly career will be summed up by future historians of the discipline in a mere footnote, if we are mentioned at all, should foster in us a humble perspective as to our own importance. Even if I spend my entire life pursuing an academic career and produce a number of scholarly writings, in the grand scheme of things I will not amount to all that much. Many of the people publishing books today will barely be mentioned by future chroniclers of a given discipline.

A second observation that occurred to me while studying the history of hermeneutics was how brilliant, prolific, learned, and accomplished many scholars of the past were. Even though we are not nearly as erudite as previous scholars, by the providence of God we are able to compensate to some extent for our lack of learning today by virtue of the advances in technology that enable us to do lexical and syntactical work in a short period of time that would have taken previous generations of scholars years, and in some cases an entire lifetime, to complete. The recognition of the vast erudition of many scholars in the past will help keep us from thinking too highly of our own contributions.

I was reminded of this just yesterday when I had the unique opportunity to look firsthand at the original copy of Erasmus's 1516 *Novum Instrumentum* at the library of St. John's College here in Cambridge.[14] As I leafed through this work in growing awe, I glanced through the lengthy Latin preface, selectively perused the presentation of the entire New Testament in the form of parallel Greek and Latin columns, and was astonished to discover a virtual commentary on the entire New Testament in the form of learned annotations toward the end of the book. Here was a man who has had few equals in any age among Bible interpreters and students of Scripture.

Humility will be a natural byproduct of being realistic and not self-focused. Don't be delusional; in the overall scheme of things, you and I are not that important. Our lives are like a mist (James 4:14), and we will soon die and take all our training, education, and knowledge with us. Recognition of this inevitable reality will foster humility. Even if we leave a meaningful legacy, it will be small in comparison to many others.

If this is true, what can we hope to achieve? Should we abandon our scholarly aspirations in light of the rather sobering note struck in my comments above? I am not suggesting this at all. While we should develop a keen awareness of our own limitations and see our work in proper perspective, we can, and should, strive to be advocates of biblical truth and endeavor accurately to teach the Scriptures.[15] This is no small calling! Beyond our teaching ministry, there is also strategic value to the vocation of writing. When you commit your thoughts to writing, you increase your potential impact over time.[16]

In fact, writing is highly strategic. I personally try to strike a balance between mentoring and writing. Writing cannot be a substitute for mentoring because the latter thrives on the more personal medium of discussion and dialogue. Jesus was able to instruct his disciples more fully than the crowds because he spent one-on-one time with them. Similarly, our students will have more access to us than those who simply pick up our books. Nevertheless, writing can be a vehicle for discipleship by extending our teaching to a wider audience. It is always gratifying for an author to hear back from someone who has read and benefited from a published book or article.[17]

Humility and Superstardom
Many Christians have the unfortunate habit, perhaps influenced by our culture, of putting their leaders on pedestals and treating them like celebrities. Don Carson, Albert Mohler, and John Piper all have large groups of ardent followers, and even though they do everything in their power to exalt Christ and point people to him, it is almost impossible to counteract acolytes who thrust them onto a pedestal in their minds. There is no way you could ever live up to the state of sainthood or superstardom that people will try to bestow on you if you are successful (though, fortunately, this is a problem few of us will ever face).

This problem is exacerbated by our small subculture. Danny Akin, the president of the seminary where I serve, is widely known among Southern Baptists, but in non-Southern Baptist circles he is known by comparatively fewer people. The same is true for many others. We can be easily deluded concerning our own importance if we are well known in our very small subculture or circle of influence. This danger became vividly real to me one day when somebody at church asked me a particular question. I remember thinking at the time, "Doesn't this person know who I am?" That was an incredibly proud thought that had been fostered by the fact that on campus, in my small subculture, most people know who I am. I was immediately convicted and asked myself, "Who do I think I am? Should that person really have known who I am?"

Even if you never characterized yourself as a superstar in our evangelical subculture, simply being a pastor or professor can lead to pride. After all, you will know more about the Bible than most of the people with whom you come in contact. You carry an exalted title such as "pastor" or "doctor," and many church members and students look up to you and expect you to have all, or at least most, of the answers. We can easily begin to think that we deserve respect or admiration. It is good and necessary to humble yourself consciously in this regard. Paul exhorted the believer "not to think of himself more highly than he ought to think, but to think with sober judgment, each according to the measure of faith that God has assigned" (Rom. 12:3).

It is helpful to have some friends to spend time with who couldn't care less that you are a professor and author. At times in the past, I have been impressed by visiting with a well-known scholar and observing his interaction with people in his church who were blissfully unaware of who that person was. Apparently, my friend had never told his fellow church members that he was a famous scholar! For them, that person was simply a brother in Christ, and he related to them as a humble fellow servant. This spoke volumes to me about that man's character.

On a personal note, having teenagers—not to mention a spouse—helps. There is no way you can be deluded about your importance with teenagers in the house. I currently have three in my home who look at me as their dad and not as a writer or scholar. They are not interested in me because I am a professor and have written a number of books, but because I am their father and am walking through life with them. They are also keenly aware of my limitations and know me for who I really am. In addition to your spouse, teenagers are a great way for God to keep you humble.

Another great way to stay humble is to present your academic work to first-rate scholars at professional meetings or other scholarly gatherings.

I just had such an opportunity, presenting a paper on the relationship between John's Gospel and the Synoptics to the Tyndale Fellowship before an audience that included scholars such as Richard Bauckham, Howard Marshall, Don Hagner, David Wenham, and Seyoon Kim, to mention but a few, as well as a number of doctoral students from various parts of Europe. This was particularly humbling because I could not presume on people agreeing with me simply because they shared my view of Scripture or were part of the same faith community. My scholarship must stand or fall on its own merits, and the ensuing discussion surfaced many important items of feedback, which to incorporate took a considerable amount of time.[18]

I can do no better than to end this chapter on humility with this delightful quotation from the writings of Martin Luther:

> If, however, you feel and are inclined to think you have made it, flattering yourself with your own little books, teaching, or writing, because you have done it beautifully and preached excellently; if you are highly pleased when someone praises you in the presence of others; if you perhaps look for praise, and would sulk or quit what you are doing if you did not get it—if you are of that stripe, dear friend, then take yourself by the ears, and if you do this in the right way you will find a beautiful pair of big, long, shaggy donkey ears. Then do not spare any expense! Decorate them with golden bells, so that people will be able to hear you wherever you go, point their fingers at you, and say, "See, see! There goes that clever beast, who can write such exquisite books and preach so remarkably well." That very moment you will be blessed and blessed beyond measure in the kingdom of heaven. Yes, in that heaven where hellfire is ready for the devil and his angels. To sum up: Let us be proud and seek honor in the places where we can. But in this book the honor is God's alone, as it is said, "God opposes the proud, but gives grace to the humble" [1 Pet. 5:5]; to whom be glory, world without end, Amen.[19]

Conclusion

Scholarly excellence demands humility. Without humility, you will be blind to your own weaknesses, unaware of the obvious holes in your arguments, and unable to be corrected or guided by others. Humility enables a scholar to truly learn through submission to the evidence and correction by the insights of others. A humble scholar will not force the evidence to fit pre-determined conclusions but will modify presuppositions, even ones dearly held, to develop hypotheses that best square with the evidence.

Humility will also enable a scholar to realize how much he or she needs other people, both scholarly colleagues and nonacademic friends. No person is an island, and we are all dependent on one another throughout our lives and careers. Scholarly excellence requires a healthy recognition of our own dependence on other people and a commitment to genuine involvement in the communities of which we are a part. This leads us to contemplate another scholarly virtue, the virtue of interdependence.

16

Interdependence

To your humility, add interdependence.

Interdependence may not seem like the most obvious topic in a book on achieving scholarly excellence. It is certainly not as self-evident as some of the other virtues I have chosen for discussion such as diligence, courage, humility, and love, and yet it is just as vital an ingredient for the achievement of true scholarly excellence. The notion of the self-sufficient, autonomous scholar who works in complete isolation from others in producing great works of scholarship, while persistent, is not borne out by the reality of the demands placed on scholars in today's academic climate. Not only is interdependence required for greater excellence and larger influence in our work, but it also reflects the reality of the scholarly task: we desperately need one another.[1]

When I arrived at Trinity as a freshly minted PhD student, I was at first taken aback by the competitiveness of many of the students there (though they would have probably told you the same thing about me). I must tell you that this observation comes from someone who is very competitive and desperately tries to win any and every contest I enter. I even hate to lose at board games. It seemed to me that in this kind of competitive environment, people actually tried to keep each other at bay so they could get the most important resources in the library, be best positioned to come out on top in a given class, or assist the most coveted professors. Through that experience, I realized how ugly that attitude was and how important it was for Christians, especially those studying theology, to have a more collaborative approach to their work and ministry. Your success does not have to be achieved at the detriment of others, and you do not have to step all over others to get ahead.

This, of course, does not take away from the fact that scholarship is at times a lonely proposition, because you can only publish and present your own work. (In another sense, of course, scholarship involves an important social dimension, allowing you to interact with the voices of many other writers.) Everything cannot be a group project. Even though much of our research takes place in the solitary confinement (that almost sounds like a prison!) of a library carrel or office, we need regular and intentional interaction with other people in order to strengthen our scholarship and to remain spiritually, emotionally, and intellectually healthy.

As I write this, I am on study leave at Tyndale House in Cambridge, England. One of the great benefits of working in this kind of environment is the balance between individual research and writing and involvement in a scholarly community. Every day at 11 o'clock in the morning and at 4 o'clock in the afternoon, people's research comes to a grinding, albeit temporary, halt, and everyone congregates for tea in the commons room. You never know with whom you might find yourself engaged in an animated conversation, whether a seasoned scholar on sabbatical or a bright PhD student working on an interesting dissertation topic.

After this exercise in community, resulting in intellectual stimulation and mutual support and encouragement, it is time to return with new vigor to one's specialized work. This kind of model reinforces the consciousness that one is not the only one doing serious academic work in one's own discipline or in a number of related areas. It fosters mutual respect, humility, and a willingness to learn from the insights of others, whether or not there is an immediate payoff for one's own academic work. This is interdependence at its best.

A Biblical Theology of Interdependence

Although one will look in vain for the entry "interdependence" in a given concordance, as the thumbnail sketch below will demonstrate, the biblical material in both Testaments is replete with examples of individuals who wrongly asserted their independence from God and/or others and of those who rightly recognized their dependence on God and their interdependence with others. The early church, in particular, seemed to model a degree of interdependence that seems largely foreign to our individualistic modern mindset. As even the most casual perusal of the book of Acts will reveal, the first Christians genuinely had a sense of mutual need and interdependence as they faced strong persecution from the unbelieving world and were bound together by a common faith and mission.

Interdependence in the Old Testament

From the very beginning, Adam and Eve were created as both dependent and interdependent beings. They were dependent on God, of course, but they were also dependent upon each other (Gen. 2:18). Human beings were not created to be independent. In fact, the woman's assertion of her independence from her Creator, and her husband, followed the Tempter's prior assertion of his own independence from God and precipitated the fall of humanity.

Positive examples of interdependence abound throughout the Old Testament. Moses felt he could not confront Pharaoh alone but with his brother Aaron found the courage to do so (Ex. 4:14–16). Ruth and Naomi supported each other through difficult times. David depended on Jonathan for his very life (1 Samuel 20) and treated Jonathan's descendants with favor (2 Samuel 9). While often praised for his epic one-on-one confrontation with Goliath, David in fact surrounded himself throughout his career with mighty men, generals, and advisors. The examples of Abigail (1 Sam. 25:30–31) and Nathan (2 Samuel 12), among others, make clear that David did not view himself as above rebuke but humbly received correction from others. Apart from God's favor, David's success was due largely to the interdependent relationships he developed and sustained with others.

Jeremiah, along with some of the other Hebrew prophets, provides us with a rather unusual example. God's calling on a person's life may sometimes require him or her to walk a lonely road, with little support from others. At times, the defense of truth can be a friendless struggle, as both John the Baptist and Jesus experienced in New Testament times.[2] This, however, should not be considered the norm for life and ministry. The group known as the "sons of the prophets," for example, indicates that many prophets did not serve and minister in isolation but worked alongside each other (2 Kings 2), and the fate of many kings significantly rested on whether they were willing to listen to their advisers.

The Old Testament narratives also provide some negative examples. Saul, as he grew older, became increasingly intransigent to instruction and cut himself off from Samuel, the only person who would genuinely confront him and offer help and correction (1 Sam. 15:35). Samson, likewise, emerges as a solitary figure who eluded accountability and failed to sustain healthy relationships that would have helped him judge and live righteously (Judg. 14:3). In his youthful folly, Rehoboam, the son of Solomon, rejected the sound advice of his elders and promptly paid a heavy price (1 Kings 12:1–24; 14:21–31). David's sin with Bathsheba was precipitated by David, at "the time when kings go out to battle," sending out his army while himself remaining in Jerusalem, a fatal mistake (2 Sam. 11:1). Sadly, the list could continue.

Interdependence in the New Testament

In the New Testament, we find John the Baptist, Jesus's forerunner, gathering a group of disciples around him to share in his ministry (Matt. 11:2; John 1:35). When it was time for John to be overtaken by Jesus in influence and scope of ministry, John graciously yielded to the divine will and famously insisted that he, as the "friend of the bridegroom," must become less, while Jesus must become greater (John 3:27–30). John realized that God had given him a ministry that was to be supportive of that of another, Jesus the Messiah, as part of God's overarching plan for Israel and the world.

Jesus himself, our Lord and our God, provides us with a strongly positive example of interdependence. This is striking indeed. If there ever was a person who should have been able to make it alone, accomplishing his mission from God without the help of other humans, it would have been Jesus. Jesus, however, was completely dependent on God the Father (John 5:19), and also intentionally chose to depend on human disciples whom he called to share in his life and ministry.

In an utter display of humility and chosen dependence, Jesus, when tired from his journey, asked the Samaritan woman for a drink (John 4:7). At other times, he solicited help from one or several of his followers when performing a variety of miracles (e.g., John 6:5, 10, 12). Even though Jesus had a missional purpose for training his disciples, as a human he desired relationship with them. In his final hour in the garden of Gethsemane, for example, he looked to them for support (though, sadly, his closest friends let him down in his hour of greatest need; Matt. 26:36–46).

In the early church, Barnabas provides an excellent model of humility and interdependence. There was a time when he was head and shoulders above Paul, but he did not allow pride or fear stop him from recruiting Paul as an ally (Acts 11:25), defending him (Acts 9:27), and subsequently working with him as an equal (Acts 13:2). What is more, any perceptive reader of the narrative in Acts will notice that what started out as "Barnabas and Saul" (Acts 13:2, 7) quickly morphed into "Paul and his companions" (Acts 13:13) or "Paul and Barnabas" (Acts 13:43, 46; 14:1, 23; 15:2, 22, 35), at least in part because Paul was the chief speaker (Acts 14:12; though see 14:14; 15:12, 25).

As Jesus and Paul did with regard to John the Baptist and Barnabas, our students or understudies may in the end surpass us, but this should not stop us from allowing God to use us in serving him and others in keen awareness of our interdependence. As my friend Chip McDaniel, a truly wise and humble man, is given to say, "Be nice to your students, because they may be your bosses one day." As Christians, we are part of a team, and we stand or fall together.

The apostle Paul, even with all his brilliance and courage as a strategist and church planter, had a strong preference to work with other people and always tried to minister as part of a team. As evidenced by the various greetings, many of his letters were written in conjunction with others (though their precise role differed; see 1 Thess. 1:1; 2 Thess. 1:1; Phil. 1:1; Col. 1:1), and from time to time he employed an amanuensis (Rom. 16:22; Gal. 6:11).[3] The lists of individuals in his various letter closings indicate an intricate web of interdependent relationships.[4] Also, even though Paul often ministered bi-vocationally (Acts 18:3), he at times received financial support from local congregations (Phil. 4:14–19) and helped organize financial assistance from Gentile churches for the poverty-stricken church in Jerusalem (Rom. 15:25–28). His actions and methodology consistently model interdependence.

The contrast between Paul and the prevailing Greco-Roman ideal of self-sufficiency is particularly pronounced in the closing section of his letter to the Philippians, where he at the same time affirms that he has learned the secret of being content (Greek *autarkēs*) in any and every situation (Phil. 4:11) but then proceeds, "Yet it was good of you to share in my troubles" (Phil. 4:14 NIV). In one sense, Paul was self-sufficient, because he found his sufficiency in "him who gives me strength" (Phil. 4:13 NIV). In another sense, Paul deliberately chose to highlight his interdependence with others, giving them an opportunity to share in God's work in and through him and allowing them to participate in his mission through giving and praying (see, e.g., Eph. 6:18–20). This is a great model to emulate, not only for missionaries but also for all of us who are engaged in carrying out God's work, including scholars.

The Interdependent Scholar

Spheres of Interdependence

The whole notion of human autonomy is a myth. Even the idea of free will must be qualified to some degree because we have little choice in many aspects of our lives, including our gene pool, our place of birth, and our family background. People may change the color of their hair or even of their eyes, but they cannot completely surmount various constraints with which they were born (including their sinful nature). In addition, we are constantly affected by the choices made by others, and we, in turn, affect other people's lives by the choices we make. Like it or not, you will depend on others throughout your career, and others will depend on you.

There are many different spheres of interdependence that require us to engage and interact with various people. These include relationships in our family, church, and work (whether administrators, colleagues, or students), as well as relationships with friends and neighbors. Scholarly excellence depends upon healthy relationships with others in these various communities.

Our family relationships are the most important of all. No career is worth the loss of our spouse or children due to busyness and neglect. God makes it clear that Christian leaders, in particular, must give proper attention to their families and lead them in a godly manner (1 Tim. 3:4–5, 12; Titus 1:6).[5]

Our work relationships should fall in line after our family. Throughout our career, our colleagues will need our help and we will need theirs. Spend time and develop relationships with other faculty members or peers, in particular those in your area, and with those serving in administration. Learn from their areas of expertise and share yours with them. If you are in a position of authority or influence, use your position to encourage and build an esprit de corps and foster mutual respect and teamwork.

Our involvement with a local church is another significant part of our relational web. It is hard to see how a theologian or biblical scholar with little involvement, ministry, or accountability in a local church can be living his life in conformity with God's will, because the New Testament makes it clear that the church is at the very heart of God's purposes in this world. Just recently I became aware of a world-renowned theologian whose name many of you would recognize who virtually never went to church and who was not a member of a local congregation.

This is an extreme example, of course, but there are quite a few others who lack strong ties with a local congregation and do not significantly contribute to the life of a particular body of believers. There may certainly be a tension between demands placed upon a busy scholar and Bible teacher and local church involvement, and there may be times when we choose temporarily to lay aside church responsibilities to meet a particularly pressing publication deadline or other commitment. But, as a norm, we should embrace local church involvement as a God-given outlet for the spiritual gifts the Holy Spirit has given us in order to use them for the good of God's people.

Speaking personally, God has increasingly deepened in me a heart for the local church, particularly in the past few years. This should not be a matter of duty or grudging compliance but a natural outflow of the joy of our salvation and of our solidarity with other believers, including those who did not have the privilege of formal Bible training or graduate education. These relationships with other Christians in the body of Christ will also ensure that we stay firmly rooted in real life, keep us in touch with the questions people are asking and the struggles they are facing, and on the whole help us avoid the ivory-tower syndrome that plagues much of academic work.

As an editor, I receive a fair share of articles that make little (if any) effort to frame a given issue as to the relevance this issue has for the church or for believers as they live their Christian life. I realize there may be exceptions in cases of highly technical scholarship, but in most instances it will be possible to write up the results of our research in such a way that it benefits not only a handful of scholarly peers but also a larger readership. Genuine, regular involvement and interaction with other Christians will also help you stay focused on the real reason for your work and scholarship and remind you of your purpose and calling in life when you've temporarily gotten off track.

Beyond these relationships, it is healthy to maintain friendships with people we have met throughout our lives and the neighbors in our local community. This may seem impossible in the midst of doctoral or scholarly work, but it is worth the effort because the gospel can only be lived out effectively in the context of everyday personal relationships. To be sure, in the age of Facebook, the line between true, close friends and the most casual of acquaintances has gotten increasingly blurred, but there is no substitute for being intimately involved in the lives of others about whom we care deeply and who deeply care about us.

Interdependence and Approachability

Many individuals in positions of authority communicate, perhaps nonverbally, that they are not approachable. They make it clear that they are too busy, or are disinterested in what you might have to say unless it would make some direct positive contribution to their work. I don't believe many of these people even realize how much their body language and attitude keep others from feeling free to approach them. It took me a little while to realize this, but for several years I used to send unmistakable nonverbal signals to those who would pass me in the hallway or on campus that I did not want to be bothered by them. "Don't bother me; I'm busy," was the message I exuded by my haste and curtness.

Once I realized this, I tried to be more relaxed and approachable, though it is, of course, also true that some people are not very considerate and have the potential of wasting a lot of our productive time. A missionary for whom I had great respect once told me that he believed all the Devil had to do to derail us is send us one or two difficult individuals every day in order to waste a lot of our time, especially early in the day when we tend to be most productive. In some cases, this will sidetrack us not only temporarily but throw and keep us off track for the rest of the day. There is some genuine insight in this. The middle ground, exemplified supremely by Jesus, is to be open to interruptions (which may turn out to be sent across our path by divine providence) and to seek to be genuinely helpful while developing and exercising discernment as to what a given person who comes to us genuinely needs and what his or her motives are in approaching us.

When I was a fairly new Christian, I once set aside several months to study in depth Jesus's interactions with people in the Gospels. I focused especially on scrutinizing how Jesus responded to a variety of requests brought to him by others. What I found was that Jesus displayed an amazing range of responses. There were times when he simply granted a petition or answered a question straightforwardly. At other times, he rejected a request or recast the question.

Take his interaction with Nicodemus, for example.[6] This rabbi came to him most likely in order to find out more about his teaching. As was customary in first-century Jewish culture (and still is the norm in many cultures today), however, Nicodemus started out their interaction with a series of flattering pleasantries (John 3:2). Jesus had little patience with this kind of small talk (assuming we have at least the essence of that historical conversation) and cut right to the heart of the matter, redefining the issue (John 3:3). It was not a matter of one's own rabbinic accomplishments or virtues; what was at issue was spiritual rebirth. You can observe the same dynamic in Jesus's conversation with the Samaritan woman.[7]

There is no inoffensive way of saying this, but many scholars do have a rather awkward personality. I don't know what came first, the awkward personality or the scholarly work. Whether there already were quirky parts to our personalities, or the academic rigor of advanced academic studies shaped us in that direction, it seems that scholarly work attracts its fair share of socially awkward people, perhaps more so than other careers (though I have certainly not done any scientific research in this regard). This requires self-awareness (if you think others are odd, they may think the same about you!) and an intentional effort to overcome social barriers, whether out of shyness, arrogance, or personality type. We need to humble ourselves and reach out to others rather than waiting for others to reach out to us or staying indifferent altogether.

Interdependence and Research
Students and scholars who are engaged in research depend on the work of other scholars. The common expression that we all stand on the shoulders of giants obtains not only for past scholars but also for contemporary ones. You can criticize dead scholars, and they can't get back at you, but it does not work that way for those who are still alive. You will develop relationships with other scholars even if only by responding to another writer's publications and presentations at scholarly meetings. Scholarly work is relational work.

In John A. D'Elia's recent biography of George Ladd, he notes how, at the height of Ladd's academic career, a harsh review of one of Ladd's books by one of his peers completely devastated him, even to the point of alcoholism.[8] This is a sad example that illustrates how interdependent and fragile all of us are. We are not superhuman beings who can stand against the world and independently overcome fear, opposition, worry, discouragement, and in some cases even bouts with depression. In addition to the strengthening and enabling of the Holy Spirit, these battles require healthy relationships in the various spheres noted above.[9]

The intense social dimension of scholarship should impact how we write book reviews and cite people in our research. Few academic works are without any merit whatsoever. When reviewing a given work, let's make sure to include positive points and not just negative ones. Even though some of my reviews have been fairly critical, I have occasionally written positive ones, and one or two were downright glowing. I remember once receiving a note from an author whose book I had reviewed. The note came perhaps six months or so after the review had appeared in print. "I usually do not contact reviewers of my books," the author wrote, "but I am making an exception in your case. Thank you very much for your positive review of my work. I especially liked the part where you say, 'I love this book!'" Needless to say, only write this when you really mean it, but when a book is deserving of praise, say so! If you don't hold back on criticism, don't hold back on praise either.

Another observation I have made with regard to reviews is that often the harshest reviews are written by younger, aspiring scholars who have as of yet not produced works comparable to the ones they are critiquing. I have often wished that the reviewer had been required to produce a work similar in scope before writing his review. The reviewer of a commentary should have written at least one commentary; the reviewer of a reference work should have had a hand in publishing a reference work; and so on. It is far too easy to criticize others, especially when you have no firsthand experience of your subject matter. It is not as easy to write a book as it might at first appear, especially a commentary. If you haven't done so, try it sometime! And then brace yourself for the reviews. Afterward, your judgment might be less harsh and more charitable next time you review a commentary.

Another facet of scholarly interdependence is our need to stay connected with the larger world of scholarship and to get fresh, new ideas that can stimulate our own research. Justin Taylor at Crossway occasionally e-mails me links to various books, pieces, and blogs that he thinks might interest me, even though we've never had a formal teacher-student relationship. This is a very thoughtful and selfless thing for him to do, and it is a reflection of Justin's commitment to scholarly collaboration and interdependence. Unfortunately, this type of noncompetitive, affirming, and empowering interaction is not all that common. Most of us are too busy doing our own work, and in some cases too indifferent toward others (if not actually competitive toward them), to affirm others in theirs. Is our vision greater than our own self-advancement? If so, we will seek to encourage others in their scholarly work and help them in their academic pursuits, whether or not this narrowly serves to advance our own agenda. Paul's words in Philippians 2:4 come to mind: "Let each of you look not only to his own interests, but also to the interests of others."

Interdependence and Collaborative Work

An interdependent scholar will pursue collaborative work. The academy is far too specialized for most individual scholars to have the breadth of knowledge to adequately cover some topics. I have become convinced of this through several collaborative projects, particularly a recent book with Mike Kruger.[10] He has strong expertise in areas where I am average at best (such as textual criticism and canon studies). Similarly, in my *God, Marriage, and Family* book, I solicited help from ethicists to fill in what was lacking in my own area of expertise.[11] With the exception of the occasional encyclopedic mind in the world of scholarship, most mere mortals, including me, cannot specialize in everything. Darrell Bock (who, incidentally, is sufficiently brilliant that it would be understandable if he were to attempt to go it alone in his scholarly work) is a good example of a scholar who understands the value of academic collaboration and consistently exhibits an encouraging, affirming, and noncompetitive attitude toward other scholars and colleagues.[12]

We should be open whenever possible to invitations from others to work on joint projects. We all have distinctive areas of interests, and as evangelical scholars we are on the same team working toward the same goal. The church is the body of Christ and functions as a unity, with the different members of the body exercising their diverse gifts in harmony for the good of the whole (1 Corinthians 12). This realization should undercut any undue sense of competition and enable us to join freely with others who are like-minded and pursue similar goals.

Some scholars can be very self-promoting. I have seen resumes that list even the most minute accomplishment, whether classes taught (in the case of teachers), baptisms performed (in the case of pastors), or a variety of other credits, honors, awards, or achievements. Some send out copies of their work to other scholars in order to induce them to cite their writings. On the whole, Scripture is clear that self-promotion is not appropriate: "Let another praise you, and not your own mouth; a stranger, and not your own lips" (Prov. 27:2). At the same time, scholarship is part of a web of relationships. We participate in scholarly meetings not primarily for the purpose of self-advancement but as being part of an affinity group where we and other scholars can sharpen and encourage one another (Prov. 27:17; Rom. 1:11–12). In the same spirit, established scholars and seminary professors should treat students and aspiring scholars with respect, training them how to think critically and teaching them the craft of scholarship by precept and personal example.

If you are a student, let me ask you: How well do you work together and get along with other students? In group presentations, are you primarily interested in tearing down the work of those in other groups, or are you making a genuine effort to encourage them? In this life, perfection is exceedingly rare (though we are to strive for perfection; see Matt. 5:48). Just because you can find flaws or faults in the work of others does not mean you should mercilessly attack them. How much better to show kindness and come alongside them to help. My wife, for example, has often pleaded the case of my students with me and encouraged me to be more gracious than would have been my natural inclination. Those of us who are further along in our academic pilgrimage will do well to remember our early days when we desperately needed the help, encouragement, and affirmation of our mentors.

Interdependence and Service

An awareness of our interdependence with other scholars should also issue in a commitment to Christian service. In some circles, servant leadership has become a mantra that is repeated almost ad nauseam. Even non-Christian theorists have recognized the importance of service as a corporate success strategy. This recognition constitutes a backhanded compliment to the veracity of the biblical teaching on servanthood.

The problem remains, however, that because all humans are sinners, a servant attitude does not come naturally for any of us.[13] It involves sacrifice and putting others ahead of ourselves. In this world, servanthood is unnatural and counterintuitive. A servant's heart does not comport with the notion of the survival of the fittest, the urge to get ahead, or the commonly felt need to assert oneself.

Not that we should be mere doormats so others can walk all over us. There are times when we may legitimately represent our own interests. This calls for discernment. My point here is that servanthood is not intuitive, nor does it simply entail externally conforming to what we think other people expect of us. Eventually, that approach will not work, and we will break down. Servanthood is about internalizing Jesus's attitude and putting others ahead of oneself for the sake of the gospel. A Christian's life should be oriented toward others rather than be centered on self.

As mentioned, Paul exhorted the believers in Philippi to "do nothing from rivalry or conceit, but in humility count others more significant than yourselves. Let each of you look not only to his own interests, but also to the interests of others. Have this mind among yourselves, which is yours in Christ Jesus" (Phil. 2:3–5). Christ demonstrated this others-centered lifestyle through his incarnation and crucifixion. The cross serves as the perennial model that calls us to live a life characterized by genuine interdependence. *We should not use people to serve us and our agendas, but rather serve others as we serve God and promote his agenda.*

In my own life, I once had an opportunity for ministry that was to involve significant financial remuneration. In prayer, I realized that I had a mixed set of motives: there were elements of greed along with genuine excitement over the ministry opportunity. There is nothing wrong with financial remuneration (the worker is worthy of his pay; Matt. 10:10 pars.; 1 Tim. 5:18), and we have a responsibility to support our family, but we must constantly evaluate our motives: is the goal to serve God and his kingdom or ourselves? We must not involve ourselves in projects primarily on the basis of monetary or material considerations. As Jesus said, we cannot serve both God and money (Matt. 6:24). We must first seek *God's* kingdom and *his* righteousness (Matt. 6:33). Paul, in various of his writings, refers to those who were proclaiming the gospel for financial or other improper motives (e.g., Phil. 1:12–18) and, for his own part, took specific steps to ensure that he was vulnerable as little as possible to the charge that he was guided by self-interest (e.g., 1 Thess. 2:9).

Conclusion

The notion of scholarly interdependence is grounded in the fact that learning takes place not in isolation but in community. Learning in community, in turn, will encourage humility, respect for others' views, and a more collaborative and less competitive spirit. The virtue of interdependence is reflected beautifully in the New Testament concept of the church as the body of Christ. We are members of one and the same body, playing on the same team, as it were, and working toward the same goal. As such, we need each other to be fully effective in fulfilling God's call on our lives to spread his gospel across the globe.

Love, the cardinal virtue of believers, serves as the essential bond of our interdependence and constitutes the distinguishing mark of all true Christians (John 13:35). The apostles John and Paul are united in presenting love as the most important virtue (e.g., John 13:1, 34–35; 15:13; 1 Corinthians 13). In the next chapter, a discussion of love will provide a fitting climax to our study of Christian virtues in general and of scholarly virtues in particular. Do you want to be a truly excellent scholar? Then let me show you a "still more excellent way" (1 Cor. 12:31): the way of love.

17

Love

To your interdependence, add love.

When it comes to scholarship, people rarely think of love as a necessary virtue. The stereotypical view is that an excellent scholar needs to be brilliant, well-read, critical, and perhaps even a bit mean for good measure. In fact, love may even be viewed by some as a liability. If scholarship consists of objective scientific analysis, facts, and evidence, there is not much room for love. Scholarship is concerned with those vital ingredients, but it consists of so much more. As I have argued throughout this book, academic work has a relational component. Cold, hard facts cannot love each other, but people can, and Christians must.[1]

Other scholars may think of love, if the thought crosses their minds at all, as more of a general Christian obligation that doesn't consciously impact their scholarship. If love, however, is the fundamental mark of a Christian, it must extend not only to our nonacademic, day-to-day lives but to our scholarly work as well.[2] I submit, therefore, that all our scholarship should be evaluated by love. This is a very high standard with far-reaching implications. It means that it is not enough simply to be right; we must also be loving. The Christian scholar should never be vindictive or mean-spirited, because such an attitude betrays the foundational ethical imperative given to us by Christ: "love one another" (John 13:34).

Too many people in academic life operate on the basis of the abovementioned scholarly paradigm that leaves little room for love. We, as Christians, need to lead the way in changing the academic culture of engagement in a positive direction and in encouraging civility of scholarly discourse. We should be the ones setting the example of love. As I have noted with several of the virtues discussed throughout this book, evangelicals are, sadly, not known particularly for their loving approach. This should convict us and motivate us to make sure that all of our work is characterized by love.

People like us, perhaps more than others, acknowledge the supreme importance of love in principle and therefore should live lives that are characterized by love in their totality. In many ways, love is not a virtue that can be added on to other virtues but one that should infuse and characterize all of them. It should holistically pervade every other trait and flavor the character of the entire person. Love cannot simply affect a part of life, nor does it operate like a switch that can be turned on and off depending upon the circumstances. Love, or the lack thereof, will affect everything we think, say, or do.

A Biblical Theology of Love

A few years ago, the chairperson of a literary study group asked me to write a scholarly paper on John's ethic, which I was to present at the annual meeting of the Evangelical Theological Society. When I started thinking about my topic, I initially drew a complete blank. I had never given any thought to John's ethic. (Those who assigned me this topic may have made the unwarranted assumption that because I had written several books on John's Gospel, I was familiar with this particular aspect of John's theology.) When this happens to you, and it likely will at some point in your career, you basically have to start from scratch in your reading of the primary and secondary literature.[3] Through a fresh analysis of the material, I came to realize that love formed the center of John's moral vision. I summed up my findings as follows:

> God, in his love, sent his Son to die so that everyone who believes in him has eternal life (John 3:16–17). Jesus expressed this love for people, and especially believers, to the fullest extent (13:1). Believers, in turn, are to emulate Jesus' example, loving one another so that the world may know

God's love through them and believe that God sent Jesus to die for them (13:34–35; 15:10–17; 17:20–25).[4]

John 13, in particular, demonstrates the centrality of love in the Gospel and gives us a glimpse of what motivated Jesus to go to the cross. In that chapter, Jesus gives his disciples a particular example for them to follow by washing their feet. This act of foot washing is not an isolated incident meant to demonstrate the virtue of love or servanthood but fits within the broader narrative and points readers ahead to the cross. It demonstrates the attitude of Jesus that drove him to the cross and that should also characterize his followers. After the foot washing, Judas departs, and Jesus speaks the following well-known words:

> A new commandment I give to you, that you love one another: just as I have loved you, you also are to love one another. By this all people will know that you are my disciples, if you have love for one another. (John 13:34–35)

Paul may be referring back to this act of service, by which Jesus provided a concrete example of what it means to love and serve others, when he discussed how Jesus "made himself nothing, taking the form of a servant" (Phil. 2:7). The apostle uses the examples of Jesus's incarnation, humiliation, and exaltation to exhort the believers in Philippi to emulate their Lord in their attitude toward one other (Phil. 2:1–11).

Love is such a rich, multifaceted, and pervasive biblical theme that the most I can hope to achieve in the following paragraphs is to discuss three major points relevant to our particular purpose.[5] First, similar to several of the other virtues, *God's love for us provides the indispensible theological foundation for our love for others*.[6] As D. A. Carson rightly observed, "Christian love can be understood, and best practiced, only when it is seen to be a reflection of God's love in its varied dimensions. . . . God's love is the motive and standard of ours."[7]

Many of us do not naturally find it easy to love others because it is far easier to live life in a self-focused and self-serving manner. Jesus's command to his disciples to "love one another: just as I have loved you, you also are to love one another" (John 13:34) provides both a rationale and a motivation to love other people. Believers must love because they have been loved by God in Christ. Genuine awareness and contemplation of the depths of God's love for us, demonstrated in Christ's sacrificial death, will—or, at least, should—result in increased love for other people.

Paul keenly felt this dynamic when he wrote, "For the love of Christ controls us, because we have concluded this: that one has died for all, therefore all have died; and he died for all, that those who live might no longer live for themselves but for him who for their sake died and was raised" (2 Cor. 5:14–15). God's love motivates our love. John exhorted his readers by employing the same logic: "Beloved, if God so loved us, we also ought to love one another. No one has ever seen God; if we love one another, God abides in us and his love is perfected in us" (1 John 4:11–12).

Second, Jesus's actions in John 13 make an additional important point about biblical love: *genuine Christian love is expressed through tangible action*.[8] Jesus demonstrated love through active service. James, likewise, linked love with action: "If you really fulfill the royal law according to the Scripture, 'You shall love your neighbor as yourself,' you are doing well. But if you show partiality, you are committing sin and are convicted by the law as transgressors" (James 2:8–9). The association of love with action, and not simply with passive feelings, explains why the Bible so often uses love to summarize its entire ethical system. As Paul wrote in his letter to the Romans:

> For the commandments, "You shall not commit adultery, You shall not murder, You shall not steal, You shall not covet," and any other commandment, are summed up in this word: "You shall love your neighbor as yourself." Love does no wrong to a neighbor; therefore love is the fulfilling of the law. (Rom. 13:9–10)

Paul also emphasizes this point in his letter to the Galatians:

> For you were called to freedom, brothers. Only do not use your freedom as an opportunity for the flesh, but through love serve one another. For the whole law is fulfilled in one word: "You shall love your neighbor as yourself." But if you bite and devour one another, watch out that you are not consumed by one another. (Gal. 5:13–15)[9]

Paul's summary of the law, in turn, can be traced back to Jesus's statement concerning the greatest commandment, which is itself based on Deuteronomy 6:4–5 ("love God") and Leviticus 19:18 ("love others"):

> And one of them, a lawyer, asked him a question to test him. "Teacher, which is the great commandment in the Law?" And he said to him, "You shall love the Lord your God with all your heart and with all your soul

and with all your mind. This is the great and first commandment. And a second is like it: You shall love your neighbor as yourself. On these two commandments depend all the Law and the Prophets." (Matt. 22:35–40)

Love is always fleshed out in terms of obedience and service, not just feelings.[10] Third and last, I close with Paul's words in his great, well-known love chapter in 1 Corinthians 13, where he makes the following point: *without love, all other human activity and effort is meaningless and empty* (1 Cor. 13:1–3). The apostle proceeds to flesh out his thesis in the ensuing memorable words:

> Love is patient and kind; love does not envy or boast; it is not arrogant or rude. It does not insist on its own way; it is not irritable or resentful; it does not rejoice at wrongdoing, but rejoices with the truth. Love bears all things, believes all things, hopes all things, endures all things. Love never ends. (1 Cor. 13:4–8a)

Indeed, it is virtually impossible to overestimate the importance and centrality of love in a Christian's life. No spiritual gift, no sacrificial service, no significant contribution will have any true, lasting effect if there is no love.

The Loving Scholar

Love and Scholarship

Virtue chooses goals, but love is the means by which believers, including Christian scholars, should aim to achieve their academic objectives. Since biblical scholarship primarily deals with the interpretation of textual and other evidence, there will often be times when we disagree with others. Love does not require that we never disagree with other people. It rather pertains to the way in which we do so. Even the most profound disagreements and the fiercest debates should be tempered with love.

My colleague at Southeastern and director of the Center for Faith and Culture, Dr. Bruce Little, is an outstanding example to me in this regard. As a philosopher and apologist, he often participates in panels and debates and frequently finds himself in a position where he must voice his strong disagreement with the beliefs and convictions of others. As he does so, he always treats others in a courteous and respectful manner and conducts himself with kindness and charity.[11] Dr. Little is a true Christian gentleman. Even though loving discourse is a general trait of Christian maturity, some scholars have either not attained to that level of personal seasoning or not allowed it to impact their scholarship.

As a general rule, we would do well to read our work with an eye toward love before sending anything out to go to print. (This is especially true for blog posts, and even e-mails.) In previous chapters, I have already discussed many of the ways in which love will express itself in our writing. A loving scholar will give others the benefit of the doubt, will treat them with respect, and will refuse to exploit glaring weaknesses in their argument or pounce on infelicitous turns of phrase.

That said, correction can be the most loving stance toward fellow scholars, because the refusal to correct or help others when they are in the wrong is tantamount to indifference toward them, which falls short of Jesus's command to love. Whether people respond positively to correction depends both on their level of maturity and on whether we succeeded in correcting them in a loving way. This applies equally to colleagues and students (though attempting to correct the former may be more difficult because of their established status).

I recently came across a paper that was graded by a certain professor. The professor critiqued the paper in a completely negative manner. The tenor was that this was a terrible paper; the student had gotten it all wrong and should hang his head in shame. Few (if any) who looked at the professor's remarks would have concluded that love constrained his assessment of the student's work. Even if the evaluation were true, the way in which the professor communicated seemed rather uncaring. Especially if your appraisal of another person's work is negative, make sure you state your verdict in a way that is redemptive, not devastating and deflating.

One good test of love in our written remarks is to imagine the person right there in front of us. Would we word things in the same way? It is easy to take cheap shots in our writing and teaching because the opposing side is not represented. I have particularly noticed this in sermons where we tend to preach to the converted—that is, to people who we know already agree with us—which makes it easy to caricature or even ridicule opposing views held by people who are not in the audience and cannot defend themselves. Not only is the use of straw-man arguments or misrepresentation unloving, but it is also cowardly, not to mention arrogant and even rude.

Love and the Truth of the Gospel

I believe some scholars work with the following, possibly subconscious, presupposition: God will forgive us if we are mean because the opposition is so obviously wrong and, after all, we are only defending the truth of the gospel. We often demonize the opposition and rationalize our lack of love because those on the other side are, of course, the enemies and are undermining God's truth and opposing his kingdom. Our defense of the truth, however, must never leave love behind. It is not an either-or dichotomy but rather a both-and proposition. It is possible both to stand firmly for the truth of God's Word and to have genuine love for those with whom we differ.

In his biography of Francis Schaeffer, *Truth with Love: The Apologetics of Francis Schaeffer*, Bryan A. Follis argues that even though Schaeffer labored to defend truth, he genuinely loved people, and it was often that love that made a greater impact than rational arguments. In an exemplary fashion, Schaeffer combined both truth and love in his attempt to reach out to unbelievers:

> Francis Schaeffer, with all his commitment to rational apologetics, remained convinced that love between Christians was "the final apologetic." . . . Again, we need to emphasize that the love being displayed by the Schaeffers was not just a tool being used to commend their apologetics. Indeed I would maintain that the apologetics of Francis Schaeffer flowed from his love for people. Furthermore, it is clear that long before he engaged in a ministry of apologetics he (and Edith) had a deep love for individuals.[12]

Love is capable of breaking down barriers to the gospel where rational arguments are unable to penetrate. One reason for this is the lack of genuine love in the world. People are generally out to serve themselves, protect themselves, and gain things for themselves. Love doesn't particularly carry much freight in a survival-of-the-fittest cultural mindset and is therefore relatively rare. This is one reason why the Bible's command to love our enemies appears to be so counterintuitive (Matt. 5:44; Luke 6:35; 1 Pet. 3:9). Why would we want to love our enemies or those who cannot do anything for us in return? We do so in order to demonstrate God's love to them, the love that reached out to us and rescued us from our wretchedness and sin (John 3:16; Rom. 5:8). Even the most hardened sinner can be softened by genuine, selfless love.

Conclusion

Without exception, the scholars I respect the most among those whom I have come to know at a deeper personal level are those who demonstrate love in their scholarship. They are not vindictive or narrow-minded and demonstrate a generosity of spirit and strength of conviction. These scholars exhibit scholarly excellence by joining their love for God and other people to solid research and good writing. They are not out to settle scores or go after people. They hold no double standard with regard to their personal lives and their scholarly careers. Their conduct is not compartmentalized: rude as scholars and loving at home (or vice versa). They are genuinely consistent and approachable. They don't live for scholarship to the point that their family is neglected. This kind of holistic love will earn the respect of friend and foe alike and will result in both excellent scholarship and excellent scholars. And with this, it is time to conclude.

CONCLUSION

Pursuing Excellence

Are you committed to excellence? If so, are you willing to do what it takes to achieve greater excellence for the glory of God and for the good of his people? In this book, I have taken you on a journey traversing various areas of Christian virtue in the pursuit of excellence. In the spirit of 2 Peter 1, I have challenged all of us to make every effort to add to our faith various virtues that together comprise excellence. Think for a moment.

Human excellence apart from the excellence of God leads to idolatry, such as celebrity worship. Excellence without holiness and genuine spirituality is technical competence without character. Like a mosaic, excellence is comprised of a great number of concomitant virtues. Diligence without courage is parochial and small-minded. Courage and passion without restraint are mindless zealotry. Restraint without creativity is dull and boring.

Creativity and eloquence without integrity, faithfulness, and restraint are dangerous tools likely to be abused. Better to have integrity and be dull than to be eloquent and lead others astray. Wisdom without grace tends to elevate the wise. Humility and dependence without service and love may lead to monasticism or godly closet spirituality but fail to inspire, mentor, and impact others redemptively for the glory of God.

What is eloquence without humility? Passion without grace? Courage without love? Creativity without diligence? The list could be multiplied endlessly, but the above examples are sufficient to illustrate that the pursuit of excellence involves climbing a staircase of virtues that in the end will lead to genuine and continual progress in both the composite virtues and excellence as a whole.

What is more, as we have seen, excellence consists of vocational, moral, and relational excellence. Plenty of examples illustrate excelling in a given vocation but not matching vocational with moral and/or relational excellence. A golf star cheats on his wife. A Nobel Prize winner forsakes his marriage vows. An eloquent preacher leaves the ministry to pursue a homosexual relationship. Those who would pursue excellence must combine vocational with moral and relational excellence.

This balance, of course, is hard to achieve. It is much easier to spend long hours in one's study and to ratchet up an impressive record of scholarly publications while neglecting one's family. Conversely, someone may be a great father and husband but only a mediocre scholar (though, if a choice has to be made, the latter is, of course, to be preferred over the former). But does a choice have to be made? If God has called you to scholarship, he has also called you to excel in your work.

How do you excel in *both* your scholarly calling *and* your personal life? As we have seen, there is no magic formula (other than utter reliance on God's grace in all things), but for a start, we must commit ourselves to the pursuit of excellence in the vocational, moral, and relational realms.

While dangers are doubtless lurking ahead, commit yourself to excellence. The God you serve is himself characterized by excellence, and that same God has called you to the pursuit of excellence for his glory and for the good of others. If you pursue excellence and progress in it, you and others will be blessed, and God will be glorified:

> For if these qualities are yours and are increasing, they will keep you from being ineffective or unfruitful in the knowledge of our Lord Jesus Christ. . . . Therefore, brothers, be all the more diligent to make your calling and election sure, for if you practice these qualities you will never fall. For in this way there will be richly provided for you an entrance into the eternal kingdom of our Lord and Savior Jesus Christ. (2 Pet. 1:8, 10–11)

Select Annotated Bibliography

Baird, William. *History of New Testament Research*. 2 vols. Minneapolis: Fortress, 1992–2003.

    A highly instructive survey of the history of New Testament research from the time of the Reformation and the Enlightenment, setting biblical scholarship within the larger context of intellectual and cultural history. Best read in conjunction with Neill and Wright (see below).

Beale, G. K. *The Erosion of Inerrancy in Evangelicalism: Responding to New Challenges to Biblical Authority*. Wheaton, IL: Crossway, 2008.

    Greg Beale's defense of inerrancy over against the Old Testament scholar Peter Enns, formerly of Westminster Theological Seminary, where Beale now teaches.

Blaising, Craig A. "Faithfulness: A Prescription for Theology." In *Quo Vadis Evangelicalism? Perspectives from the Past, Direction for the Future: Select Presidential Addresses from the First Fifty Years of the Journal of the Evangelical Theological Society*. Edited by Andreas J. Köstenberger. Wheaton, IL: Crossway, 2007, 201–16.

    Blaising's ETS presidential address on theological faithfulness, particularly over against Bart Ehrman and other scholars who have recently proposed novel theses on the history of early Christianity.

Bonhoeffer, Dietrich. *The Cost of Discipleship*. 2nd ed. New York: Macmillan, 1963.

    A classic work on Christian discipleship from a courageous Christian witness who lost his life at the end of World War II resisting the Nazi regime in the Third Reich.

Carson, D. A. *Exegetical Fallacies*. 2nd ed. Grand Rapids, MI: Baker Academic, 1996.

A classic work on interpretive fallacies: what they are, some examples, and how to avoid them.

———. "The Trials of Biblical Studies." In *The Trials of Theology: Becoming a 'Proven Worker' in a Dangerous Business*. Edited by Andrew J. B. Cameron and Brian S. Rosner. Fearn, Ross-shire: Christian Focus, 2010.

Some indispensable tips for aspiring, and practicing, biblical scholars from a seasoned veteran scholar.

———. "When Is Spirituality Spiritual? Reflections on Some Problems of Definition," *JETS* 37 (1994): 381–94.

Helpful reflections by this eminent evangelical scholar on the definition and nature of Christian spirituality.

D'Elia, John A. *A Place at the Table: George Eldon Ladd and the Rehabilitation of Evangelical Scholarship in America*. New York: Oxford University Press, 2008.

An insightful, albeit sobering, biography on George Ladd, one of the eminent evangelical scholars of the twentieth century: his life, his achievements, and his shortcomings.

Duce, Philip, and Daniel Strange, eds. *Encountering God's Word: Beginning Biblical Studies*. Foreword by D. A. Carson. Leicester: Inter-Varsity, 2003.

Sequel to *Keeping Your Balance* (see below) with four essays on beginning to study the Old and New Testaments (Peter Williams, Alistair Wilson), encountering biblical interpretation (Antony Billington), and the role of faith and evidence (David Gibson).

———. *Keeping Your Balance: Approaching Theological and Religious Studies*. Foreword by Howard Marshall. Leicester: Inter-Varsity, 2001.

Collected essays on relevant topics for beginning students of theology, including treatments by Nigel Cameron on evangelical foundations for doing theology and by Carl Trueman on approaching theological study.

Dyer, Charles H. *Character Counts: The Power of Personal Integrity*. Foreword by Charles Swindoll. Chicago: Moody, 2010.

Accessible introduction to Christian character traits including honesty, compassion, wisdom, self-control, trust, faithfulness, balance, sexual purity, endurance, and joy.

Erickson, Millard J. "Evangelical Theological Scholarship in the Twenty-First Century." In *Quo Vadis, Evangelicalism?* Edited by Andreas J. Köstenberger. Wheaton, IL: Crossway, 2007.

Excellent, sage advice for scholars of all ages from one of evangelicalism's leading theologians.

Harrington, Daniel J., and James F. Keenan. Jesus and Virtue Ethics: Building *Bridges between New Testament Studies and Moral Theology*. New York: Rowman & Littlefield, 2002.

A helpful introduction to virtue ethics with reference to Jesus's teaching and New Testament studies.

Hughes, R. Kent. *Disciplines of a Godly Man*. Wheaton, IL: Crossway, 1995.

A classic work on the pursuit of godliness, taking its point of departure from Paul's command to Timothy to discipline himself to be godly.

Köstenberger, Andreas J. *The Marks of a Scholar*. Wake Forest, NC. N.d.

A short booklet on selected marks of a scholar that formed the impetus for the present volume.

Köstenberger, Andreas J., ed. *Quo Vadis, Evangelicalism? Perspectives from the Past, Direction for the Future: Select Presidential Addresses from the First Fifty Years of the* Journal of the Evangelical Theological Society. Wheaton, IL: Crossway, 2007.

Selected presidential addresses from the first half-decade of the Evangelical Theological Society, rich in lessons from the past. If you don't learn from history, you're doomed to repeat it.

———, ed. *Whatever Happened to Truth?* Wheaton, IL: Crossway, 2005.

Originally delivered as four plenary addresses at the annual meeting of the Evangelical Theological Society, Albert Mohler, J. P. Moreland, Kevin Vanhoozer, and I address the topic of truth from a biblical, theological-cultural, philosophical, and hermeneutical vantage point.

Luther, Martin. "Experience Makes the Theologian." In *The Trials of Theology: Becoming a 'Proven Worker' in a Dangerous Business*. Edited by Andrew J. B. Cameron and Brian S. Rosner. Fearn, Ross-shire: Christian Focus, 2010.

Vintage Luther, some very helpful advice on humility and other selected subjects for budding and blooming theologians.

———. *The Tabletalk of Martin Luther*. Fearn, Ross-shire: Christian Focus, 2003.

A serendipitous collection of many of the Reformer's trademark pithy sayings.

Mahaney, C. J. *Humility: True Greatness*. Sisters, OR: Multnomah, 2005.

A classic book on an often neglected subject by a humble man of God.

Moreland, J. P. *Love Your God with All Your Mind: The Role of Reason in the Life of the Soul*. Colorado Springs, CO: NavPress, 1997.

This is one of several helpful books on the role of the intellect in the Christian life.

Morgan, Christopher W., and Robert A. Peterson, eds. *The Glory of God*. Theology in Community. Wheaton, IL: Crossway, 2010.

A biblical-theological exploration of the glory of God, with chapters on the Old Testament, the Synoptic Gospels, Acts, and the General Epistles, John's Gospel and Revelation, Paul's Epistles, and treatments of the pastoral and missional theology of the glory of God.

Neill, Stephen, and Tom Wright. *The Interpretation of the New Testament: 1861–1986*. 2nd ed. Oxford: Oxford University Press, 1988.

A readable survey of biblical scholarship for a 125-year period. Best read in conjunction with the work of the American scholar William Baird (see above). Full of lessons to be learned by today's scholars.

Neuer, Werner. *Adolf Schlatter: A Biography of Germany's Premier Biblical Theologian*. Translated by Robert W. Yarbrough. Grand Rapids, MI: Baker, 1995.

An introductory biography of Adolf Schlatter (1852–1938), a German biblical scholar and theologian who, as a conservative, stood courageously for his positions over against Adolf Harnack, Rudolf Bultmann, and a phalanx of liberal, critical German scholarship.

Noll, Mark A. *Between Faith and Criticism: Evangelicals, Scholarship, and the Bible in America*. 2nd ed. Grand Rapids, MI: Baker, 1991.

In a readable survey of the history of evangelical scholarship in the second half of the twentieth century, Noll focuses especially on the tension between faith and critical scholarship, an issue that continues to be hotly debated today.

Peterson, David. *Possessed by God: A New Testament Theology of Sanctification and Holiness*. NSBT 1. Grand Rapids, MI: Eerdmans, 1995.

An important treatment of the biblical theology of sanctification that significantly critiques and corrects common misconceptions and provides a constructive, biblical alternative.

Piper, John. "Is There Christian Eloquence? Clear Words and the Wonder of the Cross." In *The Power of Words and the Wonder of God*. Edited by John Piper and Justin Taylor. Wheaton, IL: Crossway, 2009, 67–80.

As the title suggests, a helpful discussion of the question of whether there is room for eloquence in Christian life and ministry, with an answer in the affirmative, albeit properly qualified.

———. *Think: The Life of the Mind and the Love of God*. Wheaton, IL: Crossway, 2010.

Excellent challenge to evangelicals to think hard and well, with a response to the challenges of relativism and anti-intellectualism and reflection on the relationship of knowledge to humility and love.

Schaeffer, Francis A. *True Spirituality*. Wheaton, IL: Tyndale, 1971.

A classic work on spirituality by the leading North-American evangelical apologist of the twentieth century.

Sire, James W. *Habits of the Mind: Intellectual Life as a Christian Calling.* Downers Grove, IL: InterVarsity, 2000.

A classic work on the Christian life and intellectual pursuits (see also J. P. Moreland's work, above).

Spurgeon, C. H. *Lectures to My Students.* Fearn, Ross-shire: Christian Focus, 1998.

A classic collection of this prince of preachers' lectures to his college students.

Syed, Matthew. *Bounce: Mozart, Federer, Picasso, Beckham, and the Science of Success.* New York: HarperCollins, 2010.

As one endorser puts it, "A cutting-edge dissection—and ultimate destruction—of the myth of innate talent in the pursuit of excellence." An interesting but controversial book.

Warfield, Benjamin B. *The Religious Life of Theological Students.* Phillipsburg, NJ: Presbyterian & Reformed, 1911.

A well-known, brief discussion of desiderata for students of Christian theology.

Webb, Robert L., and Duane F. Watson, eds. *Reading Second Peter with New Eyes: Methodological Reassessments of the Letter of Second Peter.* Library of New Testament Studies 382. London: New York: T&T Clark, 2010.

Contains several insightful essays on 2 Peter, including Peter's list of Christian virtues in chapter 1.

Williams, Joseph M. *Style: Toward Clarity and Grace.* Chicago: University of Chicago Press, 1990.

An unconventional and refreshingly practical treatment of important virtues for writers and researchers.

Wood, W. Jay. *Epistemology: Becoming Intellectually Virtuous.* Contours of Christian Philosophy. Downers Grove, IL: InterVarsity, 1998.

The standard work on Christian epistemology and virtue.

Wright, N. T. *After You Believe: Why Christian Character Matters.* New York: HarperOne, 2010.

Yet another major work by this acclaimed Anglican author on a (for him) new subject, the pursuit of Christian virtue and character.

Notes

Preface

1. http://www.samuelmiller.org. Samuel Miller was the second president of Princeton Theological Seminary.

2. See, e.g., *Excellence: Inspiration for Achieving Your Personal Best*, ed. J. Pincott (New York: MJF Books, 2008).

3. See esp. Thomas J. Peters and Robert H. Waterman, *In Search of Excellence: Lessons from America's Best-Run Companies* (New York: Harper & Row, 1982); Jim Collins, *Good to Great: Why Some Companies Make the Leap . . . and Others Don't* (New York: HarperCollins, 2001).

4. As N. T. Wright, *After You Believe: Why Christian Character Matters* (New York: HarperOne, 2010), 63, observes, scriptural teaching on "grace, which meets us where we are but is not content to let us remain where we are, [is] followed by direction and guidance to enable us to acquire the right habits to replace the wrong ones." However, several reviewers have taken Wright to task for misrepresenting the Reformers' teaching, in particular Martin Luther. Others have even charged that Wright neglects the gospel of grace.

5. The passage features two of the four New Testament instances of the Greek word for "virtue," *aretē*. Another legitimate starting point, taken by R. Kent Hughes in his classic *Disciplines of a Godly Man* (Wheaton, IL: Crossway, 1995), are Paul's words to Timothy, "Train yourself for godliness" (1 Tim. 4:7), which requires careful reflection on the word groups related to "discipline" (Greek *paideia*) and "godliness" (*eusebeia*).

Introduction

1. Dietrich Bonhoeffer, *The Cost of Discipleship*, 2nd ed. (New York: Macmillan, 1963), 99.

2. C. S. Lewis, *Surprised by Joy: The Shape of My Early Life* (London: Harvest, 1966), 228–29.

3. Selected stanzas. The lyrics were written by Charles Wesley in 1738.

4. Ken Kantzer, Tom McComiskey, Carl Henry, and Joe Brown are now all deceased, having left a tremendous legacy of scholarship for succeeding generations.

5. A revised version was published as *Jesus and the Feminists: Who Do They Say That He Is?* (Wheaton, IL: Crossway, 2008).

6. Thanks are due to John Sailhamer, who during his brief tenure as director of PhD and ThM studies at Southeastern Seminary asked me to prepare a brief presentation, "The

Marks of the Scholar," for the doctoral Integrative Seminar. A slightly edited version of this material was subsequently published in booklet form by Southeastern. In due course, Justin Taylor saw a reference to this booklet on my website, http://www.biblicalfoundations.org, and encouraged me to develop some of the material in greater detail.

7. For a humorous illustration of the havoc wreaked on a well-loved text by a practitioner of historical criticism, see Edmund Clowney's delightful parody, "Bultmann Reads Mother Goose," http://primalsubversion.blogspot.com. Clowney's spoof has spawned a host of imitators, most recently Jason Hood, "Tom Wright Reads Humpty Dumpty," http://www.set-online.org.

8. By calling the slide from conservative to liberal to agnostic a "slippery slope," I am not engaging in an invalid "slippery slope" argument, as if I were suggesting, for example, that everyone who moves from conservative to liberal will inexorably go on to move from liberal to agnostic, or the like. Not at all. Some have done so, while many others have not. That said, the slope is still slippery, and the best way not to start slipping is to get off that slippery slope!

9. This, I believe, is well illustrated by the history of the Evangelical Theological Society, on which see a volume I edited, *Quo Vadis, Evangelicalism? Perspectives from the Past, Direction for the Future: Select Presidential Addresses from the First Fifty Years of the Journal of the Evangelical Theological Society* (Wheaton, IL: Crossway, 2007).

10. Zeugma creates grace, clarity, and rhythm for the virtues in Peter's list. The beauty marks the verse for notice and the rhythm for memory.

Chapter 1: The Excellence of God

1. L. Gregory Jones and Kevin R. Armstrong, *Resurrecting Excellence: Shaping Faithful Christian Ministry* (Grand Rapids, MI: Eerdmans, 2006), register the following insightful comment as they discuss excellence in relation to pastoral ministry from an ecumenical perspective: "During our conversations, we struggled with whether 'excellence' is the right word to describe what we wanted to commend in Christian ministry. We eventually agreed that it is an important and life-giving notion, so long as the primary referent for excellence is God. We discussed the importance of excellence as it is patterned in the life, death, and resurrection of Jesus Christ. And we focused on 'resurrecting excellence' in order to place the primary accent on the hope and new life of Easter. The image also reminds us of the perennial call to discover in God's excellence a vocation for the life-giving character of Christian discipleship and, more particularly, the vocation of pastoral ministry" (p. *xi*).

2. Millard J. Erickson, *Christian Theology*, 2nd ed. (Grand Rapids: Baker, 1998), 289–323, divides God's attributes into attributes of greatness (spirituality, personality, life, infinity, and constancy) and attributes of goodness (moral purity: holiness, righteousness, justice; integrity: genuineness, veracity, faithfulness; love: benevolence, grace, mercy, persistence). Wayne Grudem, *Systematic Theology: An Introduction to Biblical Doctrine* (Grand Rapids, MI: Zondervan, 1994), 156–225, adopts the traditional language of communicable (spirituality, invisibility, knowledge, wisdom, truthfulness, goodness, love, mercy, holiness, peace, righteousness, jealousy, wrath, will, freedom, omnipotence, perfection, blessedness, beauty, and glory) and incommunicable (independence, unchangeableness, eternity, omnipresence, unity) attributes. John Feinberg, *No One Like Him: The Doctrine of God* (Wheaton, IL: Crossway, 2001), 233–374, divides them into God's nonmoral (aseity, infinity, immensity and omnipresence, eternity, immutability, omnipotence, sovereignty, omniscience, wisdom, unity, and simplicity) and moral (holiness, righteousness, love, grace, mercy, longsuffering, goodness, lovingkindness, and truth) attributes.

3. Grudem, *Systematic Theology*, 211. For a book-length exposition of the glory of God, see Christopher W. Morgan and Robert A. Peterson, eds., *The Glory of God*, Theology in Community (Wheaton, IL: Crossway, 2010).

4. Grudem, Systematic Theology, 218.

5. Ibid.

6. Ibid., 220–21.

7. Webster's dictionary defines excellence as "the quality of being excellent; state of possessing good qualities in an eminent degree; exalted merit; superiority in virtue"; and excellent as "excelling; surpassing others in some good quality or the sum of qualities; of great worth; eminent, in a good sense; superior" (http://www.webster-dictionary.net/definition/Excellence).

8. Holiness is also a closely related attribute. God's holiness, among other things, indicates his complete uniqueness, otherness, and set-apartness from all else. I will explore this connection further in chapter 3 below.

9. I will discuss the Greek word translated "excellence" (*aretē*) in more detail in the following chapter, but for now I will note its connection with praise. In the LXX, *aretē* is used six times: Isa. 42:8, 12; 43:21; 63:7; Hab. 3:3; and Zech. 6:13. Each use in Isaiah translates the Hebrew word *těhillāh* ("praise"). In Hab. 3:3 and Zech. 6:13, it translates *hôd* ("splendor," "honor").

10. Erickson, *Christian Theology*, 312.

11. Grudem, *Systematic Theology*, 157, writes, "God's *wisdom* would usually be called a communicable attribute, because we also can be wise. But we will never be infinitely wise as God is. His wisdom is *to some extent* shared with us, but it is never *fully* shared with us. Similarly, we can share God's *knowledge* in part, yet we shall never share it fully, for God's thoughts are higher than ours 'as the heavens are higher than the earth' (Isa. 55:9). We can imitate God's love and share in that attribute to some degree, but we will never be infinitely loving as God is. So it is with all the attributes that are normally called 'communicable attributes': God does indeed share them with us *to some degree*, but none of these attributes is completely communicable. It is better to say that those attributes we call 'communicable' are those that are more shared with us" (emphasis original).

12. Andreas J. Köstenberger with David W. Jones, *God, Marriage, and Family: Rebuilding the Biblical Foundation*, 2nd ed. (Wheaton, IL: Crossway, 2010), 23–24 (emphases original).

13. Bruce K. Waltke with Charles Yu, *An Old Testament Theology* (Grand Rapids, MI: Zondervan, 2007), 218–19, writes, "'Image' entails more than human form and the capability of social relationships; it confers the functional notion of duty and authority. . . . Genesis 1 confers this authoritative status of God's image to all human beings, so that we are all kings, given the responsibility to rule as God's vice-regents over the earth. . . . In other words, humankind is created to establish the rule of God on earth." Cf. Eugene H. Merrill, *Everlasting Dominion: A Theology of the Old Testament* (Nashville: B&H Academic, 2006), 170.

14. In terms of attaining to a certain skill level, this is true also for unbelievers. A Tiger Woods, for example, may excel in golf. For those who are unregenerate, however, there are limitations as to the extent to which unbelievers are able to reflect God's moral excellence.

15. See, e.g., Mark A. Noll, *Between Faith and Criticism: Evangelicals, Scholarship, and the Bible in America*, 2nd ed. (Grand Rapids, MI: Baker, 1991); John A. Elia, *A Place at the Table: George Eldon Ladd and the Rehabilitation of Evangelical Scholarship in America* (New York: Oxford University Press, 2008).

16. Though there are many fine examples, as we will see throughout this volume.

17. Thanks are due to participants of the Integrative Seminar class of fall 2010 who helpfully suggested including a section on rest in this volume as well as recommended various other improvements.

18. A classic expression of this malaise, especially with regard to Christians' participation in the arts and the media, is Franky Schaeffer, *Addicted to Mediocrity: Contemporary Christians and the Arts* (Wheaton, IL: Crossway, 1981).

19. Some even believe that, on a secondary level, this passage also alludes to Jesus's experience with his earthly father, Joseph, from whom he learned the trade of carpentry (Matt. 13:55; cf. Mark 6:2).

20. Classic treatments include A. B. Bruce, *The Training of the Twelve: Timeless Principles for Leadership Development* (Grand Rapids, MI: Kregel, 1971); and Robert Coleman, *The Master Plan of Evangelism* (Grand Rapids, MI: Revell, 1963).

Chapter 2: The Pursuit of Excellence

1. Franky Schaeffer, *Addicted to Mediocrity: Contemporary Christians and the Arts* (Wheaton, IL: Crossway, 1981).

2. For a recent exploration of the proper pursuit of Christian virtue, see N. T. Wright, *After You Believe: Why Christian Character Matters* (New York: HarperOne, 2010). Wright sets the pursuit of Christian virtue within the larger context of Jesus's proclamation of the kingdom of God and relates it to the larger aims of worship and mission (but note that Wright's work, as mentioned, has been subjected to rather severe criticism). See also the socio-rhetorical study by Dennis D. Sylva, "A Unified Field Picture of Second Peter 1.3–15: Making Rhetorical Sense Out of Individual Images," in *Reading Second Peter with New Eyes: Methodological Reassessments of the Letter of Second Peter*, ed. Robert L. Webb and Duane F. Watson, LNTS 382 (London/New York: T&T Clark, 2010), 91–118, where the author argues that "the individual images of 2 Pet. 1.3–15 are developed into a coherent larger picture of a journey in ways designed to inspire the reader to undertake the rigors of the moral life rather than sink into self-serving sensuality" (p. 91).

3. Note that while I take my cue from 2 Peter 1:3–11, the virtues singled out for discussion in this book are not identical to those listed in that passage, in the understanding that the list there is not meant to be exhaustive or to specifically address the calling to scholarship.

4. The dative case in the Greek construction *idia doxē kai aretē* at the end of verse 3 could be translated "to" (direct object) or "by" (instrumental dative) his own glory and excellence. Richard J. Bauckham, *Jude, 2 Peter*, WBC 50 (Waco, TX: Word, 1983), 178, opts for "by," contending that "to" would seem to require the preposition *eis* plus the accusative, as in 1 Pet. 5:10. Gene L. Green, *Jude and 2 Peter*, BECNT (Grand Rapids, MI: Baker, 2008), 183–84, favors "to," adducing 1 Thess. 2:12 and 2 Thess. 2:14 as possible parallels. I will refrain from taking a position on this matter here, because regardless of the meaning of the phrase in the present passage, both truths are affirmed in Scripture elsewhere (see, e.g., 1 Thess. 2:12: "God, who calls you into his own kingdom and glory"; 1 Pet. 5:10: "the God of all grace, who has called you to his eternal glory in Christ"; and 1 Pet. 2:9: "that you may proclaim the excellencies of him who called you").

5. Daniel J. Harrington and James F. Keenan, *Jesus and Virtue Ethics: Building Bridges between New Testament Studies and Moral Theology* (New York: Rowman & Littlefield, 2002), 40.

6. See Al Wolters, "'Partners of the Deity': A Covenantal Reading of 2 Peter 1:4," *CTJ* 25 (1990): 28–44, for a cogent defense of the translation "partners of the deity" for the difficult expression normally translated as "partakers of the divine nature." If so, the expression indicates participation in God's activity rather than ontological inclusion in God's being or essence.

7. The NIV translates *aretē* as "goodness" in both verses 3 and 5. For primary texts, see Green, *Jude and 2 Peter*, 183; Bauckham, *Jude, 2 Peter*, 185; and Otto Bauernfeind, "ἀρετή," *Theological Dictionary of the New Testament*, ed. Gerhard Kittel; trans. Geoffrey W. Bromiley (Grand Rapids, MI: Eerdmans, 1964), 1:457–61.

8. Bauckham, *Jude, 2 Peter*, 185, is certainly correct when he notes, "Doubtless because of its typically Greek connotations—virtue as the achievement of human excellence, rather than as obedience to God—it is rarely used in the LXX or in the NT (only here and Phil. 4:8 in the moral sense), and only slightly more common in the Apostolic Fathers." Wright, *After You Believe*, 60, observes that Paul never used *aretē*. Wright's own volume compares and contrasts Aristotle's concept of virtue (including his teaching on the pursuit of eudaimonion, "happiness") with Jesus's proclamation of the kingdom of God and his call to self-denial and sacrificial service.

9. For technical discussions see the relevant commentary literature, especially Green, *Jude and 2 Peter*, 190 (cf. 183–84); and Bauckham, *Jude, 2 Peter*, 185–86.

10. Alasdair MacIntyre, *After Virtue: A Study in Moral Theory* (Notre Dame, IN: University of Notre Dame Press, 1981).

11. See, in particular, the studies by Gilbert Meilaender, *The Theory and Practice of Virtue* (Notre Dame, IN: University of Notre Dame Press, 1984); Joseph Kotva, *The Christian Case for Virtue Ethics* (Washington, DC: Georgetown University Press, 1996); James W. Sire, *Habits of the Mind: Intellectual Life as a Christian Calling* (Downers Grove, IL: InterVarsity, 2000); W. Jay Wood, *Epistemology: Becoming Intellectually Virtuous*, Contours of Christian Philosophy (Downers Grove, IL: InterVarsity, 1998); J. P. Moreland, *Love Your God with All Your Mind: The Role of Reason in the Life of the Soul* (Colorado Springs, CO: NavPress, 1997); and now Wright, *After You Believe*, along with a host of other monographs and articles.

12. Harrington and Keenan, *Jesus and Virtue Ethics*, 3.

13. Wood, *Epistemology*, 45.

14. Moreland, *Love Your God with All Your Mind*, 106.

15. Jesus's teaching, for its part, reflects Old Testament wisdom (see, e.g., Prov. 27:19 NIV: "As water reflects a face, so a man's heart reflects the man").

16. Harrington and Keenan, *Jesus and Virtue Ethics*, 23.

17. The question of the end goal can be answered in different yet congruent terms. Harrington and Keenan, *Jesus and Virtue Ethics*, 40–45, for example, identify the end goal as the kingdom of God and the means as discipleship. Their point of departure is the Synoptic Gospels, while my major point of reference is the list of virtues in 2 Peter 1.

18. Chapter 4 will return to this question by discussing spiritual disciplines.

19. Wood, *Epistemology*, 20.

20. Though see for an evangelical "defense" of individualism, D. A. Carson, "Editorial: Contrarian Reflections on Individualism," *Them* 35 (2010): 378–83.

21. Wood, *Epistemology*, 51.

22. Wright, *After You Believe*, 18, 21 (emphasis original).

23. Ibid., 29. On pp. 40–41, Wright cites the learning of a second language as an example and produces a quote by C. S. Lewis on how to learn (or not to learn) ancient Greek. On pp. 62–63, he gives the illustration of a choir being taken over by a new conductor who really teaches the choir members how to sing.

24. Ibid., 83.

25. Ibid., 92.

26. Ibid., 107.

27. Wright's rendering of *teleios*, "perfect," in Matt. 5:48 (ibid., 108, also citing Matt. 19:21; James 3:2).

28. Ibid., 109 and 112.

29. Ibid., 114, with reference to Wright's teacher G. B. Caird. Thus the dichotomy between what Wright calls "Gospel" and "epistles people" (i.e., those who focus unilaterally on Jesus's teaching on the kingdom or on his death and resurrection) is false.

30. Ibid., 116.

31. Ibid., 124.

32. Ibid., 117. Wright also makes much of Jesus's calling as king and priest and of believers' calling to be rulers and intercessors with Christ, in keeping with Israel's calling to be a "kingdom of priests" or "royal priesthood" (Ex. 19:4–6; cf. 1 Pet. 2:5, 9). See ibid., chap. 3: "Priests and Rulers."

33. In any case, virtue ethics by itself does not represent a comprehensive moral theory but rather constitutes part of a biblical moral theory that also incorporates insights from natural law ethics and divine command theory. Cf. Steven B. Cowan and James S. Spiegel, *The Love of Wisdom: A Christian Introduction to Philosophy* (Nashville: B&H Academic, 2009), 368–70. For a brief description of virtue ethics and some necessary cautions, as well as an alternate proposal, see Dennis Hollinger, "The Trials of Christian Ethics," in *The*

Trials of Theology: Becoming a 'Proven Worker' in a Dangerous Business, ed. Andrew J. B. Cameron and Brian S. Rosner (Fearn, Ross-shire: Christian Focus, 2010), 177–85, esp. 177–79.

34. A similar passage in Paul's writings, Gal. 5:19–23, contrasts the works of the sinful human nature with the fruit of the Spirit. It is abundantly clear there that increase in the fruit of the Spirit is not due to human self-effort at moral improvement but to the powerful and gracious activity of the Holy Spirit. In view of the Spirit's activity, Paul exhorts believers to "walk by the Spirit" (Gal. 5:25).

35. Ruth Anne Reese, *2 Peter and Jude*, Two Horizons New Testament Commentary (Grand Rapids, MI: Eerdmans, 2007), 187.

36. See Gene Edward Veith, *God at Work: Your Christian Vocation in All of Life*, Focal Point Series (Wheaton, IL: Crossway, 2002); Gustaf Wingren, Luther on Vocation, trans. Carl Rasmussen (Eugene, OR: Wipf & Stock, 2004).

37. Moreland, *Love Your God with All Your Mind*, 174.

38. Benjamin B. Warfield, *The Religious Life of Theological Students* (Phillipsburg, NJ: Presbyterian & Reformed, 1911), provides a classic exposition of the duty and vocation of the theological student. With reference to a certain professor he writes, "'Vocation'—it is the call of God, addressed to every man, whoever he may be, to lay upon him a particular work, no matter what. And the calls [sic], and therefore also the called, stand on a complete equality with one another. The burgomaster [sic] is God's burgomaster; the physician is God's physician; the merchant is God's merchant; the laborer is God's laborer. Every vocation, liberal, as we call it, or manual, the humblest and the vilest in appearance as truly as the noblest and the most glorious, is of divine right" (p. 4).

39. This goal is similar in many ways to that of Sire, *Habits of the Mind*, 9, who states, "The central goal of this book is to identify, describe and encourage those habits of the mind that are central to fulfilling our call to glorify God by thinking well."

Chapter 3: Holiness

1. Eugene H. Merrill, *Everlasting Dominion: A Theology of the Old Testament* (Nashville: B&H Academic, 2006), 56. Cf. Ex. 15:11; 2 Kings 19:22; Job 6:10; Pss. 29:2; 89:35; Isa. 1:4; 29:23; 40:25; 43:3, 15; Jer. 50:29; 51:5; Ezek. 39:7; Hab. 1:12; 3:3.

2. Merrill writes, "By holy at least two things are meant: (1) that God is separate from all else that exists . . . and (2) that his holiness is translated into moral and ethical perfection" (ibid.; emphasis original).

3. David Peterson, *Possessed by God: A New Testament Theology of Sanctification and Holiness*, NSBT 1 (Grand Rapids, MI: Eerdmans, 1995), 17 (emphasis original).

4. Ibid., 20.

5. The two key words are *paroikos* ("alien," "foreigner," "sojourner") and *parepidēmos* ("sojourner," "stranger"); both terms are found together in 1 Pet. 2:11. J. H. Elliot, *A Home for the Homeless: A Sociological Exegesis of 1 Peter, Its Situation and Strategy* (Philadelphia: Fortress, 1981), argues for a strictly sociological understanding of the words as a description of the actual experience of the Christian community. Moses Chin, "A Heavenly Home for the Homeless: Aliens and Strangers in 1 Peter," *TynBul* 42 (1991): 96–112, cogently argues, against Elliot, that the words indicate believers' status on their cosmological and spiritual journey as pilgrims on earth toward their heavenly home.

6. Chin, "A Heavenly Home for the Homeless," 110.

7. It is not necessary to name specific individuals. Any thoughtful reader can immediately think of recent examples of public figures, whether in the athletic, political, or religious arena, who failed in the area of sexual purity.

8. Paul could easily have leveled the same charge against today's church that he brought against the Jewish people in the book of Romans: "For, as it is written, 'The name of God is blasphemed among the Gentiles because of you'" (Rom. 2:24).

9. See particularly Andreas J. Köstenberger and David W. Jones, *God, Marriage, and Family: Rebuilding the Biblical Foundation*, 2nd ed. (Wheaton, IL: Crossway, 2010), 188–91; Stephen Arterburn and Fred Stoeker, *Every Man's Battle: Winning the War on Sexual Temptation One Victory at a Time* (Colorado Springs, CO: WaterBrook, 2000); and Stephen Arterburn, Fred Stoeker, and Mike Yorkey, *Every Man's Battle Guide: Weapons for the War against Sexual Temptation* (Colorado Springs, CO: WaterBrook, 2003). For resources, see http://www.pureintimacy.org and http://www.settingcaptivesfree.com.

10. For D. A. Carson's reflections on "lone rangers" in scholarship, see "The Trials of Biblical Studies," in *The Trials of Theology: Becoming a 'Proven Worker' in a Dangerous Business*, ed. Andrew J. B. Cameron and Brian S. Rosner (Fearn, Ross-shire: Christian Focus, 2010), 127. According to Carson, lone rangers in scholarship are prone to oscillate, ironically, between abject despair and unmitigated arrogance.

11. Köstenberger and Jones, *God, Marriage, and Family*, 190 (emphasis original).

12. Martin Luther, "Experience Makes the Theologian," in *Trials of Theology*, 29. For Luther's theology of good works, see *A Treatise on Good Works* (Rockville, MD: Serenity, 2009).

13. Ibid., 29–30.

14. For a thorough, Reformed treatment of the subject, see Herman Bavinck, *Reformed Dogmatics*, vol. 4: *Holy Spirit, Church, and New Creation*, trans. John Vriend (Grand Rapids, MI: Baker, 2008). A recent popular work is Tim Chester, *You Can Change: God's Transforming Power for Our Sinful Behavior and Negative Emotions* (Wheaton, IL: Crossway, 2010).

15. Michael Fox, "Biblical Scholarship and Faith-Based Study: My View," http://www.sbl-site.org/publications/article.aspx?articleId=490; Jacques Berlinerblau, "The Unspeakable in Biblical Scholarship," http://www.sbl-site.org/publications/article.aspx?articleId=503.

16. For a response, see Albert Mohler, "Can Believers Be Bible Scholars? A Strange Debate in the Academy," http://www.albertmohler.com/commentary_read.php?cdate=2006-03-20.

17. Cf. Andreas J. Köstenberger, ed., *Whatever Happened to Truth?* (Wheaton, IL: Crossway, 2005), esp. the epilogue.

18. The role of the Holy Spirit will be discussed in greater detail in the following chapter.

19. For further discussion of the virtue of humility, see chapter 15 below.

20. John M. Frame, in a pamphlet entitled "Studying Theology as a Servant of Scripture," published by Reformed Theological Seminary Bookstore and accessible at http://www.frame-poythress.org/frame_articles/2000Studying.htm, makes the point that "we must make a conscious attempt to achieve a *balance*—to find some place in our life for every command of God, to the exclusion of none. We must decide what must be done at a certain time, what must be postponed until later, what demands a lot of time, what demands only a little, etc. Each of us must have a scale of *priorities*. The top priority, at seminary as everywhere else, is the glory of God" (p. 8; emphasis original).

21. I will have more to say about this in the following chapter.

22. Andreas J. Köstenberger and Peter T. O'Brien, *Salvation to the Ends of the Earth: A Biblical Theology of Mission*, NSBT 11 (Downers Grove, IL: InterVarsity, 2001), 240.

23. See my published revised dissertation *The Missions of Jesus and the Disciples according to the Fourth Gospel* (Grand Rapids, MI: Eerdmans, 1998).

24. See on this Andreas J. Köstenberger and Michael J. Kruger, *The Heresy of Orthodoxy: How Contemporary Culture's Fascination with Diversity Has Reshaped Our Understanding of Early Christianity* (Wheaton, IL: Crossway, 2010).

Chapter 4: Spirituality

1. D. A. Carson, "When Is Spirituality Spiritual? Reflections on Some Problems of Definition," *JETS* 37 (1994): 387.

2. Ibid.

3. Ibid. He further notes that "only rarely are such matters made explicit."

4. Quoted from Saint Augustine, *Confessions: A New Translation by Henry Chadwick*, Oxford World's Classics (Oxford: Oxford University Press, 1998), 3. Chadwick remarks in a footnote that this sentence "announces a major theme of his work" (p. 3).

5. Carson, "When Is Spirituality Spiritual?," 384.

6. Ibid., 390–94.

7. For helpful discussions of the Holy Spirit in Scripture, see esp. René Pache, *The Person and Work of the Holy Spirit* (Chicago: Moody, 1954); Leon J. Wood, *The Holy Spirit in the Old Testament* (Grand Rapids, MI: Zondervan, 1976); Paul D. Feinberg, "Charismatic Theology and Neo-Pentecostalism: The Baptism in the Holy Spirit," in *Theology and Mission*, ed. David J. Hesselgrave (Grand Rapids, MI: Baker, 1978), 39–54; J. I. Packer, *Keep in Step with the Spirit* (Old Tappan, NJ: Revell, 1984); Michael Green, *I Believe in the Holy Spirit*, rev. ed. (London: Hodder & Stoughton, 1985); and Gordon D. Fee, *God's Empowering Presence: The Holy Spirit in the Letters of Paul* (Peabody, MA: Hendrickson, 1994).

8. Andreas J. Köstenberger, "Abiding," in *Dictionary of Jesus and the Gospels*, rev. ed., ed. Nicholas Perrin, Jeannine Brown, and Daniel G. Reid (Downers Grove, IL: InterVarsity, forthcoming).

9. Francis A. Schaeffer, *True Spirituality* (Wheaton, IL: Tyndale, 1971), 3, rightly connects spirituality with salvation by writing, "The first point which we must make is that it is impossible even to begin living the Christian life, or to know anything of true spirituality, before one is a Christian. And the only way to become a Christian is neither by trying to live some sort of Christian life nor by hoping for some sort of religious experience, but rather by accepting Christ as Savior."

10. Fee, *God's Empowering Presence*, 721–22; Green, *I Believe*, 189–90.

11. Andreas J. Köstenberger, "What Does It Mean to Be Filled with the Spirit? A Biblical Investigation," *JETS* 40 (1997): 233.

12. Cf. Peter T. O'Brien, "The Church as a Heavenly and Eschatological Entity," in *The Church in the Bible and the World*, ed. D. A. Carson (Grand Rapids, MI: Baker, 1987), 98–105; R. J. McKelvey, *The New Temple: The Church in the New Testament* (Oxford: Oxford University Press, 1969); and R. Y. K. Fung, "Some Pauline Pictures of the Church," *EvQ* 53 (1981): 89–107.

13. N. T. Wright, *Justification: God's Plan and Paul's Vision* (Downers Grove, IL: InterVarsity, 2009), despite many possible areas for disagreement, rightly draws attention to the centrality of the Holy Spirit in Paul's theology and the tendency for evangelicals to minimize the Spirit's importance: "But there is something missing—or rather, someone missing. Where is the Holy Spirit?" (p. 10).

14. A similar connection is made between sanctification and the Spirit in 2 Thess. 2:13: "But we ought always to give thanks to God for you, brothers beloved by the Lord, because God chose you as the firstfruits to be saved, through sanctification by the Spirit and belief in the truth."

15. For a helpful discussion of Eph. 5:18, see Chip Anderson, "Rethinking 'Be Filled with the Spirit': Ephesians 5:18 and the Purpose of Ephesians," *EvJ* 7 (1989): 57–67.

16. Köstenberger, "What Does It Mean to Be Filled with the Spirit?," 235.

17. I have heard this expressed as the four Cs: constant, conscious communion with Christ.

18. Leon Morris, *1 and 2 Thessalonians*, rev. ed., TNTC (Grand Rapids, MI: Eerdmans, 1984), 107.

19. Carson, "When Is Spirituality Spiritual?," 393.

20. The phrase "hermeneutic of consent" is derived from Peter Stuhlmacher, *Historical Criticism and Theological Interpretation of Scripture: Towards a Hermeneutics of Consent*, trans. Roy Harrisville (Philadelphia: Fortress, 1977). James K. Mead, *Biblical Theology: Issues, Methods, and Themes* (Louisville: Westminster, 2007), 51, aptly describes this approach as one "which employs a critical reading of the Bible but also asks that the Bible

be read in light of the claims it appears to be making upon humanity." Among other things, this requires openness to transcendence.

21. See "Ascertaining Women's God-Ordained Roles: An Interpretation of 1 Timothy 2:15," *BBR* 7 (1997): 107–44; abridged in "Saved through Childbearing? A Fresh Look at 1 Timothy 2:15 Points to Protection from Satan's Deception," *CBMW News* 2/4 (1997): 1–6; and "The Seventh Johannine Sign: A Study in John's Christology," *BBR* 5 (1995): 87–103, respectively.

22. See, e.g., Anthony T. Selvaggio, *The Seven Signs: Seeing the Glory of Christ in the Gospel of John* (Grand Rapids, MI: Reformation Heritage, 2010), esp. 4–5.

23. R. R. Reno, "Virtue and Intelligence," http://www.firstthings.com/blogs/firstthoughts (July 7, 2010). I am grateful to Justin Taylor for bringing this blog post to my attention.

24. Ibid.

25. Ibid.

Chapter 5: Diligence

1. Ex. 15:26; Lev. 10:16; Deut. 4:9; 6:7, 17; 13:14; 17:4; 19:18; Ezra 5:8; 6:12, 13; 7:17, 21; Pss. 64:6; 77:6; 119:4; Prov. 1:28; 8:17; 10:4; 11:27; 12:24, 27; 13:4, 24; 21:5; Isa. 21:7; 55:2; Jer. 12:16; Zech. 6:15; Matt. 2:8; Luke 15:8; 2 Pet. 1:10; 3:14. Of these, only the last four passages are found in the New Testament.

2. The words are *mĕ'od* ("very"; Deut. 4:9; Ps. 119:4); *yatab* (hiphil: "be thorough"; Deut. 13:15; 17:4; 19:18), *'aspparnah* ("with diligence, eagerly"; Ezra 5:8; 6:12, 13; 7:17, 21), *shakhar* (piel: "earnestly seek"; Prov. 1:28; 8:17; 11:27); and *kharuts* ("diligent; persistently industrious"; Prov. 10:4; 12:24, 27; 13:4, 24; 21:5).

3. The Hebrew verb could be repeated and intensified in a similar way for emphasis without the infinitive (see, e.g., Isa. 21:7). For further examples of the infinitive absolute translated as "diligently," see Lev. 10:16; Deut. 6:27; Ps. 64:7 MT; Isa. 55:2; Jer. 12:16; and Zech. 6:15.

4. An invitation is also issued to the nations to listen and diligently learn the ways of God's people (Jer. 12:16).

5. These include *akribōs* ("accurately, with exactness"; Matt. 2:8; Luke 1:3; Eph. 5:15); *epimelōs* ("carefully, diligently, thoroughly"; Luke 15:8); *spoudazō* ("make every effort, be diligent"; 2 Pet. 1:10; 3:14); *spoudē* ("eagerness, diligence"; contrasted with *oknēros*, "lazy, idle" in Rom. 12:11 and *nōthros*, "lazy, sluggish, slothful" in Heb. 6:11–12); *proskartereō* ("persist, keep on with devotion"; Rom. 12:12); *hypomenō* ("continue, endure, persevere"; Matt. 10:22; 24:13; Mark 13:13; Rom. 12:12); *hypomonē* ("endurance, perseverance"; Heb. 10:36); *meletaō* ("continue to do"; 1 Tim. 4:15); *katadiōkō* ("diligently seek or search for"; Mark 1:36); *anakrinō* ("examine carefully, study thoroughly"; Acts 17:11); *prosechō* ("continue to give oneself to"; 1 Tim. 4:13); *epimenō* ("continue, keep on"; 1 Tim. 4:16); and *parakoloutheō* ("investigate carefully and diligently"; Luke 1:3).

6. For a thorough exposition, see Darrell L. Bock, *Luke*, 2 vols., BECNT (Grand Rapids, MI: Baker, 1994), 1:54–67.

7. The historical reliability of Luke has, of course, been questioned by historical-critical scholarship. For a defense of Luke's accuracy, see Andreas J. Köstenberger, L. Scott Kellum, and Charles L. Quarles, *The Cradle, the Cross, and the Crown: An Introduction to the New Testament* (Nashville: B&H Academic, 2009), 340–47.

8. See Andreas Köstenberger, *The Marks of a Scholar* (Wake Forest, NC, n.d.).

9. Not to mention learning and keeping up with the biblical languages, Greek and Hebrew, on which see John Piper, "Brothers, Bitzer Was a Banker," in *Brothers, We Are Not Professionals* (Nashville: B&H, 2002), 81–88; cf. Heinrich Bitzer, ed., *Light on the Path: Daily Scripture Readings in Hebrew and Greek* (Grand Rapids, MI: Baker, 1982).

10. See Charles E. Hummel, *Tyranny of the Urgent*, rev. ed. (Downers Grove, IL: InterVarsity, 1999), for guidance in prioritizing and time management.

11. Joseph M. Williams, *Style: Toward Clarity and Grace* (Chicago: University of Chicago Press, 1990) and Wayne C. Booth, Gregory G. Colomb, and Joseph M. Williams, *The Craft of Research*, 2nd ed. (Chicago: University of Chicago Press, 2003) provide helpful guidance for revision.

12. D. A. Carson, "The Trials of Biblical Studies," in *The Trials of Theology: Becoming a "Proven Worker" in a Dangerous Business*, ed. Andrew J. B. Cameron and Brian S. Rosner (Fearn, Ross-shire: Christian Focus, 2010), 115–16.

13. Ibid., 116.

14. The study of the etymology of the word *plagiarism* is instructive here. The word derives from the Latin *plagiarius*, which means "kidnapper, seducer, or plunderer." The Latin writer Martial first used the word in the sense of "literary thief" (Ep. 1.52.9). The Latin *plagium* means "kidnapping" and stems from *plaga*, "snare, net," from *p(e)lag-*, "flat, spread out." The English word *plagiary* is attested from the 1590s. See *Online Etymology Dictionary*, http://www.etymonline.com, s.v. "plagiarism"; J. Mira Seo, "Plagiarism and Poetic Identity in Martial," *American Journal of Philology* 130/4 (2009): 567–93.

15. I also like to collect ancient coins and rare books, activities that are not so much time consuming as they are taxing on the wallet, especially for a poor seminary professor like me! On a more mundane note, I also enjoy hiking, traveling, and sipping quality green tea.

Chapter 6: Courage

1. D. A. Carson calls this temptation "the seduction of applause" in a recent address entitled "The Scholar as Pastor." The audio and video of his address can be accessed at the websites of the Henry Center, Desiring God Ministries, and The Gospel Coalition. He argues that "if you shy away from some topics for no other reason than the fact that these topics are unpopular in your guild, then you are in the gravest spiritual danger."

2. Carl Trueman, a professor of historical theology and church history at Westminster Theological Seminary, in an article entitled "Look, It's Rubbish!" published in the online magazine *Reformation 21* on May 2009 (http://www.reformation21.org/counterpoints/wages-of-spin/look-its-rubbish.php), discusses the broader scholarly community's perception of evangelical scholars, rightly stating, "Given the choice—and there is always a choice—I'd rather just be despised for being a brazen conservative with looney theology, than a duplicitous conservative with looney theology. That way one can still be of use to the church and still look in the mirror with some degree of self-respect."

3. D. Moody Smith, "The Contribution of J. Louis Martyn to the Understanding of the Gospel of John," in *The Conversation Continues: Studies in Paul and John in Honor of J. Louis Martyn*, ed. Robert T. Fortna and Beverly R. Gaventa (Nashville: Abingdon, 1990), 293.

4. See Andreas Köstenberger, *A Theology of John's Gospel and Letters*, BTNT (Grand Rapids, MI: Zondervan, 2009), 55–60, for further discussion of the undermining of the Johannine community hypothesis.

5. The massive changes that have regularly taken place throughout the history of biblical interpretation illustrate this point. See Stephen Neill and Tom Wright, *The Interpretation of the New Testament: 1861–1986*, 2nd ed. (Oxford: Oxford University Press, 1988); and William Baird, *History of New Testament Research*, 2 vols. (Minneapolis: Fortress, 1992, 2003).

6. Michael Fox, "Biblical Scholarship and Faith-Based Study: My View," http://www.sbl-site.org/publications/article.aspx?articleId=490; Jacques Berlinerblau, "The Unspeakable in Biblical Scholarship," http://www.sbl-site.org/publications/article.aspx?articleId=503.

7. See, in particular, Seung Ai Yang, "Courage," *NIB* 1:764–66. Courage is also discussed in Willem S. Vorster, "The Meaning of ΠΑΡΡΗΣΙΑ in the Epistle to the Hebrews," *Neot* 5 (1971): 51–59; and H. G. M. Williamson, "The Accession of Solomon in the Book of Chronicles," *VT* 26 (1976): 351–61. The following section draws on Keith Campbell, "A

Biblical Theology of Courage," PhD seminar paper, The Southeastern Baptist Theological Seminary, Wake Forest, NC, 2009.

8. These include, but are not limited to, *khazaq, lav, giburah, tharseō, tolmaō, euthymeō, parrēsia, andrizomai, tharreō,* and *parrēsiazomai.* The context determines when each of these words indicates courage rather than another English word within the term's semantic range.

9. Acts 4:13, 29, 31; 9:27, 28; 13:46; 14:3; 18:26; 19:8; 23:11; 26:26; 28:31.

10. Adolf Schlatter, *Der Evangelist Johannes: Wie er spricht, denkt und glaubt,* 2nd ed. (Stuttgart: Calwer, 1948).

11. For a massive, masterful biography of Schlatter, see Werner Neuer, *Adolf Schlatter: Ein Leben für Theologie und die Kirche* (Stuttgart: Calwer, 1996). A more accessible, popular biography is Werner Neuer, *Adolf Schlatter: A Biography of Germany's Premier Biblical Theologian,* trans. Robert W. Yarbrough (Grand Rapids, MI: Baker, 1995).

12. Judith Hartenstein, Review of Andreas J. Köstenberger, *Studies in John and Gender, Review of Biblical Literature,* http://www.bookreviews.org.

13. Tremper Longman III, "Warfare," in *New Dictionary of Biblical Theology: Exploring the Unity and Diversity of Scripture,* ed. T. Desmond Alexander et al. (Downers Grove, IL: InterVarsity, 2000), 835–39, provides a succinct introduction to this topic. He notes, "The theme of divine warfare is a pervasive and important one in biblical theology . . . found throughout the biblical narrative" (p. 839).

14. Longman, "Warfare," 839, notes, "For God's people spiritual warfare has replaced physical, and they are no longer a single nation; thus a modern war cannot be called Yahweh war."

15. See, e.g., John 18:37. On this point, see esp. Richard Bauckham, *The Theology of the Book of Revelation,* New Testament Theology (Cambridge: Cambridge University Press, 1993), 66–108, who identifies messianic war as a primary and pervasive theme in the book of Revelation.

16. Ibid., 76–80. Bauckham writes, "The whole verse requires that the reference to 'the blood of the Lamb' is not purely to Christ's death but to the deaths of the Christian martyrs, who, following Christ's example, bear witness even at the cost of their lives. . . . It shows how the element of faithful witness is essential to understanding how Christ's victory can take effect through the faithful discipleship of Christians in the world" (pp. 75–76).

Chapter 7: Passion

1. Peter T. O'Brien, *Consumed by Passion: Paul and the Dynamic of the Gospel* (Homebush West, NSW: Lancer, 1993).

2. Ibid., 135.

3. Peter T. O'Brien, *Gospel and Mission in the Writings of Paul: An Exegetical and Theological Analysis* (Grand Rapids, MI: Baker, 1995).

4. The Greek words *pathos, pathēmos, katastrēniaō, puroomai, hēdonē,* and *koilia* generally carry negative connotations.

5. Cf. Rom. 1:26, 27; 6:12; 7:5; 1 Cor. 7:9, 36; Gal. 5:24; Eph. 2:3; Col. 3:5; 1 Thess. 4:5; 1 Tim. 5:11; 2 Tim. 2:22; 3:6; 4:3; Titus 2:12; 3:3; James 4:1, 3; 1 Pet. 1:14; 2:11; 4:2, 3; 2 Pet. 2:10, 18; Jude 18; Rev. 14:8; 18:3.

6. "Zeal" or "zealous" translates the Greek words *zēlos, zēloō, zēleuō, and zēlōtēs.* The Hebrew word *qin'ah* indicates jealousy, zeal, or passion, indicating a close relationship between passion and jealousy.

7. See my *A Theology of John's Gospel and Letters,* BTNT (Grand Rapids, MI: Zondervan, 2009), chap. 10, §24.

8. See Andreas J. Köstenberger, L. Scott Kellum, and Charles L. Quarles, *The Cradle, the Cross, and the Crown: An Introduction to the New Testament* (Nashville: B&H Academic, 2009), chap. 9.

9. O'Brien, *Consumed by Passion,* 137 (emphasis original).

10. "The Mystery of Christ and the Church: Head and Body, 'One Flesh,'" *TJ* 12 NS (1991): 79–94.

11. Douglas Hyde, *Dedication and Leadership*, 10th ed. (Notre Dame, IN: Notre Dame Press, 1992).

12. If you need examples, peruse an issue of *Christianity Today* or even *World*.

13. On the virtue of eloquence, see chapter 10 below.

14. On restraint, see the following chapter.

Chapter 8: Restraint

1. Charles H. Dyer, *Character Counts: The Power of Personal Integrity* (Chicago: Moody, 2010), 75–90, helpfully discusses and illustrates the general Christian character trait of self-control.

2. See John Piper, *The Future of Justification: A Response to N. T. Wright* (Wheaton, IL: Crossway, 2007); and N. T. Wright, *Justification: God's Plan and Paul's Vision* (Downers Grove, IL: InterVarsity, 2009).

3. The Greek words *egkrateia, egkrateuomai,* and *egkratēs* are the most common words indicating restraint or self-control in the New Testament.

4. A powerful passage to meditate on in this regard is Romans 6–8, especially chapter 6 where Paul takes up the following questions: "What shall we say then? Are we to continue in sin that grace may abound?" (Rom. 6:1); and "What then? Are we to sin because we are not under law but under grace?" (Rom. 6:15). In both cases, the answer is, "By no means!" For believers have been united with Christ in his death and will certainly be united with him in his resurrection and must live their lives for God (Rom. 6:5, 10); and having been set free from sin, they have "becomes slaves of righteousness" (Rom. 6:18).

5. Despite his otherwise excellent scholarship, Bruce Waltke with Charles Yu, *An Old Testament Theology* (Grand Rapids, MI: Zondervan, 2007), 71, seems to go too far when he accuses Walter Brueggemann of "blasphemously" stating things and coming to "heretical" conclusions. This illustrates the necessary tension and ambiguity between passion and restraint. Waltke clearly feels passionate about truth and is convinced of the dangerous theological conclusions at which Brueggemann arrives. On the other hand, scholarly writing is not the place for heightened rhetoric, because it will generally only hurt one's case.

6. L. Scott Kellum, *The Unity of the Farewell Discourse: The Literary Integrity of John 13.31–16.33*, JSNTSup 256 (London/New York: T&T Clark, 2004); Gary Burge, *Review of The Unity of the Farewell Discourse by L. Scott Kellum, Bib* 87/2 (2006): 284–86.

7. Maybe I should go by "A. J."?

8. Or he with you: O'Brien disagrees with my interpretation of Eph. 5:32 but does so very gently. See Peter T. O'Brien, *Ephesians*, PNTC (Grand Rapids, MI: Eerdmans, 1999), 430–35, esp. 431–32.

9. Leaving a matter open can be appropriate when the resolution of a given matter is immaterial to the question at hand. In the present volume, see my discussion of the question of whether the dative in 2 Pet. 1:3 is to be construed in the sense of "by" or "for" God's glory, in chapter 2 above.

10. See chapter 17 on love, below.

Chapter 9: Creativity

1. Matthew Syed, *Bounce* (New York: HarperCollins, 2010), argues against a talent-based approach to competencies and skills and instead contends on the basis of psychology and science that anyone can achieve excellence in anything with the right amount of practice, training, and support. Motivation, effort, and endurance are key. This applies to growth in creativity as well.

2. Resources for writing well include Joseph M. Williams, *Style: The Basics of Clarity and Grace*, 3rd ed. (White Plains, NY: Pearson Longman, 2008); William Strunk and E.

B. White, *The Elements of Style*, 4th ed. (White Plains, NY: Pearson Longman, 2000); William Zinsser, *On Writing Well*, 7th ed. (New York: Collins, 2006); Annie Dillard, *The Writing Life* (New York: HarperPerennial, 1990); and William A. Sabin, *The Gregg Reference Manual: A Manual of Style, Grammar, Usage, and Formatting*, 11th ed. (New York: McGraw-Hill, 2004).

3. Some institutions, including The Southeastern Baptist Theological Seminary, are seeking to develop the writing ability of their students through the development and funding of writing centers.

4. My younger sister, Dorice, is a professional violinist with the Vienna Symphony Orchestra.

5. There is a growing consensus, even among evangelical scholars, that Genesis 1 does not describe God's creation of the world *ex nihilo*, because Genesis 1:1 is viewed as an introductory statement to the entire chapter and Genesis 1:2 begins with primordial matter already in existence. See John H. Walton, *The Lost World of Genesis One* (Downers Grove, IL: IVP Academic, 2009), 43–46; Bruce K. Waltke with Charles Yu, *An Old Testament Theology* (Grand Rapids, MI: Zondervan, 2007), 179–82. Nevertheless, the New Testament material does seem to imply God's creation of the universe *ex nihilo* (see esp. Heb. 11:3).

6. Genesis 1; Ps. 148:5; Isa. 42:5; 45:12; Amos 4:13; Mal. 2:10; Matt. 19:4; Mark 13:19; Eph. 3:9; 1 Tim. 4:3–4. In the book of Job, the Spirit and breath of God are creative in the way they make and give life to humankind (Job 33:4; cf. 32:8).

7. Paul explicitly connects salvation in Christ with God's original act of creation: "For God, who said, 'Let light shine out of darkness,' has shone in our hearts to give the light of the knowledge of the glory of God in the face of Jesus Christ" (2 Cor. 4:6).

8. This is similar to David's prayer that God create within him a new heart (Ps. 51:1). David acutely perceived his need to be inwardly renewed by God.

9. For a brilliant treatment, see Christopher J. H. Wright, *The Mission of God: Unlocking the Bible's Grand Narrative* (Downers Grove, IL: InterVarsity, 2006), chap. 4.

10. See, e.g., my essay "Jesus as Rabbi in the Fourth Gospel," *BBR* 8 (1998): 97–128, esp. 115–17. See also Robert Stein, *The Method and Message of Jesus' Teachings* (Philadelphia: Westminster, 1978), esp. chap. 2.

11. Any of N. T. Wright's numerous publications could be consulted. Among my personal favorites is *The New Testament and the People of God, Christian Origins and the Question of God* 1 (Minneapolis: Augsburg Fortress, 1992).

12. James D. G. Dunn, *The Theology of Paul the Apostle* (Grand Rapids, MI: Eerdmans, 2006).

13. Joseph M. Williams, *Style: Toward Clarity and Grace* (Chicago: University of Chicago Press, 1995).

14. The essay is scheduled to appear in *John, Jesus, and History*, vol. 3, ed. Paul N. Anderson, Felix Just, and Tom Thatcher (Atlanta: Society of Biblical Literature).

15. See John's reference to false teachers "running ahead" in 2 John 9 (NIV).

16. See chapter 12 below.

17. John A. Lee, *A History of New Testament Lexicography, Studies in Biblical Greek* (New York: Peter Lang, 2003). See my review of this highly recommended resource in the *JETS* 47 (2004): 485–86.

18. Andreas J. Köstenberger, *A Theology of John's Gospel and Letters: The Word, the Christ, the Son of God*, BTNT 1 (Grand Rapids, MI: Zondervan, 2009), 28.

19. From a blog post by Justin Taylor on the website Between Two Worlds, citing C. S. Lewis, "Cross-Examination," in *C. S. Lewis: Essay Collection and Other Short Pieces*, ed. Lesley Walmsley (London: HarperCollins, 2000), 555; C. S. Lewis, *Letters to Children*, ed. Lyle W. Dorsett and Marjorie Lamp Mead (New York: Collier, 1988), 64. For more good advice, from yours truly, see "The 7 W's of Writing," http://www.biblicalfoundations.org/writing/the-7-ws-of-writing.

20. "Letter to Joan Lancaster (June 26, 1956)," in *The Collected Letters of C. S. Lewis*, vol. 3, ed. Walter Hooper (New York: HarperCollins, 2006), 766.

Chapter 10: Eloquence

1. See, e.g., Augustine, *De Doctrina Christiana* 4.2.3, who asked, "If the evil usurp it [i.e., rhetoric] for winning vain and perverse causes, why should it not also be exploited for use by the good?" (see also ibid., 4.5.7, where he quotes Cicero, *De inventione* 1.1, to the same effect). Cf. William Harmless, *Augustine and the Catechumenate* (Collegeville, MN: Liturgical Press, 1995), 174, n81.

2. Robert Littlejohn and Charles T. Evans, *Wisdom and Eloquence: A Christian Paradigm for Classical Learning* (Wheaton, IL: Crossway, 2006), 13.

3. See Bruce Winter, *Philo and Paul among the Sophists: Alexandrian and Corinthian Responses to a Julio-Claudian Movement*, 2nd ed. (Grand Rapids, MI: Eerdmans, 2001).

4. Corin Mihaila, *The Paul-Apollos Relationship and Paul's Stance Toward Greco-Roman Rhetoric: An Exegetical and Socio-Historical Study of 1 Corinthians 1–4*, LNTS 402 (London: T&T Clark, 2009).

5. John Piper, "Is There Christian Eloquence? Clear Words and the Wonder of the Cross," in *The Power of Words and the Wonder of God*, ed. John Piper and Justin Taylor (Wheaton, IL: Crossway, 2009), 67–80.

6. Ibid., 75–76.

7. See John F. A. Sawyer, *The Fifth Gospel: Isaiah in the History of Christianity* (Cambridge: Cambridge University Press, 1996).

8. As mentioned, in 1 Corinthians 1–4 Paul did not oppose Apollos or his preaching style but the members in the Corinthian church who were influenced by the attitudes of the Sophists and exalted rhetoric as an end in itself. See Mihaila, *Paul-Apollos Relationship*, 3.

9. See George H. Guthrie, *The Structure of Hebrews: A Text-Linguistic Analysis*, NovTSup 73 (Leiden: Brill, 1994); Andreas J. Köstenberger, L. Scott Kellum, and Charles L. Quarles, *The Cradle, the Cross, and the Crown: An Introduction to the New Testament* (Nashville: B&H Academic, 2009), chap. 16, esp. the chart on rhetorical devices in the letter to the Hebrews on p. 679.

10. Piper, "Is There Christian Eloquence?," 76.

11. On the various speech acts in Scripture, see esp. Kevin J. Vanhoozer, *Is There a Meaning in This Text? The Bible, the Reader, and the Morality of Literary Knowledge* (Grand Rapids, MI: Zondervan, 1998), 207–14. More fully, see Vanhoozer, *The Drama of Doctrine: A Canonical-Linguistic Approach to Christian Theology* (Louisville: Westminster, 2005).

12. Amy K. Hermanson, "Religion's Rhetoric: Saint Augustine's Union of Christian Wisdom and Sophistic Eloquence," in *The Rhetoric of St. Augustine of Hippo*, ed. Richard Leo Enos et al. (Waco, TX: Baylor University Press, 2008), 311–14, notes that "Augustine breaks down the dichotomy between faith in God and human intervention. Augustine goes on to apply this example to the question of whether to place trust in God or in human rhetorical skill. Augustine's answer is, again, to break down the false dichotomy. He argues that using rhetoric does not challenge the authority of God's Word, but rather complements or enhances its efficacy" (p. 312).

13. The allusion is to the famous work by Marshall McLuhan, *Understanding Media: The Extensions of Man* (New York: McGraw Hill, 1964), in which he proposed that media itself, not the content it conveys, ought to be the proper focus of study—"the medium is the message." McLuhan believed that media affected society not by its message but by the characteristics of the medium itself. He derived this idea from Bernard Lonergan, Insight: A Study of Human Understanding (London: Longmans, 1957).

14. Case in point: Mike Bird's illustration of being hit in the face by a soggy fish at a recent public appearance. Though it is, of course, also true that illustrations can aid memory.

15. At other times, the illustrations—such as parables—may be so integrally intertwined with the message that separating the two is exceedingly difficult, if not impossible, without losing much of the intended effect. I recently listened to a preacher who tried to illustrate a point made in one of Jesus's parables by using one of his own illustrations. The effect, at

least in my perception, was that the poignancy of Jesus's original parable was weakened. By opting to convey his message in form of a parable, Jesus had already chosen a certain illustration, and Jesus's illustration was far superior to the preacher's.

16. He disregarded my advice and kept the illustration.

17. See, e.g., http://www.wordsmith.org. Cf. Anu Garg, *A Word a Day* (Hoboken, NJ: John Wiley, 2003).

18. E.g., *100 Words Every High School Graduate Should Know*, ed. Editors of the American Heritage Dictionaries (Boston/New York: Houghton Mifflin, 2003); *Essential SAT Vocabulary: 500 Flashcards* (Princeton Review, 2009); Harry Shaw, *Building a Better Vocabulary* (New York: Barnes & Noble, 1992). On matters of punctuation, see Lynne Truss, *Eats, Shoots and Leaves* (New York: Gotham, 2003).

19. Simon Winchester, *The Professor and the Madman: A Tale of Murder, Insanity, and the Making of the Oxford English Dictionary* (New York: Harper, 1999); Stephen Carlson, *The Gospel Hoax: Morton Smith's Invention of Secret Mark* (Waco, TX: Baylor University Press, 2005); Paul Johnson, *Intellectuals: From Marx and Tolstoy to Marx and Chomsky*, rev. ed. (New York: Harper, 2007); Susannah Heschel, *The Aryan Jesus: Christian Theologians and the Bible in Nazi Germany* (Princeton, NJ: Princeton University Press, 2008).

Chapter 11: Integrity

1. John MacArthur, *The Power of Integrity: Building a Life without Compromise* (Wheaton, IL: Crossway, 1997), *ix*.

2. Stephen Carter, *Integrity* (New York: HarperPerennial, 1996), discusses the importance of integrity in the realm of politics. He writes, "Integrity is the first of three books I plan to write about what I think of as 'pre-political' virtues—that is, elements of good character that cross the political spectrum and, indeed, without which other political views and values are useless. First among these virtues is integrity, which gives meaning to all the rest of what we say we believe in" (p. *ix*). See Henry Cloud, *Integrity: The Courage to Meet the Demands of Reality* (New York: HarperCollins, 2006), for a discussion of integrity in relationship to the business world.

3. See chapter 4 above.

4. Jerry B. Jenkins, *Hedges: Loving Your Marriage Enough to Protect It* (Wheaton, IL: Crossway, 2005).

5. I realize I have come dangerously close to violating this principle myself in some of my publications. This book, on the other hand, is a little different, since it is by its very nature more autobiographical.

6. Bart D. Ehrman, *Jesus, Interrupted: Revealing the Hidden Contradictions in the Bible (And Why We Don't Know about Them)* (New York: HarperOne, 2009).

Chapter 12: Fidelity

1. Eta Linnemann, *Historical Criticism of the Bible: Methodology or Ideology? Reflections of a Bultmannian Turned Evangelical*, trans. Robert W. Yarbrough (Grand Rapids, MI: Baker, 1990), provides a very negative assessment. See also Gerhard Maier, *The End of the Historical-Critical Method* (St. Louis, MO: Concordia, 1977).

2. Members of the Society of Biblical Literature often discuss and debate the relationship between confessional and nonconfessional scholarship. See the discussion at http://www.sbl-site.org/membership/farewell.aspx concerning an article by Ronald S. Hendel, where he explains that he is leaving the SBL because he feels the society has lowered its standards to include confessional groups and is no longer sufficiently focused on critical scholarship.

3. For an up-close and personal look at the lives and thoughts of believing scholars, see Steven Hays and James Anderson, eds., *Love the Lord with Heart and Mind*, http://www.triapologia.com/hays/Love_the_Lord.pdf (2008); Paul Anderson, ed., *Professors Who Believe: The Spiritual Journeys of Christian Faculty* (Downers Grove, IL: InterVarsity,

1998); John Ashton, ed., *On the Seventh Day: Forty Scientists and Academics Explain Why They Believe in God* (Green Forest, AZ: Master, 2002); Kelly J. Clark, ed., *Philosophers Who Believe: The Spiritual Journeys of 11 Leading Thinkers* (Downers Grove, IL: InterVarsity, 1993). See also Hugh T. Kerr and John M. Mulder, eds., *Conversions: The Christian Experience* (Grand Rapids, MI: Eerdmans, 1985); and, more broadly, Paul Johnson, *Intellectuals: From Marx and Tolstoy to Sartre and Chomsky*, rev. ed. (New York: Harper, 2007).

4. I am not advocating the complete uselessness of natural revelation but rather its insufficiency apart from God's written revelation. By itself natural revelation is not sufficient to lead humanity to God apart from Christ.

5. See, e.g., G. K. Beale, *The Erosion of Inerrancy in Evangelicalism: Responding to New Challenges to Biblical Authority* (Wheaton, IL: Crossway, 2008).

6. Andreas J. Köstenberger, ed., *Quo Vadis, Evangelicalism? Perspectives from the Past, Direction for the Future: Select Presidential Addresses from the First Fifty Years of the Journal of the Evangelical Theological Society* (Wheaton, IL: Crossway, 2007).

7. Craig A. Blaising, "Faithfulness: A Prescription for Theology," in ibid., 201–16.

8. Ibid., 203–6.

9. Andreas J. Köstenberger and Michael J. Kruger, *The Heresy of Orthodoxy: How Contemporary Culture's Fascination with Diversity Has Reshaped Our Understanding of Early Christianity* (Wheaton, IL: Crossway, 2010).

10. Philip Duce and Daniel Strange have edited two helpful works designed particularly to introduce young biblical studies and theology students to some of these issues: *Keeping Your Balance: Approaching Theological and Religious Studies* (Leicester: Apollos, 2001); and Encountering God's Word: Beginning Biblical Studies (Leicester: Apollos, 2003).

11. See my exposition of John 1:17 in *John*, BECNT (Grand Rapids: Baker, 2004), 47–48.

12. See especially John 20:21, on which see my published dissertation *The Missions of Jesus and the Disciples according to the Fourth Gospel* (Grand Rapids, MI: Eerdmans, 1998), chap. 5.

13. All of these individuals can be contrasted with Demas, who "in love with this present world, has deserted me and gone to Thessalonica" (2 Tim. 4:10).

14. For further development of this assertion, see Andreas J. Köstenberger, ed., *Whatever Happened to Truth?* (Wheaton, IL: Crossway, 2005), 131.

15. Steven Garber, *The Fabric of Faithfulness: Weaving Together Belief and Behavior*, exp. ed. (Downers Grove, IL: InterVarsity, 2007), 139–55, discusses the importance of mentoring in an academic setting.

16. N. T. Wright, *The Last Word: Scripture and the Authority of God—Getting Beyond the Bible Wars* (San Francisco: HarperSanFrancisco, 2006), represents an attempt to affirm the authoritative character of the Bible without adhering to its verbal inerrancy. Wright rightly emphasizes the importance and function of the grand narrative of Scripture and the fact that Scripture derives authority only from God's authority, but in my judgment it is not enough to affirm that the story of the Bible is inspired if the words are not. For a perceptive critique of this work, see D. A. Carson, *Collected Writings on Scripture* (Wheaton, IL: Crossway, 2010), 283–301.

17. Pope Benedict XVI, discussing the relationship between science and faith in a speech at the University of Regensburg on September 12, 2006, entitled "Faith, Reason and the University: Memories and Reflections," aptly notes, "The scientific ethos, moreover, is . . . the will to be obedient to the truth, and, as such, it embodies an attitude which belongs to the essential decisions of the Christian spirit" (p. 6). I do not hold my belief in inerrancy in spite of the evidence but on the basis of it. The whole text of the speech can be found online at http://www.vatican.va/holy_father/benedict_xvi/speeches/2006/september/documents/hf_ben-xvi_spe_20060912_university-regensburg_en.html.

18. Though there are hopeful trends as well, such as the resurgence of biblical theology; see below.

19. The term is Semler's: Johann Salomo Semler, *Abhandlung von freier Untersuchung des Canon*, 4 vols. (Halle: Hemmerde, 1771–76) (though I do not necessarily concur with Semler's model).

20. Johann Philip Gabler, *Kleinere Theologische Schriften*, ed. T. A. Gabler and J. G. Gabler, 2 vols. (Ulm: Stettin, 1831), 2:179–98. English trans.: John Sandys-Wunsch and Laurence Eldredge, "J. P. Gabler and the Distinction between Biblical and Dogmatic Theology: Translation, Commentary, and Discussion of His Originality," *SJT* 33 (1980): 133–58.

21. The Evangelical Theological Society (ETS) requires of its members an affirmation of scriptural inerrancy (with reference to the Chicago Statement on Biblical Inerrancy) along with belief in the Trinity. This provides at least a minimal framework for scholarly dialogue, though whether such is sufficient continues to be the subject of vigorous debate. See, e.g., the presidential address by Darrell Bock, "The Purpose-Driven ETS: Where Should We Go? A Look at Jesus Studies and Other Example Cases," in *Quo Vadis?*, 129–68.

22. See Greg Gilbert, *What Is the Gospel?* (Wheaton, IL: Crossway, 2010).

23. For an interesting study, see Paul V. Harrison, "Pastoral Turnover and the Call to Preach," *JETS* 44 (2001): 87–105.

Chapter 13: Wisdom

1. N. T. Wright, *After You Believe: Why Christian Character Matters* (New York: HarperOne, 2010), 165–69, demonstrates the early Christian connection of wisdom with Christology.

2. The anecdote is included in Jack Hyles, *Blue Denim and Lace* (Hammond, IN: Hyles-Anderson, 1972).

3. Cited in G. E. M. Anscombe, "Mr. Truman's Degree," http://www.anthonyflood.com/anscombetrumansdegree.htm. I am indebted for this reference to a comment signed only "HT" and dated July 7, 2010, on http://www.firstthings.com, in response to a blog post by R. R. Reno entitled "Virtue and Intelligence."

4. I am referring to Bill Davidson, my church history teacher at Columbia International University.

5. Charles H. Dyer, *Character Counts: The Power of Personal Integrity* (Chicago: Moody, 2010), 51–74, helpfully discusses and illustrates biblical wisdom.

6. See, e.g., 2 Chron. 1:10–12; Prov. 1:7; 2:6, 10; 9:10; 14:6; 30:3; Eccles. 2:21, 26; Isa. 11:2; 33:6; Dan. 2:21; Rom. 11:33; Eph. 1:17; Col. 1:9; 2:3.

7. Eugene H. Merrill, *Everlasting Dominion: A Theology of the Old Testament* (Nashville: B&H Academic, 2006), 623.

8. Bruce K. Waltke with Charles Yu, *An Old Testament Theology* (Grand Rapids, MI: Zondervan, 2007), 902.

9. Eckhard J. Schnabel, "Wisdom," in *New Dictionary of Biblical Theology: Exploring the Unity and Diversity of Scripture*, ed. T. Desmond Alexander and Brian S. Rosner (Downers Grove, IL: InterVarsity, 2000), 847–48, notes that this emphasis is unique to the New Testament. He identifies four other emphases of wisdom across the biblical literature. First, wisdom is a divine gift, linked with God, and is not an independent human enterprise. Second, God's wisdom is often inscrutable and defies explanation by human rationality. Third, "genuine wisdom manifests itself in proper behaviour which pleases God" (p. 847). Fourth, teaching is important, because proper behavior is not automatic and must be passed on from generation to generation.

10. Heb. 5:14 comes to mind here: "But solid food is for the mature, who by constant use have trained themselves to distinguish good from evil" (NIV).

11. Andreas J. Köstenberger and Richard D. Patterson, *Invitation to Biblical Interpretation: Exploring the Hermeneutical Triad of History, Literature, and Theology* (Grand Rapids, MI: Kregel, 2011).

12. As a personal example of such an effort, I offer my study "Jesus as Rabbi in the Fourth Gospel," *BBR* 8 (1998): 97–128, in which I contended that John's Gospel should be taken more seriously as a historical document, including in historical Jesus research.

13. See his forays into philosophy: Bart D. Ehrman, *God's Problem: How the Bible Fails to Answer Our Most Important Question—Why We Suffer* (New York: HarperOne, 2008); and biblical theology: *Jesus, Interrupted: Revealing the Hidden Contradictions in the Bible (And Why We Don't Know about Them)* (New York: HarperOne, 2009).

14. Contemporary examples of such polyglots are Don Carson, Tom Wright, and James Dunn, each of whom have contributed to almost the entire spectrum of New Testament studies and more. Others, such as Peter O'Brien or Robert Kysar, focus fairly carefully on a clearly delineated corpus of material, whether the Pauline writings or John's Gospel.

15. An example of this is the movement advocating the theological interpretation of Scripture. For a survey and critique of these and other trends, see my faculty lecture, "Of Professors and Madmen: Currents in Contemporary New Testament Scholarship," *Faith and Mission* 23/2 (Spring 2006): 3–18.

16. I could give specific examples but will refrain from doing so out of respect for these scholars.

17. I wrote my John commentary (BECNT) in about eighteen months, but that's only because I had done a lot of previous work in the area, including another more specialized commentary.

18. Scot McKnight, "The Professor as Scholar: Exiled to Eden," http://www.vanguard-church.com/the_professor_as_scholar_by_scot_mcknight.pdf, 23, makes some helpful comments regarding deadlines. He stresses that authors need to live in reality and "have realistic expectations of the time you need. I say this especially for young authors: publishers know which authors meet deadlines and which don't. And they want authors who meet the deadlines."

19. *God, Marriage, and Family: Rebuilding the Biblical Foundation*, 2nd ed. (Wheaton, IL: Crossway, 2010).

20. Posted by "Jeff" on July 7, 2010, http://www.firstthings.com, in response to a blog by R. R. Reno entitled "Virtue and Intelligence."

Chapter 14: Grace

1. Joel B. Green, "Grace," in *New Dictionary of Biblical Theology: Exploring the Unity and Diversity of Scripture*, ed. T. Desmond Alexander et al. (Downers Grove, IL: InterVarsity, 2000), 524–27, rightly focuses on the soteriological dimensions of grace throughout the canon. He concludes, "From a biblical-theological perspective, 'grace' is fundamentally a word about God: his uncoerced initiative and pervasive, extravagant demonstrations of care and favour for all. On the one hand, his favour is poured out indiscriminately ('to the ungrateful and the wicked,' Luke 6:35); on the other, those in dire straits, the poor and marginalized, can be assured that his compassion reaches especially to them. God's grace is given freely, but it also enables and invites human response, so that people are called to behave towards God with worship, gratitude and obedience; and towards one another in ways that reflect and broadcast the graciousness of God" (p. 527).

2. Bruce K. Waltke with Charles Yu, *An Old Testament Theology* (Grand Rapids, MI: Zondervan, 2007), 850–69.

3. At other times, a scholar at Tyndale House has persuaded me of his conviction on a given issue. An example of this is the late Harold Hoehner, who at one occasion spent a considerable amount of time showing me that a date of AD 33 for Jesus's crucifixion was considerably more likely than the alternative date of AD 30. See Harold W. Hoehner, *Chronological Aspects of the Life of Christ* (Grand Rapids, MI: Zondervan, 1977); Hoehner, "Chronology," in *Dictionary of Jesus and the Gospels*, ed. Joel Green, Scot McKnight, and I. H. Marshall (Downers Grove, IL: InterVarsity, 1993), 118–22; and my *John*, BECNT (Grand Rapids, MI: Baker, 2004), 11, 55–56, 72, 104, passim.

4. See on this larger issue books such as D. A. Carson, *The Gagging of God: Christianity Confronts Pluralism* (Grand Rapids, MI: Zondervan, 1996); and Andreas J. Köstenberger and Michael J. Kruger, *The Heresy of Orthodoxy: How Contemporary Culture's Fascination with Diversity Has Reshaped Our Understanding of Early Christianity* (Wheaton, IL: Crossway, 2010).

5. See chapter 6 on courage, above.

6. In this regard, you may want to check out a recent interaction between Voddie Baucham and me on the family-integrated church movement on my website, http://www.biblicalfoundations.org. I'll let you be the judge as to how well Voddie and I did on that occasion.

7. Millard J. Erickson, "Evangelical Theological Scholarship in the Twenty-First Century," in *Quo Vadis, Evangelicalism?*, ed. Andreas J. Köstenberger (Wheaton, IL: Crossway, 2007), 188–89.

Chapter 15: Humility

1. C. J. Mahaney, *Humility: True Greatness* (Sisters, OR: Multnomah, 2005).
2. Ibid., 22.
3. Ibid., 31.
4. For a brief account of my conversion, see the introduction to this volume.
5. Isa. 13:11; 16:6; 23:9; 25:11; Jer. 13:9; 48:29; 49:16; Ezek. 7:24; 16:49; 28:1–19; Hos. 5:5; 7:10; Amos 6:8; Obad. 3; Zeph. 2:10; Zech. 9:6; 10:11.
6. Todd C. Penner, *The Epistle of James and Eschatology: Re-Reading an Ancient Christian Letter*, JSNTSup 121 (Sheffield: Sheffield Academic Press, 1996), 171.
7. D. A. Carson, "The Trials of Biblical Studies," in *The Trials of Theology: Becoming a 'Proven Worker' in a Dangerous Business*, ed. Andrew J. B. Cameron and Brian S. Rosner (Fearn, Ross-shire: Christian Focus, 2010), 128–29, citing Calvin, *Institutes* 2.2.11.
8. Mahaney, *Humility*, 65–68.
9. John Piper, *Think: The Life of the Mind and the Love of God* (Wheaton, IL: Crossway, 2010), 164, writes concerning 1 Cor. 8:1–3, "So both groups had knowledge. Both groups used their minds to increase knowledge. And both groups were puffed up. What they needed was not less knowledge. The solution to their problem was not to stop thinking. The solution was the heartfelt discovery of God's grace in Jesus Christ. The Corinthians needed to see that everything they knew was a free gift of electing grace and was designed by God to feed the fires of humble love for God and man."
10. Mahaney, *Humility*, 68–71.
11. Ibid., 87–94.
12. Ibid., 97–154.
13. See Stephen Neill and Tom Wright, *The Interpretation of the New Testament: 1861–1986*, 2nd ed. (Oxford: Oxford University Press, 1988); and Werner Georg Kümmel, *The New Testament: The History of the Investigation of Its Problems*, trans. S. McLean Gilmour and Howard C. Kee (Nashville: Abingdon, 1972).
14. More people know Erasmus's first modern edition of the Greek New Testament, published in the following year (1517); his Novum Instrumentum, which represents Erasmus's preparatory work for this project, is comparatively less well known.
15. See chapter 12 on fidelity, above.
16. Just last night my family and I attended the screening of C. S. Lewis's *The Voyage of the Dawn Treader*. As I sat in a sold-out movie theater, the thought occurred to me how amazing it is that, through his published work, Lewis, though he has been dead for almost fifty years, still speaks (cf. Heb. 11:4). See also the above-mentioned book by Douglas Hyde, *Dedication and Leadership*, 10th ed. (Notre Dame, IN: University of Notre Dame Press, 1992).
17. Such as an e-mail message I received just the other day from someone in New Zealand (a place where I have never been) who was working through one of my books

(though keeping me humble was the fact that the reason this person wrote was to alert me to a typo in the book).

18. In case you're interested, the paper will be published as "John's Transposition Theology: Retelling the Story of Jesus in a Different Key," in *Earliest Christianity: History, Literature, and Theology. Essays from the Tyndale Fellowship in Honour of Martin Hengel*, ed. Michael F. Bird and Jason Maston, WUNT (Tübingen: Mohr-Siebeck).

19. Martin Luther, "Experience Makes the Theologian," in *Trials of Theology*, 30, cited from Jaroslav Pelikan et al., eds., *Luther's Works: Career of the Reformer IV*, vol. 34 (Philadelphia: Muhlenberg, 1960), 285–88.

Chapter 16: Interdependence

1. N. T. Wright, *After You Believe: Why Christian Character Matters* (New York: HarperOne, 2010), 207–18, rightly draws attention to the importance of virtue being lived out in the context of community.

2. See further the discussion below.

3. His solitary ministry in Athens serves as an exception to prove the rule since he was waiting to be joined by others (Acts 17:15–16).

4. On the interconnectedness of the early Christians, see Michael B. Thompson, "The Holy Internet: Communication between Churches in the First Christian Generation," in *The Gospels for All Christians: Rethinking the Gospel Audiences*, ed. Richard Bauckham (Grand Rapids, MI: Eerdmans, 1998), 49–70.

5. See Andreas J. Köstenberger with David W. Jones, *God, Marriage, and Family: Rebuilding the Biblical Foundation*, 2nd ed. (Wheaton, IL: Crossway, 2010), chap. 12.

6. For a very incisive piece on this, see Peter Cotterell, "The Nicodemus Conversation: A Fresh Appraisal," *ExpTim* 96 (1985): 237–42.

7. For an in-depth analysis of Jesus's interchange with the Samaritan woman, as well as his conversation with Nicodemus, see my commentary *John*, BECNT (Grand Rapids, MI: Baker, 2004), 141–48 and 117–28, respectively.

8. John A. D'Elia, *A Place at the Table: George Eldon Ladd and the Rehabilitation of Evangelical Scholarship in America* (Oxford: Oxford University Press, 2008).

9. The depiction of Ladd's relationship with his son in D'Elia's biography is instructive in this regard.

10. Andreas J. Köstenberger and Michael J. Kruger, *The Heresy of Orthodoxy: How Contemporary Culture's Fascination with Diversity Has Reshaped Our Understanding of Early Christianity* (Wheaton, IL: Crossway, 2010).

11. Köstenberger and Jones, *God, Marriage, and Family*.

12. See, e.g., the recent volume *Key Events in the Life of the Historical Jesus: A Collaborative Exploration of Context and Coherence*, WUNT 247, ed. Darrell L. Bock and Robert L. Webb (Tübingen: Mohr-Siebeck, 2009); now available in the US through Eerdmans.

13. On the intriguing question of the nature of Jesus's teaching on God's kingdom in the Sermon on the Mount, see Wright, *After You Believe*, chap. 4.

Chapter 17: Love

1. John Piper, *Think: The Life of the Mind and the Love of God* (Wheaton, IL: Crossway, 2010), 167, forcefully notes that "all thinking—all learning, all education, all schooling, formal or informal, simple or sophisticated—exists for the love of God and the love of man. It exists to help us know God more so that we may treasure him more. It exists to bring as much good to other people as we can—especially the eternal good of enjoying God through Christ."

2. N. T. Wright, *After You Believe: Why Christian Character Matters* (New York: HarperOne, 2010), chap. 6, discusses the distinctiveness of the Christian virtue of love in detail.

3. Another personal example is mission in the Second Temple period: see Andreas J. Köstenberger and Peter T. O'Brien, *Salvation to the Ends of the Earth: A Biblical Theology of Mission*, NSBT 11 (Leicester, UK: Inter-Varsity, 2001), chap. 3.

4. Andreas J. Köstenberger, *A Theology of John's Gospel and Letters: The Word, the Christ, the Son of God*, BTNT (Grand Rapids: Zondervan, 2009), 514.

5. See the helpful discussion of love in D. A. Carson, "Love," in *New Dictionary of Biblical Theology: Exploring the Unity and Diversity of Scripture*, ed. T. Desmond Alexander et al. (Downers Grove, IL: InterVarsity, 2000), 646–50.

6. Carson noted, "'God is love,' John writes (1 John 4:8), a statement the Bible makes about no other being. The truth of the statement is one of the glories of the Bible's picture of God. It rules out impersonal pantheism; it denies the cogency of the deist vision, in which God is no more than powerful and distant. The God of the Bible is a person, and love, like holiness, is so much bound up with who he is as a person that John can make this stupendous claim" (ibid., 646).

7. Ibid., 649–50.

8. It is important not to draw too much distinction between the biblical words for love, *philia* and *agapē*, because they are often used synonymously. See D. A. Carson, *Exegetical Fallacies*, 2nd ed. (Grand Rapids, MI: Baker Academic, 1996), 31–32, 51–53.

9. See also Paul's words in his letter to the Colossians: "And above all these put on love, which binds everything together in perfect harmony" (Col. 3:14).

10. The command to love your neighbor as yourself does not include a command to love ourselves. It rather assumes that we love ourselves and act in our own best interests and exhorts us to love others and act in their best interests to the same degree.

11. In part, this may be explained by the fact that Professor Little served in the pastorate for several decades before entering academic life and that he developed an interest in matters of the intellect a bit later in life. I have enjoyed hearing this humble man's testimony on more than one occasion.

12. Bryan A. Follis, *Truth with Love: The Apologetics of Francis Schaeffer* (Wheaton, IL: Crossway, 2006), 137. I should add that I had the privilege to meet and spend time with Schaeffer's son-in-law, Ranald Macaulay, who exemplifies some of the same attributes, emulating Schaeffer's love for people with a keen sense of discernment and a prophetic vision of where the world is headed and how Christians can witness to the surrounding culture.

General Index

Aaron, 151
Abednego, 162
Abigal, 211
Abraham, 170
Absalom, 179
Acts, book of, 91–92
After Virtue: A Study in Moral Theology (MacIntyre), 46
After You Believe: Why Christian Character Matters (Wright), 48–49
Ahab, 119
Ahaziah, 119
Akin, Danny, 205
Amon, 201
Anselm of Canterbury, 25
Apollos, 151, 252n8
arēt (Gk.: excellence), 43, 45–46, 239n5, 241n9, 242nn7–8
Aristotle, 50, 178
Aryan Jesus, The (Heschel), 155
Augustine of Hippo, 25, 68, 252n1; on faith in God, 252n12

baptism, 110
Barnabas, 213
Bathsheba, 162
Baucham, Voddie, 257n6
Bauckham, Richard, 207
Bauer, Walter, 168
beauty, as a reflection of God's excellence, 34
Benedict XVI, 254n17
Berea, 91–92
Bible, the, 55–56, 76, 80, 88, 108, 128, 139, 167, 168, 178, 185, 215, 226; critical reading of, 246–47n20; eloquence of, 151, 152; inerrancy of, 172, 254n16, 255n21; literary devices used in, 151

Blaising, Craig, 168
Boaz, 191
Bock, Darrell, 219
Bonhoeffer, Dietrich, 18
Briercrest Bible College, 23–24
Brown, O. J., 23
Brueggemann, Walter, 250n5
Bultmann, Rudolf, 110
Burge, Gary, 133

Calvin, John, 194, 202
Cameron, Nigel, 23
Carlson, Stephen, 155
Carson, D. A., 23, 24, 97–98, 104, 121–22, 133, 143, 202, 205, 256n14; on Christian love, 225, 259n6; on Christian spirituality, 67, 68; publishing success of, 122–23; on the "seduction of applause," 248n1; on a seminary education, 98
Chin, Moses, 57
Christianity, 38, 68, 93, 160, 168; biblical Christianity, 167; and Hellenistic/Oriental religions, 110
Christians, 27, 48, 103, 135, 139, 160; New Testament Christians, 76–77, 201, 211; persecution of, 110; as strangers/aliens/sojourners, 57, 244n5
Christlikeness, transformation into, 47, 243n17
Chrysostom, 202
circumcision, 139
Columbia Bible College and Graduate School of Missions, 22–23
Communism, 122
community, importance of to the formation of virtue, 47–48
Confessions (Augustine), 68

260

General Index

Consumed by Passion: Paul and the Dynamic of the Gospel (O'Brien), 118
Cost of Discipleship (Bonhoeffer), 18
courage, 103; basic tenets for understanding courage, 107; biblical theology of, 105; combined with trust in God, 104; examples of in the New Testament, 107–8; examples of in the Old Testament, 105–7; and faith, 108; and the fulfillment of God's mission for his people, 106–7; Hebrew and Greek words for, 105, 249n8; need for, 103–5; and obedience, 106
creativity, 137–38, 146, 250n1(ch. 9); biblical theology of, 138–40; of God and Jesus, 139, 140; human creativity in the service of God, 139–40; and innovation, 142–43; and uniqueness, 145–46. *See also* creativity, and work
creativity, and work, 140; going the extra mile, 141; leaving time for revision, 141; reading creative authors, 140; reading secondary literature on creativity and communication, 140–41

Daniel, 162
David, 59, 191, 211, 251n8; sin of with regard to Bathsheba and Uriah, 162–63, 212
Davidson, Bill, 22
deadlines, 96–98, 165–66, 256n18
Dedication and Leadership (Hyde), 122
D'Elia, John A., 217
Demas, 254n13
Deuteronomy, book of, 105
diligence, 88, 100–101; and the acquisition of godly virtues, 90–91; developing diligent habits, 99; diligence in scholarship, 94; difficulty of, 88; examples of diligence-killing time wasters, 99–100; examples of in the New Testament, 90–94; examples of in the Old Testament, 88–90; importance of, 93–94, 100; in meeting deadlines, 96–98; and obedience, 89; as a practical necessity, 89–90; in revising and correcting one's work, 96; and vices, 98–100
discipleship, 171–72
Dunn, James, 140, 256n14

education: benefits of a formal education, 178; cardinal virtues of, 148–49
Ehrman, Bart, 154, 165, 168, 183

eloquence, 147–49, 155; biblical theology of, 149–51; as a cardinal virtue of education, 148–49; and effectiveness, 153–54; importance of to the scholar, 148; nature of, 147–48; and wisdom, 152–53. *See also* eloquence, pursuit of
eloquence, pursuit of, 154; by expanding your vocabulary, 154; by reading widely, 155; by seizing opportunities, 155
Enlightenment, the, 173
Erasmus, 204, 257n14
Erickson, Millard, 36, 240n2; pledge proposals for evangelical scholars, 196–97
"eschatological authenticity," 49
Evangelical Theological Society, 181, 224, 255n21
evangelicals, 167–68; lack of character excellence in, 38
Evans, Charles, 148
excellence, 13–14, 241n7; attainment of, 37, 241n14; as a core value governing all we do, 96–97; God as the grounds for true excellence, 33–36; and holiness, 26–27; increasing excellence through rest, 38–40; lack of commitment to, 96; in relation to pastoral ministry, 240n1. *See also aretē* (Greek: excellence); excellence, pursuit of; holiness, and scholarly excellence
excellence, pursuit of, 26, 33, 40–41, 231–32; pursuing excellence because we are created in God's image, 36–38; pursuit of excellence should be grounded in God's glory, 44–46
Excellence: The Character of God and the Pursuit of Scholarly Virtue (A. Köstenberger), 24–29; approach to the reading of, 28–29; plan for the book, 26–28; purpose for the writing of, 24–26
Exegetical Fallacies (Carson), 23
"evangelical scholarship," 25–26; criticism of, 25

faith (Gk.: *pistis*), 25, 72; adding virtues to, 46–50; role of in scholarship and academic excellence, 27, 111–12; and science, 254n17
Feinberg, John, 240n2
Ferris, Paul, 22
fidelity, 167, 175; biblical theology of, 169–71; to colleagues and your institution, 174; evangelical fidelity, 167–68; to God, 171–72; to oneself, 174–75; to Scripture, 172–74

Finzel, Hans, 22, 23
Follis, Bryan A., 229
Fowler, Paul, 22
Fox, Michael, 62
Frame, John, 245n20
fruitfulness, 69

Gabler, J. P., 173
gentleness, 128, 129
Gnosticism, 110
God, 61, 76, 98, 87, 108, 186, 203, 212, 231, 232; attributes of, 34–36, 240n2, 241n11; commands of, 245n20; creative activity of, 139; developing a right relationship with, 106; faithfulness of, 170; glory of, 34, 37; grace of, 14, 87, 94, 189–90, 257n9; as the grounds for true excellence, 33–36; hatred of the proud, 200–201, 207; holiness of, 56; as love, 259n6; our creation in God's image, 36–38, 241n13; perfection of, 34–35; saving initiative of, 50–51; sovereignty of, 20; trust in, 104, 107, 162, 252n12; truth of, 63; wisdom of, 179, 180, 241n11, 255n9
God, Marriage, and Family (A. Köstenberger), 219
God's Word, study of, 27
Gospel Hoax, The (Carlson), 155
grace, 87, 94, 189–90, 197, 239n4, 250n4; biblical examples of, 191–92; biblical exhortations concerning, 192; biblical theology of graciousness, 190–91; exhibiting grace when we are criticizing others, 196–97; exhibiting grace when we are criticized, 194–96; grace in the midst of disagreements, 193–94; salvation by, 94; sanctification by, 94; soteriological dimensions of, 256n1
Green, Joel, 256n1
Grudem, Wayne, 34, 123, 240n2

Habits of the Mind (Sire), 244n39
Hagner, Don, 193, 207
Harrington, Daniel, 44–45, 46, 47
Hedges (Jenkins), 164
Hendel, Ronald S., 253n2(ch. 12)
Henry, Carl F. H., 23, 239n4
Heresy of Orthodoxy, The (A. Köstenberger and M. Kruger), 168
Hermanson, Amy K., 252n12
Hermeneutical Spiral, The (Osborne), 94
hermeneutics, 112; "hermeneutic of consent," 246–47n20

Heschel, Susannah, 155
Hezekiah, 201
History of New Testament Lexicography, A (Lee), 143
Hitler, Adolf, 153
Hodges, Igou, 22
Hoehner, Harold, 256n3
holiness, 35, 55, 65, 66, 241n8; because God is holy we must be holy, 55–57; being and becoming holy, 59–61; and scholarly excellence, 61–63
Holy Spirit, 64, 66, 69, 70, 72, 94, 163, 215, 218; appearance of to Luke, 80; corporate dimension to the work of, 71; effect of in a person's life, 72–73; fruit of the Spirit, 244n34; importance of, 246n13; and sanctification, 72; walking in the Spirit, 74
Hulbert, Terry, 22
humans: attributes of, 34; creation of in God's image, 36–38
humility, 128, 148, 182, 199–200, 207–8; biblical theology of, 200–202; and lasting significance, 204–5; pursuit of, 202–3; and repentance, 201–2; and research, 203; and superstardom, 205–7
Humility: True Greatness (Mahaney), 199, 203
Hyde, Douglas, 122

idolatry, 231
ignorance, 177
integrity, 159–60, 166; biblical theology of, 160–63; and eloquence, 153; financial integrity, 163–64; as a necessary virtue to draw closer to God, 160–61; in politics, 253n2; sacrificing integrity, 103–4; scholarly integrity, 163, 165–66; sexual integrity, 164–65
Intellectuals, The (Johnson), 155
interdependence, 209–10, 221–22; and approachability, 216–17; biblical theology of, 210–11; examples of in the New Testament, 212–14; examples of in the Old Testament, 211–12; and research, 217–19; and service, 220–21; spheres of, 214–16
Interpretation of the New Testament, The: 1861–1986 (Neill and T. Wright), 204
"Is There Christian Eloquence? Clear Words and the Wonder of the Cross" (Piper), 150
Isaiah, 118

General Index

Israel, faithlessness of, 169
Israelites, 57

Jehu, 119
Jenkins, Jerry, 164
Jeremiah, 211
Jeroboam, 119
Jesus Christ, 47, 77, 93, 110, 160, 211, 212, 241n19; abiding in, 69–70; cleansing of the Temple by, 129–30; on the commandment of love, 226–27; creativity of, 139; death of, 119, 249n16, 256n3; dependence of on God and human disciples, 212–13; divine power of provided to believers, 51; as a divine warrior, 113; forgiveness through, 150; grace of, 190; interactions of with people, 216–17; parables of, 252–53n15; passion of, 119, 125; as the pinnacle of God's wisdom, 180; restraint of, 129; and salvation, 246n9; sanctification through, 60–61, 109–10; trust in, 151; as the ultimate example of God's covenant faithfulness, 169
Jesus Interrupted (Ehrman), 165
Johannine community hypothesis, 104
John the apostle, 70; moral vision of, 224–25
John the Baptist, 92, 211, 212, 213
John, Gospel of, 65, 110, 151, 207, 224
Johnson, Paul, 155
Jonathan, 211
Joseph, 161
Joseph (husband of Mary), 241n19
Joshua, 106
Joshua, book of, 105
Josiah, 201
Journal of the Evangelical Theological Society, 168
Journey of the Mind to God, The (St. Bonaventure), 83–84
Jubilee, year of, 38
Judah, 113
Jude, 171

Kantzer, Kenneth, 23, 239n4
Keenan, James, 44–45, 46, 47
Kellum, Scott, 133
Kim, Seyoon, 207
Kingdom of God, 49, 57, 113; final consummation of, 113; Jesus's proclamation of, 242n2
knowledge, 177–78, 257n9

Köstenberger, Andreas J. (AJK), 111, 207, 257n6; books read by, 155; competitive nature of, 209–10; conversion of, 18–22, 200; courtship and marriage of, 22–23; creativity of, 138; graduate school education of, 22–23; his new life in Christ, 22–24; hobbies of, 100, 248n15; Johannine scholarship of, 183–84, 256n17; reading of the Bible by, 19–20; respect of for other scholars, 204; struggle with the concept of God's sovereignty, 20; struggle with personal sinfulness, 20, 21–22; teaching at Briercrest Bible College, 23–24; teaching at Trinity Evangelical Divinity School, 24; teenage children's effect on, 206; university education of, 22
Köstenberger, Hannes (father of AJK), 19
Köstenberger, Hans (grandfather of AJK), 22
Köstenberger, Marny (wife of AJK), 15, 22–23, 24; education of, 24; teaching of, 24
Kruger, Michael, 168
Kümmel, Werner, 204
Kysar, Robert, 256n14

Ladd, George, 217, 258n9
Larkin, William, 22
"law of Christ," 74
laziness, 89, 97–98, 99
Lee, John, 143
legalism, 56, 191
Levitical code, the, 56
Lewis, C. S., 21, 257n16; on developing a personal style of writing, 145–46
Little, Bruce, 227–28, 259n11
Littlejohn, Robert, 148
logical fallacies, 132
Lord's Supper, the, 110
love (Greek: *agapē*), 72, 148, 223–24, 230, 259nn8–9, 259n10; biblical theology of, 224–27; centrality of in the gospel, 225; as the "law of Christ," 74, 134; and scholarship, 227–28, 258n1; and the truth of the gospel, 229
Luc, Alex, 22
Luke, 63, 65, 247n7; appearance of the Holy Spirit to, 80; production of his Gospel, 92–93
Luther, Martin, 58, 133, 194, 239n4; on humility, 207; on temptation and the study of Scripture, 59

MacArthur, John, 160
Macaulay, Ranald, 259n12

MacIntyre, Alasdair, 46
Mahaney, C. J., 199, 200, 203
Manasseh, 201
Mark, 170
"Marks of the Scholar, The" (A. Köstenberger), 239–40n6
Marshall, Howard, 207
martyrs, 249n16
maturity: growth toward, 134; restraint as a mark of, 133
McComiskey, Thomas, 23, 239n4
McDaniel, Chip, 213
McKnight, Scot, 23, 143
McLuhan, Marshall, 252n13
McQuilkin, Robertson, 22
Mead, James K., 246–47n20
media/medium, as the message, 152, 252n13
meditation, and Scripture reading, 76–77
meekness, 128–29
Merrill, Eugene, 178
Meshach, 162
"Mighty Fortress Is Our God, A" (Luther), 58–59
Miller, Samuel, 13, 239n1 (Preface)
ministry, 123, 124
Mohler, R. Albert, Jr., 62, 205
Moo, Douglas, 23, 143
moralism, pagan, 49
Moreland, J. P., 46–47, 52
Morris, Leon, 76
Moses, 56, 139–40, 151, 211

Naomi, 169, 191, 211
Nathan, 211
natural revelation, 254n4
Nebuchadnezzar, 201
Neill, Stephen, 204
New Testament, 50, 57, 60, 71, 77, 183
New Testament, The: The History of the Investigation of Its Problems (Kümmel), 204
Nicodemus, 217
Novum Instrumentum (Erasmus), 204, 257n14

O'Brien, P. T., 118, 121, 123, 134, 250n8, 256n14
obedience, 70, 75, 89, 106, 113; to Scripture, 80–81
Old Testament, 57, 60, 76–77, 183
orthodoxy/heresy distinction, 169
Osborne, Grant, 23, 94

parables, 252–53n15
paradigms, changing nature of, 104

parochialism, 183
passion, 120–21, 125; biblical theology of, 118; and communication, 124; danger associated with, 125; and faith commitment, 117–18; of God, 118–19; human passion, 119–20; and truth, 124–125, 128; as zeal, 118, 249n6. *See also* passion, in scholars
passion, in scholars: passion and purpose, 122–24; passion and self-knowledge, 121–22
Pastoral Epistles, the, 128
pastors, accountability of to elders and deacons, 182
Paul, 57, 60, 70, 72, 82, 90, 110, 113, 121, 125, 192, 194, 213, 244n8, 252n8, 258n3; anger of, 129; "anti-eloquence" stance of, 149, 151, 152; on ascetic spirituality, 76; centrality of the Holy Spirit to Paul's theology, 246n13; on circumcision, 139; on the importance of fidelity to the gospel message, 169–70; instructions to Timothy, 129; integrity of, 163; on the Jews' zeal for God, 119; on the love of Christ, 226; on not quenching the Spirit, 75; post-conversion passion of, 120; on the resurrection of Christ, 109; on salvation and creation, 251n7; self-sufficiency of, 213–14; on the Spirit of God, 25–26; on spiritual growth, 74; use of eloquent rhetoric by, 149–50; on the wisdom of the world compared to the wisdom of God, 179–80; writing and ministry of, 124; as zealous in his pre-Christian life, 120
Penner, Todd, 202
Peter, 14, 26, 35, 48, 50, 57, 72, 168, 192; on the absence and presence of virtues, 52–53; exhortation to believers to add virtues to their faith, 50–51; exhortation to believers to strive for excellence, 43–44
Peterson, David, 56
Pfister, Jerry, 20
Pfister, Madeline, 19
Phinehas, 119
Piper, John, 128, 150, 204, 257n9, 258n1
plagiarism, 98–99, 248n14; as an act of selfishness, 99
Potiphar, 161
praise, 35–36
prayer, 27, 69, 77
pride, 200–201, 203
Prince, The (Machiavelli), 45

General Index

Professor and the Madman, The (Winchester), 155
publications, 123–24
publishing, and wisdom, 181–84; publish within your area of expertise, 183; using caution in the rush to publish, 181–82; utilizing spouses to critique manuscripts, 182

Quo Vadis, Evangelicalism? (ed. A. Köstenberger), 168

Reese, Ruth Anne, 51
Rehoboam, 179, 201, 212
Reno, R. R., 83
repentance, relation of to humility, 201–2
restraint, 127–28, 134–35, 148, 250n3; and avoiding inflammatory language, 132, 133; and awareness of our limitations, 133–34; biblical theology of, 128–30; as a mark of maturity, 133; reflection of in our personal attitude toward others, 131–32; related virtues of, 128–29; as a virtue, 128, 133
Revelation, book of, 113
Ruth, 169, 191, 211

Sabbath, the, 38
sabbaticals, 94–95
Sailhamer, John, 239–40n6
"saints," 60
salvation, 68, 91, 150; and the act of creation, 251n7; assurance of, 92; and God's salvific restraint, 130; by grace, 94; proclamation of the gospel of salvation through Jesus Christ, 107–8
Samson, 212
Samuel, 212
sanctification, 14, 72, 246n14; definitive sanctification, 60; interplay between the definitive and progressive aspects of sanctification, 60–61; progressive sanctification, 60
Saul, 119, 191, 212
Schaeffer, Francis, 229
Schlatter, Adolf, 110
scholars, Christian/evangelical, 64, 66, 173; exhibiting grace during disagreements, 193–94; exhibiting grace when criticizing others, 196–97; involvement of with churches, 215; and living holistically, 64–65; need for humility among, 64; need for reliance on the Holy Spirit among, 63–64; presenting work at professional meetings, 207–8; and seeking God's approval, 109–10; self-promotion among, 219–20; as set apart for spiritual warfare, 112–14, 249nn13–14; straying of from the scholarship of integrity, 25, 240n8

scholars, spiritual, 77–78, 84; and active obedience to Scripture, 80–81; the call to scholarship, 78; and the faith/reason dichotomy, 78–79; piety and poor scholarship, 79–80; the quest for scholarly significance and the mission of God, 82–84; and the scholarship of love, 81–82

scholarship: confessional scholarship, 111; confessional/nonconfessional debate, 253n2; defined as the advancement of knowledge in a given field, 95; as a form of dialogue, 130–31; personal dimension of, 131. *See also* scholarship, Christian/evangelical

scholarship, Christian/evangelical, 88; believing scholarship, 61–63; and diligence, 94; and hard work, 94–96; integrity of, 25; and interaction with those who disagree with your position, 95–96; organization and presentation of scholarly material, 144; as part of the calling to bear witness to an unbelieving world, 65–66; and the problem of secondary literature, 144. *See also* faith (Greek: *pistis*), role of in scholarship and academic excellence

science, 25; and faith, 254n17
Scripture, authority of, 173
self-control (Gk.: *egkrateia*), 72, 128
self-reliance, 64
Sermon on the Mount, 76
sexual temptation, dealing with, 57–59, 244n7; and confession, 58; pursuing virtue, 58; resisting the power of the Tempter, 58–59
Shadrach, 162
sin, 21, 37, 49, 58, 59, 70, 80, 82, 98, 118, 120, 161–63, 165, 180, 203, 226, 229; 250n4; desensitizing nature of, 99; exposure of, 200; freedom from, 19
Society of Biblical Literature (SBL), 105, 253n2
Sophists, 149
Southeastern Baptist Theological Seminary, 251n3
spiritual warfare, 112–14, 249nn13–14
spirituality, biblical, 27, 84; attainment of, 73; Christian spirituality, 68; components of, 69–71; definition of, 71; meaning of,

67–69; and the monastic/ascetic tradition, 75–76; New Testament spirituality, 75; and obedience, 70; progressive, 73–75; spiritual disciplines, 75–77; "spirituality of the Word," 77; as a theological concept, 68–69; why we need spirituality, 71–73
St. Bonaventure, 83
Stewart, Alex, 15
Style: Toward Clarity and Grace (Williams), 140
Syed, Matthew, 250n1
Synoptic Gospels, the, 207, 243n17

Taylor, Justin, 218–19, 239–40n6
Theology of John's Gospel, A (A. Köstenberger), 144
Theophilus, 92, 93
Thomas, 129
Timothy, 91, 129; fidelity of, 170
Trinity Evangelical Divinity School, 23
Trueman, Carl, 248n2
trust, 161; in God, 104, 107, 162, 252n12; in Jesus Christ, 151
Truth with Love: The Apologetics of Francis Schaeffer (Follis), 229

Unity of the Farewell Discourse, The (Kellum), 133
Uriah, 162
Uzziah, 201

virtue(s), 26, 49, 53–54, 137; and academic excellence, 27–28; as character transformation, 48; consequences of the absence and presence of, 52–53; development of, 47–48, 50; and excellence, 46–50; godly virtues, 87–88, 90–91; and intelligence, 83–84; pursuit of Christian virtue, 242n2; role of in Christian ministry, 51–52; virtue ethics, 50, 243–44n33; and wisdom, 185–86
vocation, 26, 38, 52–53, 62, 114, 232, 244n38; as a Christian scholar, 28, 44, 50, 63, 78, 87–88, 97, 100, 103, 146, 160; in pastoral ministry, 240n1; vocational excellence, 28

Waltke, Bruce, 191, 250n5
Wenham, David, 207
"Who Were the First Disciples of Jesus? An Assessment of the Historicity of the Johannine Call Narrative (John 1:35–51)" (A. Köstenberger), 141–42
Williams, Joseph, 140
Winchester, Simon, 155
Wirt, Sherwood, 145
wisdom, 177–78, 186, 255n9; and application, 185; biblical theology of, 178–80; as a cardinal virtue of education, 148–49; and commitments, 184; distinction from knowledge, 177–78; and eloquence, 152–53; and fear of the Lord, 178–79; and maturity, 180, 255n10; and publishing, 181–84; and research, 180–81; and virtue, 185–86
Witherington, Ben, 143
Wood, Jay, 46; on the development of virtue, 47–48
Wright, N. T., 48–49, 128, 133, 154, 239n4, 243n23; on the authority of the Bible, 254n16; on Christ's calling as king and priest, 243n32; creativity of, 140; on "eschatological authenticity," 49
Wright, Paul, 22
Wright, Tom, 204, 256n14
writing, 205; as a creative enterprise, 138; difficulty of, 95; formal instruction in, 138, 251n3; importance of introductions in, 141–42; purpose of, 122; strategic importance of, 122; strategic nature of, 205

Yarbrough, Robert, 123, 143

Zedekiah, 201
Zimmerman, Joan, 19

Scripture Index

Genesis
1 153, 241n13, 251n5
1–2 139
1:1 251n5
1:2 251n5
1:27 37
2 183
2:2–3 38
2:18 211
3 183
39:9 161

Exodus
4:10–17 151
4:14–16 211
15:26 88, 89
19:14 56
19:22 56
19:22, 24 57
20:8–11 38
35:30–35 140

Leviticus
10:16 89
11:44 45
11:44–45 55
19:2 55
19:18 226
20:7, 26 55
20:26 56
25:1–22 38

Numbers
25:11 119

Deuteronomy
3:14 106
4:9 89
6:4–5 226
6:7 89
6:17 89
7 113
13:14 89
15:1–3 113
17:4 89
19:18 74
20 113
28:1–14 106
28:7 113
28:15–68 106
28:64–67 106
29:20 119
31:6 105

Joshua
1:3–5 106
1:7–9 106
1:9 105

Judges
10:18, 23, 27–28 107
14:3 212
17:6 169
20:22 107
21:25 169

Ruth
1:16–17 169

1 Samuel
15:35 212
20 211
24:3–7 191
25 191
25:30–31 211
26:7–11 191

2 Samuel
9 211
10:12 107
11–12 162
11:1 212
12 211
12:13 162
15:32–34 179
21:2 119

1 Kings
3:9 179
4:30, 34 179
10:1–13 179
12:1–24 212
12:6–15 179
14:21–31 212
21:29 201

2 Kings
2 212
9:27 119
10:13–14 119
10:16 119
10:29, 31 119
19:31 118
22:19 201

1 Chronicles
28:10, 20 107

2 Chronicles
1:10 179
7:14 201
12:6–7, 12 201
19:8 107
19:9 107
19:10 107
19:11 107
26:16 201
32:25 201
33:10–13, 19 201
33:23 201
36:12 201

Ezra
5:8 89
6:12, 13 89
7:17, 21 89

Nehemiah
9 106

Job
2:9–10
32:8 251n6
33:4 251n6

Psalms
8:6–8 37
10:4 200
15 160
23 151
25:9 201
31:23 200
46:10 38
51:1 251n8
64:6 89
69:9 119
77:6 89

106:31 119
111:10 178
119 77, 151
119:4 89
135 106
136 106
139 162
147:6 200

Proverbs
1:28 89
3:34 200
6:9 89
6:16–17 200
8:17 89
8:22–31 178
9:10 178
10:4 89
11:14 179, 181
11:27 89
12:24, 27 89
13:4 89
13:24 89
14:17, 29 128
15:18 128
15:25 200
15:33 178
16:18–19 200
18:17 133
20:4 89
20:6 161
21:25 89
22:13 89
24:6 181
24:30–34 89
25:11 151
25:28 128
26:13 89
26:14 89
27:2 203, 220
27:17 220
29:23 200

Isaiah
2:11–12 201
9:7 118
21:7 89
26:11 118
37:32 118
42:3 129
42:13 118
44:6–8
55:2 89
55:9 179, 241n11

55:11 170
59:17 118
63:10–11 71
63:15 118
65:17 139
66:2 201

Jeremiah
4:9 107
49:19 35

Lamentations
2:4–5 113

Ezekiel
5:13 119
10 106
22:13–14 107
36:5 119
36:26–27 71
37 71
38:19 119

Daniel
3 162
3:17–18 162
4:37 201
6 162

Hosea
1–3 169
4:1–2 169
11:9 56

Amos
2:16 107

Habakkuk
1:4 169
3 106

Zechariah
4:6 39
6:15 89
14:3 113

Matthew
1:5 169
3:11–12 113
5:5 128
5:44 229
5:48 36, 220
6:1–15 76
6:14–15 190

6:24 112, 221
6:33 221
9:10 191
10:10 221
10:22 91
11:2 212
12:20 129
12:34 47, 192
12:36–37 38, 163
13:55 241n19
14:27 107
18:32–35 190
19:30 201
22:17–22 139
22:35–40 227
23 130, 191
24:13 91
25:21, 23 52
26:36–46 213
26:67 129
28:18–20 107, 171
28:20 107

Mark
2:8 90
2:15 191
6:2 241n19
8:36–38 18
9:28–35 129
10:31 201
10:35–40 129
11:28–33 139
13:13 91

Luke
1:1–4 63, 80, 92
1:2 92
1:3 92, 93
1:4 93
5:30 191
6:35 229, 256n1
6:40 41, 172
6:45 47
7:36–50 191
9:54 191
9:54–55 129
9:55 191
12:11–12 107
14:28–32 96
15:1 191
15:8 90
16:10 160
17:10 64
18:1 91

18:1–8 91
19:17 52
21:19 91
22:42 169

John
1:1, 14 170
1:3 139
1:17 169, 171, 190
1:35 212
1:35–51 141
1:38–39 69
2:13–17 130
2:14–22 82, 129
2:17 119
2:19–22 119
3:2 217
3:3 217
3:16 229
3:16–17 224
3:27–30 212
4:7 212
4:7–42 191
4:21–24 119
5:19 41, 212
6:5, 10, 12 212
6:56 69
6:68–69 168
7:53–8:11 191
8:31 69
8:31–32 77
8:44 130
8:48–54 129
12:25–26 109
13 226
13:1 224
13:1, 34–35 222
13:34 224, 225
13:34–35 69, 81, 225
13:35 222
14:16–26 70
15:4–7 69, 73
15:5 64, 73
15:8 69
15:9–10 69, 70
15:10–17 73, 225
15:12–13 69, 81
15:13 222
15:16 82
15:20 110
16:13 79
16:33 107
17:17 77

Scripture Index

17:17, 19 79
17:18 65
17:20–25 225
18:37 190
20:21 65
20:24–29 129
20:30–31 151

Acts
1:8 107
1:14 91
2:42 77
2:42, 46 91
4:19–20 163
6:4 77, 91
9:27 213
11:25 213
13:2 213
13:2, 7 213
13:13 213
13:43, 46 213
14:1, 23 213
14:12 213
14:14 213
15:2, 22, 35 213
15:12, 25 213
16:9 78
16:29–30 191
17:11 92
17:31 109
17:34 82
18:3 213
18:24 151
21:20 119
23:2–3 129
22:3 119, 120
24:25 128
27:10, 31 191

Romans
1:1 125
1:11–12 220
1:16 175
2:4 130
2:24 244n8
3:23 37, 191
5:1 22
5:3 91
5:8 229
6–8 250n4
6:1 250n4
6:1–11 70
6:1–14 70
6:5, 10 250n4
6:12 118
6:12–14 70
6:15 250n4
6:18 250n4
8:1–17 72
8:9 73
8:29 45, 70, 73, 78, 163
9:3 120
10:2 119
12:2 78
12:3 134, 206
12:8 120
12:11 120
12:12 91
12:19 128
13:9–10 226
14:10–12 163
15:25–28 213
16:22 213

1 Corinthians
1–2 179
1–4 252n8
1:2 60
1:17 149
1:18–25 179
1:30 60, 180
2:1–2 149
2:1–5 149
2:11–16 26
2:12–16 70
2:16 78
3:11 53
3:16 71
4:1–2 170
4:3–4 196
6:19–20 71
7:5, 9 128
8:1 177
8:1–3 257n9
9:16 120
11:1 41, 45
12 219
12:19 37
12:31 222
13:1–3 227
13:4–8a 227
15:3–4 109, 174
15:10 15, 50
15:17 109
16:12 151

2 Corinthians
1:6 91
4:6 251n7
5:10 163
5:14–15 226
5:17 139
5:20 192
6:4 91
6:16 71
7:11 120
9:2 120
10:3–5 113
10–13 163

Galatians
1:6–9 170
1:10 196
1:14 119, 120
5:13–14 74
5:13–15 226
5:14 74
5:15 74
5:16–24 72
5:16, 25 72, 73
5:19–21 19, 74
5:19–23 74, 244n34
5:23 128
5:24 118
5:25–6:5 74
5:26 74
6:1 74, 129
6:2 74
6:11 213
6:15 139

Ephesians
1:17 180
2:4–6 70
2:8–9 40
2:10 40, 139
2:15 139
2:20–21 71
4:2 201
4:3 90
4:7–8 113
4:24 139
4:29 38
4:30 73, 74
4:32 190
5:1 36, 41, 45
5:15–16
5:18 73, 74
5:32 250n8
6:5–8 52
6:12 113, 194
6:18–20 214
6:19–20 108

Philippians
1:1 213
1:6 40
1:12–18 221
1:14 108
2:1–11 225
2:3 201
2:3–5 221
2:4 219
2:7 225
2:12–13 40
2:20 170
3:6 119, 120
3:7–9 18
4:8 242n8
4:11 213
4:13 214
4:14 213
4:14–19 213
4:15 163

Colossians
1:1 213
1:9 180
1:16 139
1:28–29 39
2:3 180
2:12–13 70
2:15 113
2:18–23 76
3:1 70
3:12 129, 201
3:12–13 191
3:14 259n9
3:16 180
3:23 52, 93
4:2 92
4:5 180
4:6 192

1 Thessalonians
1:1 213
2:2 108
2:4 109
2:9 221
2:12 242n4
2:17 90
4:3, 7–8 57
4:6 128
5:13 75
5:14 75

5:15 75
5:16–18 75
5:17 76
5:19 73, 75
5:20–21 75
5:21 194
5:22 75

2 Thessalonians
1:1 213
2:13 246n14
2:14 242n4

1 Timothy
1:13–14 192
2 183
2:4 130
2:9, 15 128
2:12 111
2:15 82
3:2 128
3:2–4, 12 175
3:2, 8 53
3:3 128
3:4–5, 12 214
3:6 53
4:13–16 92
4:16 53
5:18 221
6:20 170

2 Timothy
1:3 174
1:6–7 128
1:14 166
2:2 170
2:15 91, 94
2:22 58
2:23–26 81
2:24–26 129
2:25–26 194
3:5 79
3:10–11 41
3:12 110
4:3 152
4:9, 21 90
4:11 170

Titus
1:2 170
1:6 175, 214
1:7 128
2:2 128
2:3–5 175
2:14 120
3:12 90
3:13 151

Hebrews
1:1–2 170
1:2 139
3:7–4:13 38
4:9–10 38
4:11 91
4:13 162
4:16 108
5:7 169
5:14 255n10
6:11–12 91
6:13–20 170
10:14, 29 61
10:19 108
10:19–20 61
10:32 91
10:36 91
10:39 108
11:4 257n16
12:10 61
12:14 61
13:12–15 110

James
1:3–4 91
1:12 91
1:13 56
2:8 134
2:8–9 226
3:1 53
3:1–12 38
3:9–12 192
3:13 129
3:13–17 180
4:4–10 202
4:6 200, 201

4:7 113
4:10 201
4:14 205
5:7–11 201
5:16 58

1 Peter
1:1–2 72
1:1, 17 57
1:14–16 57
1:15–16 55, 65
1:16 45
2:4–5 71
2:9 36, 45, 242n4
2:20 91
2:21 45
3:8 201
3:9 229
3:13 120
3:15–16 192
5:5 200, 201, 207
5:6 201
5:8–9 113
5:10 242n4

2 Peter
1 231
1:1 50, 51
1:1–4 47
1:2 51
1:3 44, 45, 50, 51, 250n9
1:3–4 44, 50
1:3–11 14, 26, 28, 43, 44, 50, 242nn2–3
1:4 51
1:4, 8 45
1:5 43, 45, 50, 51, 53, 90
1:5–7 28, 44, 46, 72
1:6 128
1:8 44, 51–52
1:8, 10–11 232
1:9 44

1:9–11 52
1:10 52, 53, 91
1:10–11 44
1:11 52
1:12–15 48
3:9 130
3:13–14 91
3:15–16 77

1 John
3:23 69, 81
3:23–24 73
3:24 69, 70
4:11–12 226

3 John
4 172

Jude
3 171

Revelation
1:9 91
2:2–3, 19 91
2:4 125
3:10 91
3:16 125
3:19 120
4:11 139
5:5–6 113
7:4–14 113
12:11 113
12:17 113
13:10 91
14:12 91
19:11–16 113
21:1 139
21:5 139
21:8 108

NEWLY REVISED AND UPDATED

Tackles the latest debates and challenges to the biblical foundation of marriage and family

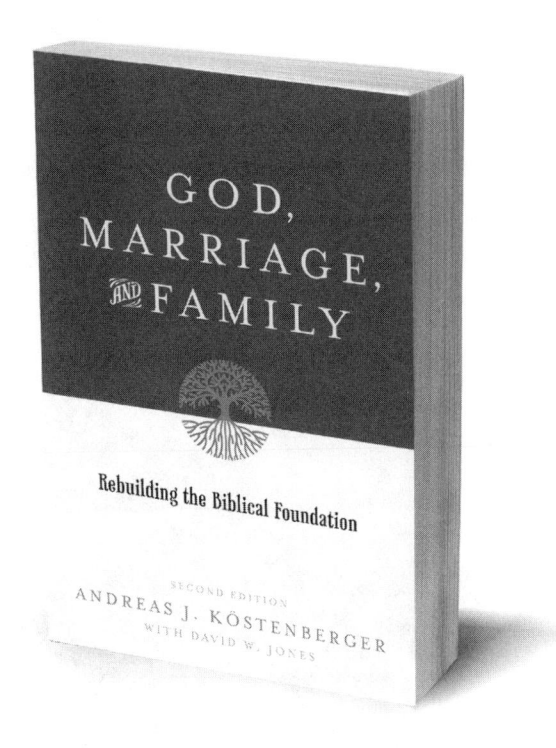

"The easy mastery with which the author threads his way through forty years' special pleadings gives this compendium landmark significance, and I recommend it highly."
  J. I. PACKER, Board of Governors' Professor of Theology, Regent College; author, *Knowing God*

"The special value of this book lies in its pervasive exposition of Scripture. We are adrift in a sea of speculation without this. I am thankful for the book. I plan to give it to my grown children."
  JOHN PIPER, Pastor for Preaching and Vision, Bethlehem Baptist Church, Minneapolis

"This is a superb book—the work of a gifted exegete whose feet are firmly planted in this world. *God, Marriage, and Family* addresses the daunting issues facing today's Christians regarding marriage, divorce, remarriage, sexuality, children, contraception, abortion, singleness, sex roles, and leadership with radical biblical fidelity and practicality. If you want the Bible on these questions, this is the book! What a gift to today's church!"
  R. KENT HUGHES, author, *Disciplines of a Godly Man*, Senior Pastor Emeritus, College Church, Wheaton, Illinois

Evaluating historical evidence, *The Heresy of Orthodoxy* **defends early Christian orthodoxy from the legacy of New Testament criticism: the modern "orthodoxy of diversity."**

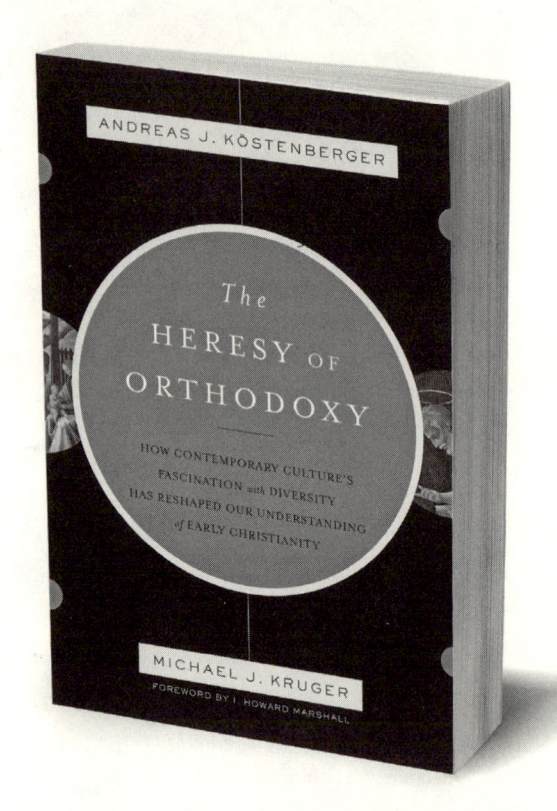

"The Bauer thesis, taken up in many university circles and popularized by Bart Ehrman and through TV specials, has long needed a thorough examination. The *Heresy of Orthodoxy* is that work."
  Darrell L. Bock, Research Professor of NT Studies, Dallas Theological Seminary

"*The Heresy of Orthodoxy* will help many to make sense of what is happening in early Christian studies today."
  Charles E. Hill, Professor of New Testament, Reformed Theological Seminary